THE NATION'S PICTURES

THE NATION'S PICTURES

A GUIDE TO THE CHIEF NATIONAL
AND MUNICIPAL PICTURE GALLERIES
OF ENGLAND, SCOTLAND AND WALES

Edited by

ANTHONY BLUNT, C.V.O.

Professor of History of Art in the University of London

and

MARGARET WHINNEY, D. Lit.

1950

CHATTO AND WINDUS

LONDON

PUBLISHED BY

Chatto and Windus

LONDON

★

Clarke, Irwin & Co. Ltd.

TORONTO

PRINTED IN GREAT BRITAIN BY
BUTLER & TANNER LTD., FROME AND LONDON
COPYRIGHT 1950 BY CHATTO & WINDUS

FOREWORD
By Anthony Blunt

IN planning this volume the publishers had in mind a quite specific object, to give visitors to the United Kingdom an idea of the paintings to be found in the various collections accessible to the public in this country. It was not planned to describe as a whole the museums of England, Scotland and Wales, but only to include those which contain a section devoted to paintings. In order to make such a handbook usable it was also decided not to aim at completeness, but only to mention galleries in which the visitor would find something of particular interest. There are many smaller museums in this country which have perhaps one room of 19th-Century English painting of not very distinguished quality, but the Editors felt that to mention them all would merely obscure the more interesting items. It is for this reason that the sub-title of the book has the form 'The *Chief* Picture Galleries'.

No book of this kind can be completely up to date at the time of its publication, since museums are constantly making new acquisitions, and a re-arrangement may mean that some pictures are put away and others brought out of store. The Editors have, however, made every attempt to make the book as up to date as possible at the time of going to Press, that is to say, in July 1950. Those who visit England in 1951 will naturally find many points of difference, owing to the large number of temporary exhibitions which are to be organised by museums and art galleries in connection with the Festival of 1951, but these will no doubt be amply advertised.

The Editors wish to thank the Directors of art galleries and all those who have prepared contributions in this volume. Without their generous collaboration such a compilation would have been impossible.

In cases where the attribution of a picture is the subject of dispute, it has not been the policy of the Editors to interfere with the views expressed by the writers of individual articles, who are, therefore, responsible for such attributions.

ACKNOWLEDGMENT

THE account of the Walker Art Gallery is based on an article by the same author published in *The Studio* in July 1946, and the author is grateful to the Editor of that periodical for his kind permission to reprint considerable parts of it.

CONTENTS

vii

LIST OF PLATES

INTRODUCTION

PUBLIC collections of pictures generally have their origin in pre-
viously existing private collections. Thus, for instance, the
Prado and the Louvre were formed out of the Spanish and French
Royal collections; the Pitti contains the princely collection of the
Medici; while museums like the Jacquemart-André in Paris are the
result of private benefactions of a later date.

In England, private collecting, though late in starting, pursued a
distinguished and varied course on lines somewhat different from
those followed in other countries, and this distinct character is reflected in the evolution of our public collections. It may be worth
while to say a few words on the development of both private and
public collecting, since it illustrates several aspects of taste in this
country and explains some of the peculiarities of English picture
galleries.

England is exceptional among European countries in that here
the Royal Collection of painting retains its original status and still
forms part of the heirlooms attached to the Crown, though the
greater part of its contents are regularly accessible to the public in
Windsor Castle and the palaces of Hampton Court, Kensington and
Holyrood. It is by far the oldest collection in the country, though
its early history is somewhat obscure. Henry VIII certainly owned
a large collection of paintings of which inventories survive, and
certain pictures can be traced back to the reign of his father,
Henry VII, whose greatest distinction in the field was to have owned
the *St. George* by Raphael, which is now in the National Gallery,
Washington. Earlier kings of England and of Scotland were certainly patrons of the art, but for our knowledge of their commissions
we are forced to rely mainly on written records and on the few
surviving works such as the *Wilton Diptych*, probably commissioned
by Richard II. The great collection formed by Charles I was largely
dispersed at his death by the Commonwealth, but those parts of
it that survived formed the nucleus round which later sovereigns,

notably George III and George IV, built up the present collection. For many years—one might almost say for several centuries—the Royal Collection fulfilled the function now performed by public galleries, in that it was the only large group of paintings to which artists and students could easily obtain access; and the influence of individual paintings in the collection—particularly the Raphael Cartoons and the Van Dycks—can be traced through generations of English painters.

Next to the Crown in order of seniority as collectors we must probably place the Universities. The colleges of Oxford and Cambridge began at a very early date to collect portraits of their founders, principal benefactors and distinguished members. In the actual formation of a museum Oxford was far ahead of Cambridge, owing to the initiative of Elias Ashmole, the founder of the museum which bears his name and which was opened in 1683. But, as Dr. Parker points out in his article on the museum, this was not a picture gallery in our sense, but rather a *Wunderkammer* or cabinet of curiosities, in which a few portraits were included for their historical rather than their artistic interest.

The next stage in the development of Academic collecting is marked by the activity of a very different character, Dr. William Hunter (1718–83), founder of the Hunterian collection belonging to the University of Glasgow. In the intervals of an active life of research in physiology and anatomy he formed a collection of books, coins, engravings and paintings in addition to the scientific specimens which were his more immediate concern. After his death the collection came to the University of Glasgow, of which he had been a prominent member. The pictures are few but include several paintings by Chardin, an artist in whom no other collector on this side of the Channel appears to have taken interest till nearly a century later.

Finally, in 1816, the Fitzwilliam Museum, Cambridge, was founded by the will of the 7th Viscount Fitzwilliam, who bequeathed to the University his collection and a large sum with which to build a gallery. Lord Fitzwilliam's collection was an example of what many English noblemen had been doing since the beginning of the 17th Century, when Lord Arundel and the Duke of

Buckingham had almost rivalled Charles I in their patronage of the arts. But it was the first of its kind to be made over to a public body.

It is significant of the social changes taking place at the beginning of the 19th Century that the two other public galleries founded at about the same time as the Fitzwilliam were due to the initiative of quite different classes of people. In 1811 Sir Francis Bourgeois, a painter but also a man of means, bequeathed to Dulwich College his collection, the greater part of which he had received through the will of his friend Noël Desenfans, a successful dealer. That is to say, the patron of the arts could now be a dealer or an amateur artist. It was not, of course, the first time that an artist had formed an important collection of pictures. Lely and Reynolds had both been collectors, but they had not left their pictures to a public body. Dealers also had naturally been in possession of important works of art, but they, too, had not felt the urge to an act of public generosity. No doubt the spread of education and the widening of the public interest in the arts was beginning to impress artists and connoisseurs with the need for supplying galleries where this interest could be satisfied. Two other artists certainly felt this need: Sir John Soane, who at his death in 1837 left his house and collection to the nation, and Sir Thomas Lawrence, who made every effort, though without success, to arrange that the nation should buy on reasonable terms his unrivalled collection of drawings.

More significant, however, of the change in temper and the widening interest in the arts are two movements which can be traced in London and in the provinces. In London agitation for the formation of a national gallery was active at any rate from before 1800, but all attempts failed till at last the Government was shamed, one might almost say, into buying the Angerstein collection, which was made the nucleus of such a gallery opened in 1824. The early struggles of the National Gallery are told in the appropriate chapter of this book, but it is worth noticing here that not everyone was in favour of it. Many thought it an unnecessary luxury and some, like Constable, thought it an actual menace in that it would distract painters from the direct study of nature. However, the fact that it was founded revealed the growing feeling for the need of picture galleries.

In the provinces the same feeling is manifested by a series of independent attempts at almost the same time to found smaller collections accessible to the public. These attempts were generally due to the intellectual societies which sprang up in the new industrial cities and which were to play such an important part in the development of English thought in the 19th Century. In the field of art Glasgow was ahead of other towns, for it had founded an academy of art in 1754, that is to say fourteen years before London formed a similar body. We have already seen that it early acquired a university gallery, but in the actual creation of a municipal gallery it was outstripped by other towns, since the present museum in Kelvingrove was not founded till 1854. Meanwhile Liverpool had been active. After many failures, lasting for about forty years, it succeeded in founding an academy of art in 1810, and seven years later a body called the 'Liverpool Royal Institution'. In 1821 this body distinguished itself by buying the collection of paintings left at his death in that year by one of its founders, William Roscoe, the historian of the Medici. Roscoe was far ahead of his time in his admiration for early Italian painting, and his collection contained paintings such as the panel by Simone Martini and the *Pietà* of Ecole Roberti, which are now recognised as masterpieces of this school. In 1877 Liverpool acquired a municipal gallery; fifteen years later the Royal Institution transferred the Roscoe pictures to it on permanent loan, and finally in 1949, when the Institution was disbanded, the pictures were presented and became part of the gallery's permanent collection.

Meanwhile, Manchester had followed suit. The year 1829 saw the foundation of the 'Royal Manchester Institution for the Promotion of Literature, Science and the Arts', which in addition to holding exhibitions soon began to form its permanent collection, which was transferred to the Municipality in 1882. A late example of the same practice can be found at Norwich, which though it possessed a museum from 1825 onwards, only began to form a picture gallery properly speaking in 1894 when its acquisitions consisted mainly of gifts from the 'East Anglian Art Society'.

The National Gallery of Scotland had its origin mainly in the same kind of individual enthusiasm. It was founded in 1859, but it incorporated the collections formed earlier by the Royal Scottish Academy, the Royal Institution and the College of Edinburgh. The two former had been collecting paintings of the Italian and Dutch schools for some time, and the College had received in 1835 a bequest from Sir James Erskine of Torrie, consisting mainly of 17th and 18th Century pictures, together with some sculpture.

The second half of the century saw the consolidation of work in the provincial galleries. The initiative of the independent societies had roused the consciences of the municipalities themselves, and most of the great industrial towns of the north formed their own museums and art galleries between 1850 and 1900. Glasgow and Liverpool, as we have seen, had galleries in 1854 and 1877, respectively, and three other towns established important foundations of the same kind: Birmingham (1867), Leicester (1885) and Leeds (1888). Besides these institutions, which developed into major provincial picture galleries, other towns endowed smaller picture galleries, or museums devoted more particularly to archæology or to some technical subject connected with local industry, such as the collections of pottery and porcelain at Derby and Stoke-on-Trent.

Meanwhile, the State had not been inactive, and various new museums had sprung up in London, mainly devoted to the satisfaction of some specialised need. The National Portrait Gallery, opened in 1856, recognised the importance of a collection of portraits based on their historical interest rather than their artistic merit. The Tate Gallery, established after many struggles in 1897, satisfied the demand for a gallery of Modern British art. Much later, in 1934, the most technical of all the museums containing pictures was founded, namely the National Maritime Museum at Greenwich, in which are housed paintings illustrating the history of the Royal Navy and the Merchant Navy.

The end of the 19th Century and the beginning of the 20th were marked by new instances of private benefactions. Not only did existing museums benefit greatly by gifts of individual pictures or of whole collections—such as the Mond bequest to the National Gallery—but new galleries were founded by private initiative both in London and in the provinces. Of this movement the most famous instance is the Wallace Collection founded by the will of Lady

Wallace, widow of Sir Richard Wallace, in 1897. In this way the Nation came into possession of the unrivalled collection of paintings and *objets d'art* formed by the Hertford family and increased by Wallace. A smaller foundation of the same kind was made by the will of Lord Iveagh, who in 1927 left Kenwood House and its contents for the enjoyment of the public. A third, of a more special character, was the Courtauld Institute, founded in 1932 by Samuel Courtauld, as part of the University of London, in which were housed for the benefit of the university and the public the pictures which he had collected of the French Impressionist and Post-Impressionist schools.

Private initiative was also active outside London, and many towns, large and small, acquired galleries by the gift or bequest of a local enthusiast for the arts. As an isolated early instance of this tendency, separated apparently by many decades from other similar cases, it is worth mentioning the town of Basingstoke, which still houses in its town hall a small collection of pictures, mainly of the 17th Century, presented to the municipality by a Mr. Sheperd of Old Basing apparently in the 18th Century. It was not till the later 19th Century, however, that this tendency became general. Barnard Castle, Yorkshire, was endowed by John Bowes (died 1885) and his wife with a museum containing important pictures and works of art. The Norwich Castle museum has benefited from the generosity of the Coleman family, first in 1898 and again in 1946, in two great bequests of paintings of the Norwich school. In 1905 Brighton received the bequest of a collection of pictures from Henry Willett which formed the nucleus of their present gallery. Bristol and Port Sunlight each received a museum from the heads of local industry, the Wills family and Lord Leverhulme, in 1904 and 1922 respectively. One of the latest municipal galleries to be founded is the Usher Art Gallery at Lincoln, due to the generosity of James Ward Usher, a local jeweller. Finally, mention must be made of the Barber Institute, Birmingham, a collection formed in 1932 by the generous bequest of Lady Barber for the benefit of the University of Birmingham.

In recent years another tendency has become visible in the policy of provincial museums. Many municipalities have acquired by gift or purchase old houses in or near the town which have been adapted as additions to the central museums. The most notable example is the acquisition by the Leeds Corporation of Temple Newsam, bought from Lord Halifax in 1921, and used primarily as a museum of applied art. In the same way Aston Hall, a magnificent Jacobean house, has been acquired by the city of Birmingham and is now fitted up as far as possible as a private house with appropriate furniture and pictures. Manchester has no less than six subsidiary museums, each assigned to a special branch of the collection, costume at Platt Hall, furniture at Wythenshawe, and so on. This extension adds greatly to the variety obtainable in museum display and has the further advantage of scattering the collection over different parts of the town and so making it more easily accessible to the population.

By acquiring such houses the municipalities are playing their part in attempting to save the great country houses of England which in present economic circumstances the owners so often have to abandon. Another organisation which contributes greatly towards the solution of this problem is the National Trust, which in recent years has become the owner of important collections of pictures. Details of the collections in their possession are given below in the chapter dealing with the National Trust, and at this point we need only notice their existence as perhaps the latest symptom in the development of public ownership of paintings in this country.

The difficulty of keeping up a great country house appears to be having another result which affects public art galleries. Many private individuals find themselves in possession of pictures which they are unable to house, but which they are also unwilling to sell. Many have found a solution of this problem by depositing their paintings on a long loan with a national or provincial gallery. So, for instance, the National Gallery of Scotland is now enjoying the finest of Lord Ellesmere's pictures, while Birmingham has on view most of those belonging to Mr. Christopher Loyd and Lord Rothschild. This can clearly only offer a temporary solution; but while it lasts it is one which has great advantages from the point of view of the public.

Those who visit the picture galleries of England expecting to find collections similar to those on the Continent will be uniformly disappointed. Among the State museums they will find nothing like the Louvre or the Uffizi; still less will they find in the provinces galleries such as exist in even the smaller towns of Italy. But, if they free themselves from these expectations, they will find much that is of interest and some things which are of the greatest beauty. The National Gallery may not have the overwhelming accumulation of masterpieces of a particular school which makes a visit to, say, the Prado unforgettable; but there are a few museums in the world which can present so complete and balanced a picture of European painting since the beginning of the Renaissance. In the provincial galleries, too, the curious will not only find many works of beauty and importance but will learn much about the English character. We can offer galleries of every kind; the old accumulation of the Royal Collection at Windsor, Hampton Court and Holyrood; the products of courageous individual enthusiasm in the Hunterian and the Roscoe collections; the results of discriminating taste in generations of a single family, as in the Wallace; and museums formed from the enlightened use of wealth newly acquired in industry as at Kenwood or the Courtauld Institute. We can show museums designed to illustrate the whole history of painting, and others which cover only a special corner of the field; museums housed in old country houses and others in up-to-date, scientifically equipped buildings; in fine, collections which embody the great tradition of the English amateur, taking the word in both its English and its French sense; galleries in which is carried on the spirit which created the private collections in the great houses of England, perhaps the greatest contribution made by this country in the field of the visual arts.

ANTHONY BLUNT

I

The Royal Collection

HAMPTON COURT PALACE

THE visitor to Hampton Court is likely to be attracted primarily by the desire to see Wolsey's mansion, Wren's great classical palace built for William III and the Gardens unrivalled in their kind in this country. But when he has soaked himself in historical memories, in the charms of nature and in the beauties of architecture, he will do well to remember that the palace contains within not only a series of magnificent rooms designed by Wren and decorated by Verrio, Thornhill and Kent, but also an important part of the Royal Collection of pictures.

Like all the English Royal Palaces, Hampton Court contains a series of paintings which have accumulated there without deliberately formed plan, in the gradual process of shifting from one house to another which takes place within the collection, as taste changes or as one palace or another is adapted to a new purpose. In general, however, it can be said that Hampton Court now contains some of the oldest surviving parts of the collection, namely the bulk of the 16th-Century portraits and the remains of the Italian pictures belonging to Charles I. To these must be added certain later groups of portraits, such as the Lely and Kneller *Beauties*, and a series of Italian paintings of the 17th and 18th Centuries, which were mainly transferred to Hampton Cout within the last hundred years.

The 16th-Century portraits are mostly displayed in the Guard Room, and the small Wolsey Rooms which lead off it. They represent the main surviving part of the collections formed by the Tudor kings and queens.

Henry VIII's collection, which is the earliest of which we have detailed records, consisted of two parts: portraits and religious paintings. Of the latter very few survive, though the exceptions include works of great importance such as Holbein's *Noli me tangere* (Pl. 3*b*) and the Mabuse *Adam and Eve*. Among them was also a painting which is of historic rather than of purely artistic interest since it is probably the one surviving example of Henry's

3

use of painting for purposes of religious propaganda. It is a small grisaille, formerly thought to be Flemish but now ascribed to the Italian painter Girolamo da Treviso who worked for Henry in this country. It depicts the prostrate figure of a Pope on whom the four Evangelists hurl down stones. The picture is full of anti-catholic symbols marked by the lack of restraint typical of all religious controversy of that time.

The portraits recorded as being in the collection of Henry VIII consisted largely of heads of the Kings of England, many of which are preserved in the private rooms at Windsor Castle, but they included also the little group by Mabuse representing the children of Christian II of Denmark, one of whom was the Princess Christina whose hand was later sought in marriage by Henry VIII and who was the subject of Holbein's great portrait, bought by the National Gallery from the Duke of Norfolk but formerly also in Henry VIII's collection (Pl. 7a). The great monument of the period, Holbein's fresco at Whitehall representing Henry VIII with his parents and Queen Jane Seymour, perished in the fire of 1698, but its composition is known to us from a copy made by Remigius van Leemput in 1667, which hangs in the Tapestry Gallery at Hampton Court. In the same gallery may be seen three interesting historical paintings connected with Henry VIII, but probably painted at the end of the 16th Century. They represent the meeting of the King and the Emperor Maximilian, the embarkation of Henry at Dover, and his meeting with Francis I at the Field of the Cloth of Gold. All three are admirable examples of the type of pageant painting in which the Tudors particularly delighted.

Henry VIII's features are ably recorded in the half-length portrait by Joos van Cleef, to which hangs as a pendant, somewhat surprisingly, a similar portrait of Queen Eleanor of France, sister of Charles V and wife of Francis I. Two portraits of the great humanists Erasmus and Frobenius, by a very close follower of Holbein, present an interesting technical point. Charles I had them both altered by the addition of an architectural background painted to his order by Steenwyck. Recently this background was removed from the portrait of Frobenius but it is still visible in the Erasmus.

The spread of Holbein's influence in England can be seen in two portraits of the middle of the century, a full-length of Edward VI, and a remarkable portrait of an unknown young man in red, one of the most impressive and puzzling pictures in English painting of this period.

The reign of Elizabeth produced little that was new in English painting, but the Queen appears at Hampton Court in one exquisite example of the adaptation of painting to delicate court flattery. This is the panel by Hans Eworth (Pl. 3a) depicting the Queen taking part in a sort of Judgment of Paris and defeating Juno in power, Minerva in wit and Venus in beauty.

James I and his Queen, Anne of Denmark, can be seen in formal full-length portraits by their court painter, Paul van Somer, and their eldest son, Henry Prince of Wales, in a hunting scene probably by Marc Gheeraerts, to whom is also attributed the enchanting portrait of a lady in a flowered Persian dress usually called Lady Arabella Stuart (Pl 1a). The fancy dress and the melancholy mottoes inscribed on the portrait convey vividly the atmosphere of the early Stuart masque.

The cycle of English portraits is closed, as far as Hampton Court is concerned, with the two series of *Beauties*. The first are the so-called *Windsor Beauties*, painted by Lely in the 1660's for the Duke of York and representing the most celebrated women of the court of his brother Charles II. The second, less distinguished in quality, are the *Hampton Court Beauties*, commissioned in emulation of the first series by Queen Mary from Kneller in the last decade of the century.

The rooms leading out of the Guard Room along the south front of the palace are decorated with Italian, mainly Venetian pictures of the 16th Century, almost all of which came from the collection of Charles I. They represent only a fragment of his whole collection, the greater part of which was sold by the Commonwealth, but they give us some slight idea of what it originally contained.

On the death of his elder brother Henry in 1612, Charles became Prince of Wales and inherited the small collection of pictures which Prince Henry had formed with the advice of Lord Arundel and Inigo Jones; but as he was only twelve at the time he can hardly have taken any active steps to increase it for some years. In 1623, on the fantastic journey to Madrid with the Duke of Buckingham, the Prince of Wales had his first opportunity of seeing some of the masterpieces of European painting. Not only did he see the works of Titian in the collection of the Spanish king, but he brought back with him to England several important works of art. Philip IV presented him with the celebrated *Venere del Pardo* and the full-length portrait of Charles V by Titian, and the Prince bought other paintings from Spanish private collections.

On his accession in 1625, Charles I began immediately to take steps for the enlargement of his collection through agents, diplomatic or private, all over Europe. In 1627 one of these agents, Daniel Nys, made his most important acquisition for the King by buying a great part of the collection of Vincenzo Gonzaga, Duke of Mantua. The details of the transaction are tortuous, and the negotiations were rendered more complicated by the necessity of secrecy, imposed by the fear of rival purchasers, such as the Grand Duke of Tuscany or Cardinal Richelieu. After long discussions, however, the finest pictures from the collection were shipped to England. They included masterpieces by Titian, Correggio, Raphael and Andrea del Sarto, as well as many other works of importance. Two years later a further purchase was made of the *Triumphs* of Mantegna, also belonging to the Gonzagas.

In addition to these large-scale purchases, Charles I bought or exchanged pictures singly or in smaller groups. In 1637 he acquired the collection of Daniel Fröschl, or Frosley, miniature painter to the Emperor Rudolph II, which contained a number of interesting Italian and Flemish pictures. Many paintings can further be traced as gifts to the King from members of the court, or from ambassadors who had bought them on their travels abroad.

It is only in imagination that the collection of Charles I can be reconstructed; but a mere list of some of the great Italian masterpieces which it contained and which are now scattered as a result of the Commonwealth sale will in itself give an impression of its quality. Of all painters Titian was the most magnificently represented, and it is not too much to say that almost all the best works of that master now in the Louvre, as well as many fine ones in Vienna and Madrid, were in the possession of Charles I. The list of the most important runs as follows: the twelve Emperors (now destroyed); the *Entombment*, the *Supper at Emmaus*, the so-called *Alfonso d'Este with Laura de' Dianti*, the *Jupiter and Antiope* (the *Venere del Pardo*), the *Davalos Allegory*, the *Man with a Glove*, another portrait and a *Holy Family*, as well as probably the *Vièrge au Lapin* (all in the Louvre); the *St. Margaret*, the portrait of Charles V, the *Venus with an Organ Player* (in the Prado); probably the *Girl in a Fur* in the Museum at Vienna and the *Doge Andrea Gritti* in the Czernin collection; *Alexander VI before St. Peter* at Antwerp.

Round this astonishing nucleus were grouped other works scarcely less important. Giorgione's *Concert Champêtre* (Louvre); Raphael's *La Perla* (Prado); several works by Correggio, the *Education of Cupid* (National Gallery), *Jupiter and Antiope* and two allegories (Louvre); Andrea del Sarto's *Holy Family* in the Prado.

It is tempting to be romantic about the collection of Charles I, especially on account of the tragic fate of its creator and the disastrous dispersion of the Collection itself. But when every allowance has been made, it remains undeniable that the King can rank as one of the great collectors of all time. He missed no opportunity of obtaining the great works of the past, and he displayed the essential qualities of the collector: enthusiasm and discrimination. No doubt his collection contained many paintings which modern criticism has condemned as copies or imitations; but the essential fact remains that, in the relatively short period of twenty years, he brought together a collection of works of art hardly to be paralleled by any other collector with similar opportunities.

After the execution of Charles I in 1649 Parliament declared all his possessions and those of the Queen confiscate to the State. A great part of the gold and silver plate was melted, and the metal sent to the Mint. Of the remaining objects, pictures, statues and tapestries, detailed inventories were prepared for the ultimate purpose of selling the Collection.

The details of the Commonwealth sale are complicated, and in some points obscure. But the outline is as follows: A value was placed on every item; a few were then retained for the use of the State; a large number were allotted to persons connected with the court to whom salaries or payments for work were due; and finally, the remainder were offered for sale.

Pictures in the first two categories remained for the most part in England. It appears even that some of the paintings allotted to creditors in lieu of payment were never collected, and remained in the Palaces till the Restoration. Of those offered for sale, some were bought by English collectors, and many by dealers such as de Critz, who sold them to foreign buyers, of whom the principal were the King of Spain, Archduke Leopold William, Cardinal Mazarin and the banker Jabach. The correspondence of Mazarin shows the complicated negotiations of his agent in London to obtain particular prizes. Gradually treasure after treasure crossed the Channel, many of them never to return. Those bought by the King of Spain are now in the Prado; those by the Archduke in Vienna; and those which passed to Mazarin and Jabach mostly entered the collection of Louis XIV and are now in the Louvre. Others, however, passed eventually to collections such as that of the Duke of Orleans, returned to this country and are now in private collections or in the National Gallery.

The works reserved by the State for official use form a curious list. The most important items are the Mantegna *Triumphs*, which were reserved in order that tapestries should be woven from them, but the list also includes several Madonnas and an Assumption. It seems unlikely therefore, as has been suggested, that the Commonwealth only sold paintings of which it disapproved on religious or moral grounds. Indeed, the only works which were not included in the inventory for eventual sale were the portraits of the mediæval Kings and Queens of England, which may have been excluded on historical grounds.

At the Restoration, Charles II at once began to recover as much as possible of his father's scattered collections. Those paintings which had crossed the Channel were for the most part lost. However, as a courteous gesture to the newly returned King the Dutch States General bought and presented to him the collection of van Reynst, and in this way a number of important Italian paintings entered the Royal Collection, including the magnificent portrait of Isabella d'Este, now attributed to Giulio Romano (Plate 1*b*),

1.*b* GIULIO ROMANO Isabella d'Este

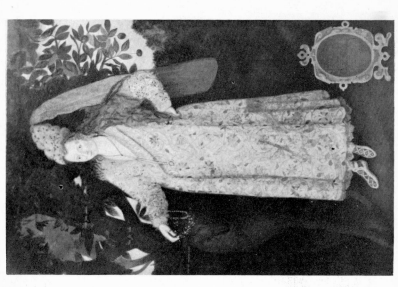

1.*a* ANON Lady Arabella Stuart

2.*a* MANTEGNA Triumph of Caesar   *Hampton Court Palace*

2.*b* TINTORETTO Esther before Ahasuerus *Hampton Court Palace*

For the pictures which had remained in England, however, the case was different. A Royal Commission was set up to direct the recovery of the missing goods, and by an ingenious method of 'voluntary' gifts, stimulated by reports supplied by special informers, a great part of the Collection was reconstituted—a great part, that is to say, in quantity, for the foreign buyers had carried off the majority of the masterpieces. Nevertheless the manuscript inventory of Charles II's paintings shows that he had a collection of which no king need have been ashamed.

If we turn from the melancholy contemplation of what has been lost from the collection of Charles to the study of what has survived, we shall find at least a number of works of the highest quality. The Venetian series opens with the Mantegna *Triumph of Cæsar*, a set of nine decorative paintings in tempera, at present on view in the Orangery (Pl. 2*a*). These paintings display the various stages in the triumphal march of a Roman emperor, and were executed by Mantegna between 1484 and 1494 for one of the rooms in the castle of the Gonzagas at Mantua, where he had already painted his celebrated *Camera degli Sposi*. They display to the full the passion for archæology of north Italian humanists of the time, but also Mantegna's genius in transmuting his material into a great imaginative whole. In spite of the damage which they have suffered and of the difficult conditions under which they are exhibited, we can still realise that they are one of the most splendid monuments of Renaissance art in this country.

The first phase of Venetian painting in the 16th Century can be seen in two pictures connected with the last years of Giovanni Bellini, the lovely portrait of a young man, and the *Concert*, which, if not certainly from his hand, bears at any rate the strong marks of his personality. The mellow poetry of his pupil, Giorgione, can be felt in the *Shepherd with a Pipe*, in spite of its damaged condition. The Titians surviving in the collection are only two: the portrait of a man, generally called Jacopo Sannazaro, and the *Lucretia*. The former shows Titian still under the influence of Giorgione but already moving towards his mature style. The *Lucretia* was formerly considered to be a studio work, but the recent cleaning, and the removal of disfiguring additions to the canvas, have made it certain

C

that, though in bad condition, it is an original painting probably executed about 1530. This figure, of which the pose goes back to Raphaelesque models, illustrates well the classical style which was evolved by Titian in the decades after the death of Giorgione. A minor practitioner of the same phase was Titian's contemporary, Palma Vecchio, whose *Holy Family* and *Sibyl* illustrate his personal and more sensuous version of the style.

The last generation of 16th-Century Venetian painters is brilliantly represented in two great canvases by Tintoretto, the poetical *Apollo and the Muses*, and the dramatic *Esther and Ahasuerus* (Pl. 2b), and by the rich *Holy Family* of Veronese. The third member of this generation, Jacopo Bassano, was also a favourite of Charles I, and the greater part of the paintings by him escaped sale by the Commonwealth. His early *Adoration of the Shepherds* makes an interesting comparison and contrast with the late *Jacob's Journey*. Venetian portraiture is also a notable feature of this collection which is rich in portraits by Lotto, whose *Andrea Odoni* is one of his masterpieces, Tintoretto, Leandro Bassano and even his brother Jacopo. Finally, the visitor should not miss a landscape, which still bears the name of Titian, though it is probably a work of a younger artist; in any case it is one of the first Italian paintings in which the landscape dominates the composition to the almost complete exclusion of the figures.

Renaissance painting of the rest of Italy is not widely represented at Hampton Court, though there are interesting examples of two great masters, Andrea del Sarto and Correggio. From the hand of the former is a small *Madonna*, typical of his mature style, while a panel of the *Virgin and Child with St. John* shows the style connected with his studio in his last years. It may be a version of one of his own designs painted by his ablest pupil, Rosso, with whose early paintings it has strong affinities, particularly in colour. Both the Correggios belonged to Charles I; both have suffered much, but the little *Holy Family* has recently been restored and has regained much of its original delicacy of colour.

The first generation of Raphael's followers can all be seen here, Pierino del Vaga in two fragments of an altarpiece painted for S. Maria sopra Minerva; Polidoro in a charming set of playfully classical decorative panels; and Giulio Romano in a magnificent portrait of Isabella d'Este (Pl. 1*b*). This picture is perhaps the most important member of a remarkable group of Mannerist portraits which included the nervous Parmigianino *Portrait of a Boy* (often but wrongly called an *Officer of the Papal Guard*), the picturesque Franciabigio *Gardener of the Duke of Florence*, a rather heavy *Lady with a Lap-dog and an Armillary Sphere*, perhaps by Vasari, and finally the romantic and brooding *Lady in Green*, attributed to many different artists and probably coming from the school of Ferrara. The work of this school can also be seen in the paintings by Dosso, including several portraits and the strident but exciting *Holy Family with St. Anne*.

The later Stuart and Hanoverian kings acquired a small collection of Italian paintings of the 17th century. This opens with the little *Holy Family* by Annibale Carraci, once very famous under the title of *The Silence* from the gesture with which the Virgin checks St. John from waking the Christ child. His followers Domenichino, Guido Reni and Guercino can all be seen in typical works, while the rival tradition of naturalism is represented by a copy of the lost *Road to Emmaus* of Caravaggio. Of the school founded by the latter, the most interesting members from the English point of view are the two Gentileschi, Orazio and Artemisia, since they both came to England and worked for Charles I. Orazio's *Joseph and Potiphar's Wife* shows his delicate sense of colour, and Artemisia's *Self-portrait* must count as one of her most direct and successful works. The style of the Roman Baroque can be seen in Pietro da Cortona's *Augustus and the Sibyl*, perhaps painted for Philip IV of Spain. Another artist unusually well represented is Domenico Feti, who was court painter to the Gonzagas, and whose works were naturally frequent in the Mantua collection. There are no less than 15 paintings by him at Hampton Court, including a set of half-length figures of saints, an exceptionally fine portrait of Vincenzo Avogadro and a small *Sacrifice of Elijah*, so unusual in style that it was formerly attributed to Aert de Gelder.

The rooms devoted to Italian painting end with two containing works by the Venetian 18th-Century artists, Sebastiano and Marco Ricci. These all came from the collection of Joseph Smith, British

consul in Venice and the friend of Canaletto, which was bought
in 1762 by George III. The two artists, who were uncle and nephew,
seem to have worked mainly in collaboration, Sebastiano executing
the figures and Marco the landscape and architecture. The paintings
at Hampton Court consist of two kinds, first a series of small
sketches, remarkable for their freshness in handling, and secondly
the big finished compositions. We may regret that Smith preferred
Ricci to Tiepolo, whose works he might have bought, but this must
not blind us to the merits of these fine decorations.

The schools of northern Europe do not play a great part in the
collection at Hampton Court, except in the field of portraiture
which has already been dealt with. There are a few interesting
specimens of French art of the 17th Century, including a severely
classical composition by Le Sueur of *Nero depositing the Ashes of
Germanicus*, and two paintings by Vouet, a *Diana* and an early
Caravaggesque portrait.

The most important examples of Flemish painting of the 16th
Century—two panels by Mabuse—have already been referred to,
but these are accompanied by other works of interest. The most
important is a fine version of Pieter Bruegel the Elder's *Massacre of
the Innocents*, of which the original is in Vienna. The Hampton Court
picture must have been executed in the artist's studio, but was un-
happily altered in the 17th Century when the more violent incidents
were painted over so that the murdered children were transformed
into dead animals. Unfortunately, when the picture was cleaned
recently it was found impossible to remove these alterations. The
tradition is carried on into the 17th Century by two typical pictures
of Jan Bruegel the Elder (*Velvet Bruegel*), a *Kermesse* and the *Garden
of Eden*, and ends with dignity with Van Dyck's poetical *Cupid and
Psyche*, painted for Charles I.

Apart from the Holbein *Noli me tangere* already mentioned, German painting can be seen in important works by Lucas Cranach, and
in portraits attributed to Hans Brosamer and Ulrich Apt. One room
is devoted to Dutch painting of the 17th Century, though the
artists represented hardly go beyond the first half of the century,
the most important being Honthorst, Terbrugghen and Jan de
Bray.

Finally, the visitor must not miss the pictures displayed in the Prince of Wales' Rooms, which, though not part of the permanent collection, are among the most interesting exhibits. They consist of Italian and Flemish Primitives normally housed at Buckingham Palace but temporarily deposited at Hampton Court by gracious permission of H.M. the King. These include the most important pictures collected by the Prince Consort between the years 1845 and 1850, that is to say at a time when these schools were almost entirely neglected by connoisseurs. By his insight and independent judgment the Prince Consort was able to acquire fine examples of early 15th-Century Florentine painting, such as Gentile da Fabriano's *Madonna* from the Quaratesi altarpiece, of which the side panels are in the Uffizi, and the little Fra Angelico *St. Peter Martyr*. But, even more remarkably, he bought works of the despised Trecento, Bernardo Daddi's exquisite *Marriage of the Virgin*, and, the masterpiece of the whole group, Duccio's triptych with the Crucifixion. Beside these the Flemish paintings seem to be of not quite the same standard, but they include several 15th-Century works of importance, such as an early copy of Hugo van der Goes' *Coronation of the Virgin*.

Hampton Court Palace has not been used as a royal residence since the reign of George II, but for two hundred years, from the reign of Henry VIII till the middle of the 18th Century, it was regularly inhabited or visited by the Kings and Queens of England. In spite of changes, gradual or violent, which have passed over them, the gardens, the palace and the pictures which it contains still call up with singular completeness the mode of life and the taste of that great period in our history.

The Palace is open daily, except on Sunday mornings, in summer from 10 a.m. to 6 p.m.; in winter 10 a.m. till dusk.

ANTHONY BLUNT,
Surveyor of the King's Pictures.

WINDSOR CASTLE

WINDSOR CASTLE has been one of the principal residences of the Kings and Queens of England since the Norman Conquest. The earliest of the surviving buildings date from the reign of Henry II, but the castle has been continuously altered at later dates, and in the interior at any rate it owes its present appearance more to George IV than to any previous sovereign. There are, however, certain rooms which retain earlier decoration, notably three decorated for Charles II, who restored a great part of the castle and employed the Italian, Antonio Verrio, as his ceiling painter and Grinling Gibbons for his ornamental woodwork. For the rest, however, the rooms are due to Sir Jeffry Wyattville, the architect of George IV, who remodelled the castle between the years 1820–30.

As in most of the Royal Palaces, the pictures fall clearly into two sections: historical portraits, associated with the Kings and Queens of England and their courts, and paintings collected purely for their merits as works of art.

The earliest portrait exhibited at Windsor is one of Louis XII of France, now attributed to Jean Perréal, and almost certainly the actual painting brought over by that artist when he was sent by the French King with the embassy to Henry VIII in 1514 to ask for the hand of Henry's sister Mary.

Henry VIII himself appears in a copy of the central figure of Holbein's destroyed fresco in the palace of Whitehall. Round him is a group of original Holbeins, which are among the great treasures of the castle. Some of these represent members of Henry VIII's court. The third Duke of Norfolk, one of the most powerful nobles of the time, son-in-law of Edward IV, and uncle to two of Henry VIII's queens, appears wearing the Garter chain and holding the insignia of his two offices of Earl Marshal and Lord High Treasurer. In the portrait of Sir Henry Guildford, Comptroller of Henry's Household, Holbein has caught the sitter's arrogant self-confidence, and has given us some of his most exquisite painting in the vine-

14

leaves behind the figure. The third court portrait is more modest and represents William Reskimer, who was a Page of the Chamber in 1532. This simpler and more delicate type of portraiture leads on to the other group which consists of two portraits of German merchants, members of the Hansa Steelyard in London, who were Holbein's best patrons in the years after his arrival in England and before he had gained the favour of the court. These two portraits, of Hans of Antwerp and Derick Born (Pl. 6a), have none of the formal grandeur of the court portraits, but they reveal to the full Holbein's psychological insight and his combination of strict naturalism with linear beauty.

The later Tudor sovereigns are all represented here, Edward VI in an undistinguished portrait by a follower of Holbein, Queen Mary in a free version of the familiar original by Antonis Mor, and Queen Elizabeth in a lovely portrait painted about 1546 before her accession to the throne by an artist whose identity is obscure but whose style was certainly formed in France in the circle of François Clouet, the court painter to Francis I.

Early Stuart portraiture was not in general very distinguished, but its main practitioners can be seen to advantage at Windsor. Queen Anne of Denmark, consort of James I, is the subject of an unusual and interesting painting by Paul van Somer, which depicts the Queen in 1617 standing in front of her palace of Oatlands with a horse and a negro groom and surrounded by five greyhounds. Her son Charles appears as Prince of Wales in a fine full-length by Mytens, and the third painter of the time, Honthorst, is represented by an exceptionally romantic portrait of Charles I's son-in-law, William II of Orange, as a boy. James I himself is depicted in a full-length portrait which hangs in St. George's Hall and may be the earliest English portrait by Van Dyck painted on his short visit to this country in 1621 after an original executed some years earlier by van Somer.

Windsor is, however, principally associated with the portraits painted by Van Dyck when he settled in England in 1632, to remain there with the exception of short journeys till his death in 1641. During the nine years of his stay in England he not only became the favourite painter of the King, but invented a new formula for portraiture which influenced English painting directly for the next half-century and indirectly for a much longer period. He invested Charles himself, his Queen and the members of the court with a restrained elegance and a dignified distinction which to posterity has become an integral part of the vision which is conjured up by this court. How far the King and his courtiers really possessed these qualities and how far they were due to the adroit and subtle flattery of the artist it is now impossible to say, but no portraits can convey as intensely as Van Dyck's the peculiar characteristics of the English gentleman.

At Windsor the full range of Van Dyck during his English period can be seen. His mastery of formal composition is shown in the sketch for the big equestrian portrait of Charles I now in the National Gallery; but the most revealing rendering of the King is the triple portrait (Pl. 4b) painted at the request of Bernini so that he might make a marble bust of the King without having seen him. A similar bust of the Queen was planned and for this Van Dyck painted three separate portraits, two in profile and one full face, two of which are still at Windsor and again convey with intensity the personality of the sitter. Other more formal portraits of the Queen, half-length and full-length, are not entirely from the hand of Van Dyck but their composition is certainly due to him. Van Dyck also painted the King's family, first in 1635 when there were only three children, and again in 1637 when two more had been born.

To these portraits of the Royal Family must be added those depicting members of the court. The two finest of these are straightforward double portraits, one showing the sons of the Duke of Buckingham, and the other Thomas Killigrew and Thomas Carew, poets and wits of the court. Two others of interest are in the allegorical vein, one showing the Duchess of Richmond and Lennox as St. Agnes, and the other Lady Digby as Prudence, a quality in which this lady appears to have been singularly lacking. Van Dyck's portraits painted before he settled in England are naturally rarer in the Royal Collection, but his early style, still influenced by Rubens, can be seen in the *Man with a Ruff* painted while he was working in Genoa, and his manner during the second Antwerp period in the full-length portrait of Béatrice de Cusance, the mistress of Charles, Duke of Lorraine.

Van Dyck's principal successors in England were Dobson and Lely. Dobson who painted supporters of the Royalist cause during the civil wars is responsible for the charming portrait of James II as a boy, and Lely continued the tradition after the Restoration as shown by his characteristic portrait of Prince Rupert. Queen Catherine of Braganza is depicted by Jacob Huysmans in the guise of a shepherdess according to the tradition of pastoral and allegorical portraiture deriving from Van Dyck. The same artist executed the group of James Duke of York, later James II, with his first wife, Anne Hyde, and their children, including the two princesses, later Queen Mary and Queen Anne. From the same period dates a very interesting social document, a portrait by John Riley of Bridget Holmes, who was 'Necessary Woman', that is to say chambermaid, to James II. The artist has shown her at the age of ninety-six wearing her apron and holding a broom, while a page peeps at her from behind a curtain.

Eighteenth-Century portraiture is sparsely represented in the State Rooms at Windsor, but the thread of continuity is maintained by a series in St. George's Hall, in which are depicted the Sovereigns from James I to George IV in Garter robes. With the exception of the James I already mentioned and the Charles I which is by Van Dyck, the pictures are studio versions of portraits of which the originals are in other parts of the Royal Collection. A similar but smaller series is to be found in the Garter Throne Room. This, however, is continued to a later date and ends with a fine pair of full-length portraits of Queen Victoria and the Prince Consort by Winterhalter.

The last important monument of English painting at Windsor, however, is the set of portraits which decorate the Waterloo Chamber. These were painted by Sir Thomas Lawrence at the order of the Prince Regent, and they represent all those who took part in the defeat of Napoleon, either in the political or the military field. After the battle of Leipzig and the abdication of the Emperor many of the great figures engaged in the campaign came to England to visit the Prince Regent, who saw in these visits a fine opportunity of obtaining a record of so distinguished a company. He therefore commissioned Lawrence to paint a series of portraits of his visitors, but this work was soon interrupted by the return of Napoleon from Elba. After Waterloo the project was again taken up and for some years Lawrence visited the various towns of Europe in which Peace Congresses were taking place. He encountered many difficulties, the most considerable being the reluctance of many of his subjects to devote the time necessary to sittings; but finally the portraits were completed and incorporated in the room specially prepared for them by Wyattville, which, however, was not completed till after the death of both George IV and the artist himself.

Lawrence painted his portraits in two sizes, full-length for the Sovereigns, the Pope and the most prominent generals, such as the Duke of Wellington, and small half-lengths for the minor characters in the piece. Most dramatic of all is the vast portrait of Wellington, who has the place of honour in the middle of the gallery facing the principal entrance. For this portrait Lawrence has used a pattern favoured by Van Dyck, for instance in his equestrian portrait of Charles I, and has shown his hero under an arch, though here he appears standing and not on horseback. Among the most effective full-lengths are the portraits of the Emperor Alexander of Russia and the Archduke Charles, both boldly placed against a dramatic background of sky alone. The portrait of Pope Pius VII shows rather the subtle politician than the spiritual head of the church. Among the smaller portraits one of the duc de Richelieu, Foreign Minister of Charles X (Pl.5a), is remarkable for the freedom of its technique, which almost recalls Goya; and that of Count Capo d'Istria is an interesting example of a swaggering type of romantic portrait unusual in Lawrence.

The other pictures in the Castle are more miscellaneous in character than the portraits but in no way inferior in quality. The Picture Gallery contains the earlier paintings, which include two Italian panels of interest, the charming portrait of a lady with a lap-dog by Lorenzo Costa, and an unfinished head of a lady by Andrea del Sarto, unusually strong in its handling. Another picture of particular interest from the historical point of view represents Federico da Montefeltre, Duke of Urbino, and his son Guidobaldo listening to a discourse. It has been attributed to various artists but is now generally thought to be by Justus of Ghent, a Fleming who worked at the court of Urbino. Both Federico and his son were given the Order of the Garter at different times, and in this picture the father is shown wearing the cloak of the Order. It has been plausibly suggested that the artist has depicted the actual presentation of the Garter to the Duke, a ceremony at which the ambassador bringing the Order made an oration to the recipient, in the manner here depicted.

In the same gallery hangs a small group of North European paintings of the 15th and early 16th Centuries, including three portraits of unusual quality: a small head of a man by Dürer painted in 1506 on his second journey to Venice and representing a sitter who appears in the *Feast of the Rose Garlands* (Pl. 6b); a sensitive head by Memlinc; and a half-length of a man holding a copy of Petrarch, one of the very rare oil paintings by Jean Clouet, painter to Francis I and the creator of the series of portrait drawings of members of his court which rival in beauty those made by Holbein at the court of Henry VIII. Among these drawings, the bulk of which are at Chantilly, is a direct study for the picture at Windsor. In the same gallery are a few other Flemish pictures which deserve mention. One is a *Calling of St. Matthew*, by an Antwerp Mannerist of about 1525, which is said to have been taken in the raid on Cadiz by Lord Essex in 1596. The two portraits of the artist and his wife by Joos van Cleef are characteristic of the portraiture practised by the Antwerp school in the first half of the 16th Century. From the same period are two Flemish paintings, both from the Mantua collection, one a triptych by Jan Prevost and the other the popular *Money Lenders* by Marinus Reymerswael, a somewhat caricatural version of a theme treated earlier by Quentin Matsys.

The Dutch school is represented in three early pictures by Rembrandt, two of which came to the Royal Collection from Consul Smith, whose activities as a patron will be mentioned below in connection with the Canalettos. The third is a portrait of the artist's mother, dated 1631, which belonged to Charles I and is probably one of the very first Rembrandts to come to this country. It is a remarkable testimony to the taste of the King that he should have acquired this picture at a time (before 1639) when Rembrandt was still a relatively little-known artist, at least outside Leyden and Amsterdam. A fourth painting, a portrait of a young woman, hanging with these three, was formerly attributed to Rembrandt, but is now thought to be by a skilful imitator of his style in the 1650's.

The other important group of northern paintings at Windsor consists of works by Rubens. In the Picture Gallery are three portraits by him. The most striking is the self-portrait painted in 1623 at the request of Charles I, then Prince of Wales (Pl. 5a). In the swagger of its conception and in the brilliance of its brushwork it must rank with the finest portraits that Rubens ever painted. Similar in format but less spectacular in quality is a portrait which probably represents the artist's sister-in-law, Elizabeth Fourment. Finally, the visitor must not miss the head of Van Dyck by Rubens, a painting which was long thought to be a studio work, because it had been enlarged and repainted. The recent restoration of the picture, however, has shown it to be a fine painting by the master himself.

This series of paintings is continued in the Rubens Room, which is decorated with eight large canvases, all except one being by Rubens. The one exception is the *St. Martin dividing his Cloak*, which was till recently attributed to Rubens but is now recognised as one of Van Dyck's finest early religious compositions, executed when he was still dominated by the influence of the older artist. These paintings were brought together by Frederick Prince of Wales, son of George II and father of George III, who played a considerable part in the formation of the Royal Collection. In addition to acquiring the canvases in the Rubens Room he was responsible for buying several of the English portraits by Van Dyck and for adding to the collection paintings by Claude and drawings by Nicolas Poussin. The variety of Rubens' achievement can be well gauged in the pictures here displayed. The big *Holy Family* is an admirable example of his power as a religious painter; the equestrian portrait of Archduke Albert, painted about 1610, is characteristic of his full-dress formal portraits, and the two landscapes of *Summer* and *Winter* give an idea of his manner in this field, though it is unlikely that they are entirely from his own hand.

The last group of pictures at Windsor to be mentioned consists of a series of 18th-Century Venetian paintings bought by George III with the collection of Joseph Smith. Smith was a wealthy English merchant who lived in Venice from the early years of the 18th Century, and in 1740 became British Consul there. From about 1720 he began to form a library and a collection of paintings, drawings, medals and gems, all of which eventually passed to George III. The library now forms the bulk of the King's Library in the British Museum; the drawings are in the Royal Library at Windsor, and the paintings are scattered in the various palaces. For a time Smith had almost a monopoly of certain contemporary Venetian artists. Between 1724 and 1729 Sebastiano Ricci and his nephew, Marco, executed for him a set of large religious compositions, now at Hampton Court, and among other contemporary artists Smith was also a regular patron of the painter of pastel portraits, Rosalba Carriera, and of Zuccarelli who also came to England and executed for George III a series of landscapes on view at Windsor. But the most important works of this type in his collection were the landscapes by Canaletto. For some twenty-five years Smith seems to have been almost a business manager to the painter, introducing him to English travellers and probably arranging his visit to this country. George III acquired from Smith 53 paintings and over a hundred drawings by Canaletto, most of which are still in the Royal Collection. They cover every phase of the artist's work, though the greater part of them belong to the period before the visit to England in 1746. They include some of his most romantic views of Venice on the grand scale, a series of smaller paintings of the Grand Canal, executed before 1735, and a set of large views of Rome, painted from sketches made many years earlier. Nowhere can the talent of this painter be seen to such advantage as in these works collected, so to speak, at the door of the studio by a personal friend possessed of discriminating taste. It must, however, be said that Smith's selection of Venetian art was strangely one-sided. Incomparably rich in Canaletto and the two Ricci's, it contained only one drawing by Tiepolo and no work by Guardi, though it must be remembered that Guardi in his lifetime was generally held to be no more than a cheap imitator of Canaletto.

A considerable number of Smith's Canalettos are on view in the Queen's Closet. The most popular and probably the earliest is the romantic *View of Murano* (Pl. 4a) which has a freedom of handling and a sense of atmosphere not to be found in the later works. Several small canvases of views on the Grand Canal show Canaletto's familiar manner and remind us that, however much he may have fiddled with topographical detail, his sense of tone remained in control so that the coherence of the spatial design is never lost. Two other pictures are of the type known as *Capricci*, based on a species of witty juxtaposition of unexpected objects. In one the statue of Colleoni is depicted in a setting of ruins which include the Roman arch and one of the tombs of the Scaligers at Verona. In the other the horses of St. Mark are supposed to have been taken down from above the porch of the church and placed on four pedestals in front of it. The views of Rome, however, are topographically accurate in spite of having been executed long after the artist's return to Venice.

Visitors to Windsor will in the course of their tour have the opportunity of seeing much fine furniture and porcelain as well as bronzes and armour. They will also do well to remember that there is always on view a large selection of drawings from the vast collection in the Royal Library. This display is changed from time to time and it is impossible to say exactly what may be on view on a particular occasion. But it is safe to predict that the exhibition will include a selection from the drawings by Leonardo and the portraits by Holbein, in both of which Windsor has no rival. In addition there will certainly be specimens from the important groups by Raphael and Michelangelo, Poussin and Claude, as well as those illustrating the history of drawing in this country, among which we may mention the sketches by Hogarth and the views of Windsor by Paul Sandby.

The State Apartments are shown to the public whenever the court is not in residence, but are closed on Fridays and Sundays. From November to March the Apartments are open from 11 a.m. to 3 p.m.; in April, May and October 11 a.m. to 4 p.m.; from June to September 11 a.m. to 5 p.m.

ANTHONY BLUNT,
Surveyor of the King's Pictures.

KENSINGTON PALACE

KENSINGTON is perhaps the least known, as it is also one of the smallest, of the Royal Palaces, but it is nevertheless full of historical associations. The earlier Nottingham House which stood on this site was bought by William III, who built the new palace which was then at an appreciable distance from London. He also brought to Kensington most of the best pictures in the Royal Collection and Kensington remained the richest of all the palaces in this connection until the time of George III. Queen Anne shared William's affection for Kensington and the first two Georges greatly altered the palace, commissioning William Kent to redecorate the earlier building. His work has survived practically untouched. Finally, Queen Victoria was born at Kensington, spent her early days there and received there the news of her accession.

Some of these associations are reflected in the pictures which are on show at Kensington. The best portraits of William III are to be found in the other palaces, but there are two portraits by Michael Dahl, a Swedish artist who settled in this country, of George of Denmark, husband of Queen Anne. One of these is a large equestrian portrait, painted in 1704, with a view of ships at sea in the distance painted by Van de Velde. There is an attractive portrait by Sir Godfrey Kneller of the young Duke of Gloucester, and Kneller, who is naturally particularly associated with this period, is also represented, not only by more conventional portraits of the Emperor Charles VI and Peter the Great, but also by the very striking *Portrait of a Chinese convert* painted with a striking reminiscence of contemporary Roman portraiture: 'Of all his works', wrote Horace Walpole, 'Sir Godfrey was most proud of the converted Chinese.'

There is also an important group of pictures by Benjamin West, an artist who was greatly admired by George III; the four large heroic canvases of the *Death of Bayard*, the *Death of Epaminondas*, the *Departure of Regulus* and the *Oath of the Young Hannibal* hang in the King's Drawing Room and show clearly how West's classical training in Italy enabled him to satisfy the King's fondness for subjects of a strongly didactic and moralising nature. West's *Death of General Wolfe*, which hangs nearby, is inferior to the version in Ottawa but is a vital document in the development of English history painting.

The Palace is open on Saturday and Sunday afternoons from the Saturday before Easter to the end of October.

ANTHONY BLUNT,
Surveyor of the King's Pictures.

3.a EWORTH   Queen Elizabeth and the Graces   *Hampton Court Palace*

3.b HOLBEIN   Noli me tangere   *Hampton Court Palace*

4.*a* CANALETTO Murano   *Windsor Castle*

4.*b* VAN DYCK Charles I   *Windsor Castle*

THE PALACE OF HOLYROODHOUSE

THE importance of Holyrood lies mainly in its historical and romantic connection with the house of Stuart. It has, however, considerable architectural interest as a palace largely built by James IV and V and then almost completely remodelled by Charles II who employed Sir William Bruce, the Scots architect, for the purpose.

The pictures which are shown in the apartments normally open to the public are, for the most part, portraits of those people most closely connected with the Palace. The great *Trinity Altarpiece* by Hugo van der Goes, which represents James III and his Queen, is on loan to the Scottish National Gallery. Of the portraits of Mary Queen of Scots the most amusing is perhaps the full length by Daniel Mytens which was commissioned by Charles I as a posthumous tribute to his grandmother. An even more fantastic example of the same practice is the remarkable series of 100 Scottish kings painted by Jacob De Wet in 1684. The sitters range from 'Fergus I' to Charles II and are in many cases wholly mythical. There is an interesting full-size version, dated 1562, of Hans Eworth's small double portrait of Lord Darnley and his brother which hangs at Windsor and is dated 1563. Among the later pictures is the large *Arrival of George IV at Holyrood* in 1822 painted by Sir David Wilkie, an artist who was greatly patronised by George IV, primarily because the King's fondness for Dutch painting led him to appreciate Wilkie's own great interest in genre painting.

The State Apartments and the Historical Apartments are open to the public daily, including Sundays.

ANTHONY BLUNT,
Surveyor of the King's Pictures.

II

London and Neighbourhood

THE NATIONAL GALLERY

WHEN we look round at the well-balanced assembly of pictures which decorate the walls of the National Gallery in Trafalgar Square, it is difficult to imagine how inauspicious were the beginnings of the national collection. Commencing life as a hasty gesture of protest, it survived and somehow thrived on the methods of trial and error which have characterised the existence of so many British institutions. Alternately humoured and scolded by the country at large, it was not until the early years of the 20th Century that it attained a position of dignity suitable to its importance in the life of the community.

The formation of the National Gallery owes its inception to Sir George Beaumont, who offered in 1823 to give his fine collection of pictures to the nation, provided that suitable accommodation was found for it by the Government. The Rev. W. Holwell Carr also announced a similar intention. The idea of a National Gallery was not new; Reynolds and Barry had both suggested such a collection. Furthermore, the Bourgeois Bequest to Dulwich in 1814 had given practical shape to the idea. There was, however, powerful opposition at the outset. Constable in one of his more bitter moments had written to Archdeacon Fisher at Salisbury declaring:

> Should there be a National Gallery (which is talked of) there will be an end of the art in poor old England, and she will become, in all that relates to painting, as much a nonentity as every other country that has one. The reason is plain: the manufacturers of pictures are then made the criterion of perfection, instead of nature.

For the moment he seems to have forgotten how much he owed to seeing the fine Claudes and the *Château de Steen* by Rubens, which belonged to Sir George Beaumont. The loan exhibitions organised by the British Institution had also proved their value to British artists and public alike. Sir George Beaumont's offer was further underlined when the matter was mentioned in Parliament in July 1823, for it was revealed that the famous Angerstein collection would be sold during the following year.

Angerstein's collection reached its zenith about 1803 and an evening spent at his gallery was something of an event in the social life of London. The country was therefore momentarily shocked when it was known that under the terms of Angerstein's will the collection was to be dispersed. Furthermore, it became known that it was on offer to the Prince of Orange for £70,000. Though Lord Liverpool's government was struggling with the aftermath of a long and exhausting war, the House of Commons was persuaded to vote £60,000 for 'the purchase, preservation and exhibition of the Angerstein collection'. As a result 38 pictures from the collection became the property of the nation and on May 10th, 1824, the infant National Gallery was opened at 100, Pall Mall, the late owner's house.

The Gallery stood on the south side of Pall Mall where now are Carlton Gardens and part of the Reform Club, and the charge of the premises devolved upon the Treasury, which still controls the Gallery. William Séguier, who was a dealer in partnership with his brother John, was appointed Keeper of the Gallery. Séguier was also Superintendent of the British Institution and had a considerable reputation as a dealer. Until July 2nd Séguier and Colonel Thwaites, the Assistant Keeper and Secretary, held undisputed sway over the Gallery. Then a 'Commitee of Six Gentlemen' was nominated by the Treasury 'to undertake the superintendence of the National Gallery of Pictures and to give such directions as may be necessary from time to time, for the proper conservation of them, to Mr. Séguier, who will be instructed to conform to their orders'. Lords Liverpool, Ripon, Aberdeen and Farnborough with Sir George Beaumont and Sir Thomas Lawrence were nominated. In 1827 the number was increased to eight by the nomination of Lord Dover and Sir Robert Peel.

For the first three and a half years after their appointment the members of the Committee contented themselves with occasional visits to the Gallery and in bestowing such pieces of desultory advice upon the Keeper as happened to occur to them. No meetings were held, nor were any official records kept, but under the terms of his appointment the duty of negotiating the purchase of pictures was placed upon the Keeper. As the collection increased, the powers of the Committee were gradually augmented and the members acquired the title of Trustees. The Angerstein collection which at this time comprised the whole National Gallery was not very strong in Italian painting according to modern standards. The most important Italian pictures were the huge *Raising of Lazarus* by Sebastiano del Piombo (1), the *Venus and Adonis* (34) by Titian and the attractive little *Bacchus playing to Silenus* (94) by Annibale Carracci. France was represented by the fine *Bacchanal* (42) by Nicholas Poussin and five works by Claude. *The Rape of the Sabines* (38) by Rubens, three Van Dycks including the portrait of *Cornelius van der Geest* (52), two Rembrandts and a Cuyp made up the Flemish and Dutch contribution. England was represented by seven Hogarths, including the *Marriage à la Mode* scenes and Reynolds' *Lord Heathfield* (111). During 1825 the Treasury bought *The Madonna of the Basket* by Correggio. This silvery little masterpiece must have come like a breath of fresh air into the rather sombre atmosphere of the national collection. In 1826 the Treasury scored a brilliant success. For £9,000 it bought from Thomas Hamlet the *Domine quo vadis?* (9) by Annibale Carracci, the *Bacchanalian Dance* (62) by Nicholas Poussin and lastly Titian's *Bacchus and Ariadne* (35) (Pl. 10a) a picture of far-reaching importance in the history of painting and one of the glories of the National Gallery.

This was not all, however, for during 1826 Sir George Beaumont fulfilled his promise and handed over his own pictures to the Gallery. The gift included the grand portrait of *A Jew Merchant* (51) by Rembrandt, Canaletto's masterly *View in Venice* (127) and Rubens' *Château de Steen* (66), a keystone in the history of landscape painting. The strength of Beaumont's collection lay in landscape and in addition to the above it included *The Return of the Ark* (64) by Sebastien Bourdon, a landscape attributed to Nicholas Poussin (40) and two works by Richard Wilson. The little *Angel appearing to Hagar* (61) by Claude was returned by the Trustees to the generous donor, at his particular request so that he could enjoy the picture during the rest of his life.

On February 27th, 1828, the Trustees held their first regular meeting, largely owing to the business-like methods of Sir Robert Peel, who had joined the Board in the previous autumn. Three meetings were held this year but it was not until June 1840 that a resolution was passed summoning a meeting on the first Monday of every month during which Parliament was sitting. In the spring of 1828 came the first complaint that the premises in Pall Mall were too small for the collection. The Trustees proposed either adding to the number of rooms in the existing Gallery or the adaptation of part of the King's Mews on what is now the north side of Trafalgar Square. The complaint passed unheeded by the Government, and thereafter until the turn of the century the Trustees became involved in a ceaseless struggle with a reluctant Parliament to find room for the growing collection of the nation's pictures. Successive governments procrastinated and tinkered with the problem until it became chronic.

In September 1830 the Commissioner of Woods and Forests required the demolition of 100, Pall Mall in connection with the widening of Pall Mall Court. The Trustees hunted feverishly about them for new premises and suggested that the most suitable place for a new Gallery was a site left vacant at St. James's Palace which had been partly destroyed by fire. No notice was taken of this suggestion and in 1831 the Trustees approved Wilkins' plan for 'the application of the King's Mews for the reception of the pictures'. Again no notice was taken of the recommendation in spite of some pungent criticism made by members of the public about the heat and dirt in the Gallery and the serious damage done to the pictures. The problem of overcrowding was further aggravated this year by the splendid bequest made by the Rev. William Holwell Carr. This famous collection contained some great treasures including Titian's *Holy Family with Shepherd Boy adoring* (4), Tintoretto's *St. George and the Dragon* (16) and Rembrandt's wonderful *Woman Bathing* (54).

In December 1833 the Commissioner of Woods and Forests dropped another bombshell among the Trustees by announcing that the site adjoining 100, Pall Mall on the west was let for building and that the National Gallery was in danger not merely from lime dust but from undermining. Robert Smirke, the architect of the Carlton Club, added further discomfiture by warning the Gallery

5.a RUBENS Self-portrait   *Windsor Castle*

5.b LAWRENCE Duc de Richelieu   *Windsor Castle*

6.a HOLBEIN Derick Born   Windsor Castle

6.b DÜRER A young man   Windsor Castle

7.*a* HOLBEIN
Christina,
Duchess of Milan
National Gallery

7.*b* JAN VAN EYCK
Jan Arnolfini
and his wife
National Gallery

8.a REMBRANDT Self-portrait *National Gallery*

8.b RUBENS Chapeau de Paille *National Gallery*

Trustees that they would remain in their present quarters at their peril. The collection was hurriedly removed to 105, Pall Mall and reopened to the public on March 3rd, 1834. Nobody was happy, however, and the only hope of a satisfactory solution to the problem lay in the speedy erection of Wilkins' new gallery on the site of the King's Mews, Trafalgar Square. The Mews had been built by William Kent in 1732 and had been demolished in 1830–31. Wilkins' building was commenced in 1833 and was sufficiently completed for the pictures to be removed from 105, Pall Mall by December 1837. There was a further complication, however, because the Royal Academy had to be accommodated in part of the New Gallery in place of the quarters it had vacated at Somerset House. Sir Martin Archer Shee, the President of the Royal Academy and an ex-officio Trustee of the National Gallery, stated his belief that the Academy 'was a much more important institution to the nation than the National Gallery'. The East Wing of the new building was therefore allotted to the Academy and the National Gallery was left with the West Wing. The sharing of the premises was to be a constant source of irritation to both bodies until the Academy moved to Burlington House in 1869.

In 1834 the Treasury bought two works by Correggio, the *Ecce Homo* (15) and the *Mercury instructing Cupid before Venus* (10) for the then enormous sum of £11,500. Contemporary painting was introduced by the gift of three portraits by Lawrence from William IV and in 1837 Constable's *Cornfield* (130) was presented to the nation by a group of his admirers. Lord Blessington also gave *The Graces decorating a Term of Hymen* (79) by Reynolds. At this time the narrow range of choice in the purchase of pictures began to cause comment and in 1836 a Committee of the House recommended that pictures by Raphael and earlier Italian artists should be sought for. No serious notice appears to have been taken of this recommendation for some years after, chiefly owing to the opposition of Sir Robert Peel. Nor did there appear to be any plan for the purchase or historical arrangement of pictures according to schools. In 1837 there took place the last abortive effort to try to retrieve what remained of Sir Thomas Lawrence's wonderful collection of Old Master drawings. Lawrence had offered them to the nation on

most generous terms, but the Government had consistently refused
to provide the necessary money since the owner's death in 1830.
The Trustees recommended the Government in 1837 to buy the
remainder of these fine drawings, but the recommendation was
turned down and the nation lost for ever a collection of drawings
which was one of the finest of its kind in Europe.

The anxieties of the Trustees were not lessened by the move to
Trafalgar Square, and very soon complaints began to arrive as to
the foul atmosphere, the smoke and the deposits of dirt which were
begriming not only the floors but the walls, frames and unglazed
surfaces of the pictures as well. The Gallery staff did their best.
Mr. Séguier went round dusting the frames and polishing the pictures with a handkerchief. He also washed the pictures and oiled and
varnished them as well. When he found that the mastic varnish
'bloomed' he mixed his varnish with oil. The varnish darkened and
the oil did likewise, absorbing as it did so quantities of grime and
dust. Starting as a glowing golden colour it rapidly became deep
in hue and almost opaque.

On November 5th, 1843, Séguier died and was succeeded by
Charles Locke Eastlake, R.A. But meanwhile two or three notable
pictures had been acquired by the Gallery. In 1838 Lord Farnborough had bequeathed the lovely *Landscape; Sunset* (157) by
Rubens and this was followed by the purchase in 1839 of the Gallery's first Raphael, the *St. Catharine of Alexandria* (168). 1842 saw
one of the best bargains ever made for the nation when the Board
purchased Jan Van Eyck's *Portrait of Arnolfini and his wife* (186)
(Pl. 7b), one of the gems of the collection, for £630.

Charles Eastlake, the new Keeper, was an admirable choice.
Although his talents as a painter were not very great, his knowledge
of the history and technique of painting in Italy had already brought
him distinction. In his first season at the Gallery in 1844 he advised
the Trustees to buy the *Doge Loredano* (189) by Giovanni Bellini,
one of the most famous Venetian portraits in the Gallery. At the
same time he recommended another famous picture to the Trustees,
namely the *Madonna and Child with Angels* (809) by Michelangelo.
Eastlake believed that this painting was the work of Ghirlandaio
and suggested that £250 should be offered for it. The price was

refused and the Trustees declined to raise their offer. In 1870 the nation had to pay £2,000 for the picture when it was bought from Lord Taunton.

In 1844 the *Judgment of Paris* (194) by Rubens was acquired for £4,000. Just before the Parliamentary vacation Eastlake raised the question of cleaning some of the dirtiest pictures, which were in a most depressing state, as a result of Séguier's treatment. Cleaning was not the only worry at this time, for in the following year Eastlake published a statement dealing with the unfitness of the Gallery for its purpose and setting out the desirable conditions of a properly constituted Gallery. The remedies put forward were either a considerable enlargement of the existing building or the removal of the collection to some new site where there would be room for expansion. This year saw one of the very few blunders committed by Eastlake, who advised the Trustees to purchase a reputed Holbein *A Medical Professor* (195). Almost immediately the signature was found to be a forgery; the reputation of the Trustees received a further setback by the purchase of yet another Guido Reni, *Susanna and the Elders* (196). By this time the emphasis on the 17th Century was very marked in the national collection and Reni was more than adequately represented. Ruskin described the new purchase as being 'devoid alike of art and of decency'. As a result of the purchase of the forged Holbein the Treasury issued instructions that the Trustees were desired to consult outside authorities as to the condition and desirability of pictures offered to the nation.

During the vacation, 1846, Eastlake cleaned four of the pictures, *Peace and War* (46) by Rubens, *Cattle and Figures* (53) by Cuyp, *Bacchus and Ariadne* by Titian and *The Boar Hunt* by Velasquez. The cleaned pictures were back in their places among their much darkened companions at the end of October when the Gallery was reopened to the public. On October 29th a stinging attack on cleaning appeared in *The Times* over the signature of 'Verax' (J. Morris Moore) followed by another in December on the buying policy of the Trustees. In January 1847 the young Ruskin replied to Morris Moore's abusive attack in more moderate terms. He deplored the personal attacks made on Eastlake, but counselled a modest cleaning of the most discoloured pictures. He attacked the many purchases of works by Guido Reni and appealed for a wider and more representative choice of pictures. He ended:

> Let agents be sent to all the cities of Italy: let the noble pictures which are perishing there be rescued from the invisibility and ill-treatment which their position too commonly implies, and let us have a national collection, which, however imperfect, shall be orderly and continuous, and shall exhibit with something like relative candour and justice the claims to our reverence of those great and ancient builders whose mighty foundation has been for two centuries concealed by wood, hay and stubble, the distorted growing and thin gleaning of vain men in blasted fields.

'Verax' treated Ruskin to a further outburst of vituperation and so the 'row' went on until Eastlake drew up an official report on the cleaning he had carried out and submitted it to the Trustees. The Prime Minister and the Trustees expressed their confidence in the Keeper, but the attacks continued and in November 1847 Eastlake resigned.

He was succeeded by Thomas Uwins, R.A., who was Surveyor of the Queen's Pictures and something of a miniaturist. The new Keeper did not possess the accomplishments of Eastlake and seems to have been somewhat overawed by the Board. Shortly after Uwins' appointment Mr. Robert Vernon's gift of 157 pictures of the English School was received by the Gallery. Once more the Trustees found themselves at their wits' end to find room for them and for the time being they had to leave the pictures at Vernon's house, No. 50, Pall Mall. Urgent representations had been made to the Treasury to secure the bare decencies of security and space but once more procrastination was the order of the day. The Board recommended Pennethorne's plan for enlarging the Gallery, but thirteen years passed before any practical result was forthcoming. In February 1848 a Select Committee of Parliament reported that Wilkins' Gallery lacked space, dignity and elevation and they considered that the solution lay in turning out the Royal Academy and by adding a new front to the Gallery with space at the back for future extensions. Wilkins' building had been adapted from William Kent's design for the Royal Mews and consisted of a single line of rooms from East to West. The Commission recommended that a competition be held for designs of an appropriate monument to

Art. The recommendations were never put into effect, for in 1849 Marlborough House became vacant by the death of Queen Adelaide. The Trustees immediately rushed in and secured the house and in July 1850, the Vernon bequest together with the rest of the British pictures were deposited there.

In 1848 the first Italian Primitives were added to the National Collection, two *Groups of Saints* by Lorenzo Monaco. These panels were the gift of Mr. W. Coningham and at that time were attributed to Taddeo Gaddi. Between 1850 and 1853 the Trustees came under constant criticism on account of the wretched state of the pictures and the question of glazing came up for serious consideration. Very little was done however, though enquiries on the Continent revealed that the Gallery at Dresden was the only one that used glass extensively to protect the pictures.

At about the same time Ruskin offered to negotiate for two great pictures by Tintoretto in Venice *The Marriage at Cana* (Salute) and *The Crucifixion* (S. Cassiano). The proposal was peremptorily declined. The question of space was further aggravated by the great bequest by J. M. W. Turner which had to be disposed of wherever there happened to be room. As a result it was impossible to carry out Turner's instructions that the collection should be kept together. In August 1852 the Trustees consulted John Séguier as to the cleaning of some of the dirtier pictures. During the six weeks' vacation that year, Séguier cleaned 9 pictures which were in position again in the Gallery when the collection was reopened.

Almost at once the outcry against the cleaning of pictures broke out again and early in 1853 William Dyce, R.A., wrote a letter to the Prince Consort in which he criticised the general management of the Gallery in no uncertain terms. He cited the want of system which characterised the actions of the Trustees in administration, their errors of judgment and their failure to build up a collection representing the whole field of painting. Dyce's letter was followed by such a spate of criticism from other directions that the House of Commons appointed a Select Committee to enquire into the affairs of the Gallery. The Committee sat from April until August and the report which was issued in August was a document of real importance in the history of the Gallery. To summarise very briefly: the

Committee reported that the methods of cleaning pictures used by William Séguier were undesirable and they condemned the 'Gallery Varnish' which he had employed. The Committee was unanimous upon the want of method in selecting pictures for the Gallery. There was no proper representation of 15th-Century art and recent buying had laid far too much emphasis on the 17th-Century Bolognese School. The Committee also criticised the doubtful pictures which had been bought and the number of opportunities that had been missed to make the national collection really representative. Lack of co-ordination and divided responsibility for the purchase of pictures was considered to be responsible for most of these faults.

On the subject of the Gallery itself, opinion was unanimous. Foul air, dirt and the continual presence of the 'idle and unwashed' was roundly condemned. The collection was held to be far too large for the five rooms to which it was limited and the Trustees were criticised for their reluctance to claim the rooms occupied by the Royal Academy. In their Report the Committee recommended that the Gallery should be removed to a new site in Kensington Gore. It was further recommended that the Keepership should be abolished and that purchases of pictures should be made on the advice of a properly qualified Director, whose salary should not be less than £1,000 a year. A fixed annual grant should be placed at the disposal of the Trustees for the purchase of pictures.

In 1854 the Chancellor of the Exchequer bought the Kruger collection of early German pictures at Minden. Some of the pictures were later redistributed to Edinburgh and Dublin but the residue still forms the bulk of our representation of German painting previous to 1500. Meanwhile, the affairs of the Gallery continued much as before until in March 1855 it was announced that Sir Charles Eastlake, P.R.A., had accepted the Directorship of the National Gallery. With the Director came the new constitution of the Gallery recommended by the Select Committee. For thirty years the Gallery had been the victim of caprice, subject almost entirely to the will and taste of statesmen and distinguished amateurs. In the place of policy there had been casual selection and desultory method.

Eastlake's tenure of office is one of the great periods in the history of the Gallery. He wielded complete authority in administration, and his decision as to the buying of pictures was final. The Trustees became a body whose function it was to make liaison between the Gallery and the Government and to keep in contact with all lovers of art. The Director was also assisted by R. N. Wornum as Keeper and Secretary and a travelling agent, Otto Mündler, was appointed to tour Europe in search of suitable pictures. From this time forward methodical records were kept of the activities of the Gallery staff and the Director's Annual Reports furnish a continuous and useful source of information which had been lacking in the previous years of the Gallery's existence.

But Eastlake left his mark on the Gallery even more clearly by his fine and independent taste. Like the Prince Consort, to whose support he owed much, he admired the Italian Schools of the 14th and 15th Centuries, the merits of which were still not generally recognised. It was due to his initiative that the National Gallery began to acquire works of this type at a time when they could be acquired for a fraction of their present value.

1855 was an auspicious year. Samuel Rogers bequeathed three Italian pictures to the nation, which included Titian's fine *Christ and the Magdalen* (270) and Giorgione's little *Knight in Armour* (260). Eastlake himself toured Italy and came back with Botticelli's *Madonna and Child* (275), the *Madonna* (274) by Mantegna, Veronese's *Adoration of the Magi* (268), the Bellini *Madonna* (280) and Benozzo Gozzoli's *Madonna with Angels and Saints* (283). In 1856 works by Perugino, Antonio Pollaiuolo and Filippino Lippi were added to the national collection. Towards the end of this year the Court of Chancery finally delivered all the Turner pictures and drawings to the Gallery. The bequest consisted of 283 oil paintings and some 19,049 drawings and sketches.

Eastlake's energy in buying pictures quickly led to a crisis in accommodation. The recommendations of the Commission of 1853 for rebuilding the Gallery had gone the same way as all previous suggestions for the rapidly growing collection. Eastlake seems to have had some idea of a separate gallery for Modern Art, somewhat on the lines of the Luxembourg, but he was thinking too far ahead of his time.

Early in 1857 negotiations were concluded for the purchase of Veronese's *Family of Darius before Alexander* (294) for £13,650. Eastlake and Mündler were responsible for the transaction and there was an immediate outcry in the House of Commons. Lord Elcho declared that the country was paying an enormous price for a second-rate specimen of a second-rate artist, and he added later that the picture would not fetch £2,500 under the hammer. However, all criticism was suddenly stilled when Lord Palmerston disclosed that Napoleon III had been on the point of offering a good deal more than £13,650. As a result of this purchase Parliament abolished the post of 'travelling agent', much to Eastlake's disgust. Otto Mündler did his work thoroughly well but the House of Commons signally failed to see how useful he was and he was dismissed.

The winter of 1857–58 saw one of Eastlake's most brilliant successes in his acquisition of the Lombardi-Baldi collection of 22 pictures for £7,035. In a single transaction examples of the earlier phases of Italian painting were added to the Gallery and a great gap was closed. Margaritone, Agnolo di Taddeo Gaddi and Orcagna are some of the names included in the collection, but perhaps the gem of the whole array is Uccello's *Rout of San Romano* painted for the Medici Palace in Florence. The next year Eastlake continued his success by acquiring such works as Cossa's *St. Vincent Ferrer* (597), Giovanni Bellini's *Madonna of the Meadow* and a *Pietà* (602) by Carlo Crivelli. In an effort to find room for these great purchases the Vernon and Turner pictures were removed to a room adjoining the South Kensington Museum and screens were provided at Trafalgar Square for the exhibition of small pictures.

In 1860 Eastlake purchased the Beaucousin collection in Paris. Among the 46 pictures in this collection were Titian's *Madonna and S. Catherine* (635) and Bronzino's *Venus, Cupid, Folly and Time* (651) but more important from the point of view of the Gallery was the strength of the collection in early Flemish work. Rogier van der Weyden's *Reading Magdalen* (654), two portraits by Robert Campin and the *Death of the Virgin* (658) possibly by Hugo van der Goes helped to strengthen a weak section in the Gallery. The acquisition of *The Entombment* (664), a rare work in tempera on linen by Dirk Bouts perhaps after a design by Rogier van der

Weyden, added further lustre to the Flemish collection. The predella panels representing Christ surrounded by angels and saints (663) by Fra Angelico were also procured with considerable difficulty. The highlight of 1861 was the buying of Piero della Francesca's *Baptism* (665) (Pl. 9*b*) for £241, the Rembrandt *Self Portrait* (672) and Antonello da Messina's *Salvator Mundi* (673).

In October 1861, in order to try to fulfil the terms of Turner's will, his pictures were moved back to Trafalgar Square and 100 of them were crowded into one room by the device of substituting narrow gilt flats for the existing frames. 1862 and 1863 saw further additions to the Gallery including Reynolds' *Captain Orme* (681) and Gainsborough's masterly portrait of Dr. Schomberg, M.D. (684) in the former year and Giovanni Bellini's *Agony in the Garden* (726) and Crome's *Mousehold Heath* (689) in the latter. The newly discovered Pettenhofer process of renewing varnish was also used upon several pictures in the Gallery during 1864 and during the same year Lord Taunton presented Crivelli's *Annunciation* (739). In June 1865 Eastlake was re-appointed for a further term of five years as Director, but during his usual autumn tour for the Gallery he was taken ill at Milan and died at Pisa on December 24th. Just before his illness he had crowned his years of office as Director by purchasing Velasquez' *Philip IV* (745), a Ruisdael (746) and the lovely little *Garvagh Madonna* by Raphael (744). Eastlake's achievements as Director were remarkable. Not only was he an able and far-sighted administrator, but he had taste and imagination as well. Of the 139 pictures which he bought for the Gallery, nearly all were real masterpieces and he raised the general status of the collection to a position of importance in Europe.

The accommodation at Trafalgar Square at the end of 1865 was once more hopelessly overcrowded. The Trustees did their best in the face of governmental indifference to find room for the constantly growing collection of pictures, but at every turn they met procrastination and objections. The nation apparently had no policy for housing its great collection of paintings. But after various projects had been proposed it was decided in 1868 that the Academy should turn out and E. M. Barry was asked to prepare designs for rebuilding the Gallery in Trafalgar Square.

Meanwhile, in 1866 William Boxall, R.A., succeeded Eastlake as Director. He was well liked by everybody who had anything to do with him and was a widely travelled man with many friends among the artistic and literary circles of the day. His first purchases for the Gallery included the lively *Portrait of a Lady* (758), now attributed to Baldovinetti. He next bought for £7,000 *Christ blessing Little Children* (757) which he believed to be by Rembrandt. It was soon recognised to be only a school piece and Boxall was too harshly criticised for his purchase. In 1867 the Gallery acquired on very favourable terms from Lady Eastlake a number of pictures from Sir Charles Eastlake's private collection. Most of them were Italian but among them were the *Madonna Enthroned* (774) by Dirk Bouts, and the fine *Portrait of an Old Lady* (775) by Rembrandt. Lady Eastlake herself presented Pisanello's *SS. George and Anthony* (776). 1868 was made memorable by the purchase of Michelangelo's *Entombment* (790) for £2,000 and in the same year the nation's collection of Crivelli's became unrivalled by the acquisition of the Demidoff altarpiece (788).

By February 8th, 1869, the Royal Academy had left the Gallery, though the Academy Sculpture Hall and the remaining ground-floor rooms in the East Wing were not cleared until some years later. The Trustees were so elated at this sudden access of elbow-room, that after rehanging the Gallery during March and April, they immediately applied for a large selection of pictures from Hampton Court. Fortunately the Queen somewhat stiffly declined the application. In a very short time the congestion in the Gallery once more became chronic. Pictures were still being acquired steadily by gift and purchase and among the principal acquisitions in 1870 were Michelangelo's *Holy Family with Angels* (809) and Lady Eastlake's gift of the *Death of S. Peter Martyr* (812) by Giovanni Bellini. In 1871 the Peel collection was bought for £75,000 by means of a Special Grant from the Treasury. Out of a total of 77 pictures, 55 were Dutch, 12 Flemish; the remaining 10 consisted of 8 Reynolds, 1 Lawrence and 1 Wilkie. Sir Robert Peel's interest lay primarily in Dutch painting and although he was not a great connoisseur he could appreciate meticulous workmanship and 'purity'. His Dutch pictures, therefore, not only made the national collection very strong in this branch of painting, but also made it remarkable for the quality and condition of the pictures. Among the Dutch pictures *The Avenue, Middleharnis* (830) (Pl. 11*a*) by Hobbema, *The Interior* (834) and *The Courtyard* (835) by Pieter de Hooch are outstanding. The Flemish pictures contained among others Rubens' *Chapeau de Paille* (852) (Pl. 8*b*) and the glowing *Triumph of Silenus* (853) by Rubens and Van Dyck.

On May 20th, 1872, the foundations of Barry's new East Wing were laid. A year later Boxall made his last great purchase *The Triumph of Scipio* (902) by Mantegna; early in 1874 he retired from the Directorship. His acquisitions for the Gallery were by no means negligible and the brilliant purchase of the two panels by Michelangelo far outweigh his error in the case of the Rembrandt in 1866.

Boxall was succeeded by Frederick William Burton in February 1874. In June of the same year he purchased 14 important pictures at the Alexander Barker sale, which included Botticelli's *Mars, Venus and Satyrs* (915) and works by Vivarini, Tura and Pintoricchio. In addition he acquired Piero della Francesca's *Nativity* (908) at the same sale largely at the instigation of Disraeli. The Wynn Ellis Bequest came to the Gallery at the close of 1875. Ninety-four pictures out of some 400 were selected by Burton and exhibited during the next year. Among them were Filippino Lippi's *Angel Adoring* (927), Canaletto's *Scuola di San Rocco* (937) and Antonio Pollaiuolo's *Apollo and Daphne* (928). The purchases this year included three portraits by Moroni and a fine Moretto (1025). Burton also bought the Gallery's first Frans Hals the *Portrait of a Woman* (1021) for the astonishing sum of 100 guineas. The merits of Hals were not generally appreciated at this time.

August 1876 saw the opening of E. M. Barry's additions, which added seven new rooms to the Gallery. At this time the Gallery consisted of the long strip of rooms virtually one room deep, which lay behind Wilkins' façade, and Barry's square block at the east end, comprising the dome and its four crossings with Rooms VII, IX and X. Immediately behind Wilkins' building lay St. George's Barracks, which was to cause endless friction between the Trustees and the Government during the next twenty-four years. On the completion of Barry's rooms the British pictures which had been sent to South Kensington in 1859 were brought back to Trafalgar Square. Before the end of the year it was estimated that some 670,000 people had visited the Gallery. Meanwhile, pictures were still being acquired steadily and Burton was maintaining the high standard which he had set at the outset of his career at the Gallery. In 1878 Botticelli's *Nativity* (1034) and the circular *Adoration of the Kings* (1033) were acquired from the Fuller Maitland collection and from the Novar sale came Veronese's *S. Helena* (1041). The year 1880 was notable for the purchase of Leonardo da Vinci's *Madonna of the Rocks* (1093) (Pl. 9*a*) from Lord Suffolk for £9,000.

The next notable landmark was the National Gallery Loan Act of 1883, which enabled the Trustees, after a certain period, to lend works given or bequeathed to the nation. It gave a further respite to the Trustees, who were once more faced with the problem of overcrowding among the pictures, for they forthwith released a flood of less-important pictures upon the provincial galleries. It was the only expedient they could adopt, as the Government refused to commit itself to further extensions to the Gallery. In 1882 no less than 22 pictures were bought. They included works by Cotman, Ercole Grandi, Signorelli, Tintoretto and Pontormo and, more surprisingly, Blake and El Greco whose merits were at that time unrecognised; but the outstanding acquisition was the full length *Philip IV* (1129) by Velasquez from the Hamilton sale. *Christ at the Column* (1148) by Velasquez was bequeathed to the nation by Sir John Savile Lumley in 1883. Among the purchases in the same year were Andrea dal Castagno's sombre little *Crucifixion* (1138), two panels by Duccio (1139) and (1140) and the *Portrait of a Man* (1141) by Antonello da Messina. In 1884 Burton distinguished himself by negotiating for a group of 12 pictures at Blenheim, which included the *Ansidei Madonna* by Raphael, Van Dyck's *Charles I* and 7 large Rubens. After considerable bargaining the Raphael and the Van Dyck were bought for £87,500, but the sum was so large that the Government stopped the annual Grant-in-Aid of £10,000 for the next two years and only restored it gradually. During 1884 Matteo di Giovanni's *Madonna of the Girdle* (1155), *The Crucifixion* (1166) by Antonello, and Hogarth's popular *Shrimp Girl* (1162) (Pl. 12*b*) were also bought for the Gallery.

Fortunately in this year the Government made up its mind to undertake the extension of the Gallery. The work was entrusted to Sir John Taylor, who designed the new central staircase, the vestibules at the top and Rooms I, II, III, V and VI. This new extension which was completed in 1885 entailed the demolition of Pennethorne's long room which had been built in 1866 on the site now occupied by the main staircase. However, the Trustees had learnt by bitter experience and informed the Treasury at once that the new rooms could only be regarded as a temporary alleviation of the problem. In fact, it was another twenty years before the Treasury could persuade the War Office to remove the St. George's Barracks and so provide the necessary room for further expansion behind Wilkins' façade. Three important gifts were made to the Gallery in 1886, Constable's *Haywain* (1207) by Mr. Henry Vaughan, Domenico Veneziano's *Madonna* (1215) by Lord Crawford, and Spinello's *Fall of the Rebel Angels* (1216) by Sir Henry Layard. The purchases for the year included Gentile Bellini's *Mathematician* (1213), Ercole di Roberti's *Israelites gathering Manna* (1217), and Rossetti's *Ecce Ancilla Domini* (1210). 1887 saw the purchase of Giovanni Bellini's *Blood of the Redeemer* (1233) and the gift by Miss Isabel Constable of three sketches by her father followed in the next year by the *Cenotaph* and *The Glebe Farm*.

By 1889 the normal Grant-in-Aid had been restored to the Gallery and in 1890 three important pictures were acquired from Longford Castle, Holbein's *Ambassadors*, *Admiral Pulido Pereja* by Velasquez and the *Italian Nobleman* (1316) by Moroni. Lord Rothschild, Sir Edward Guinness and Mr. Charles Cotes each contributed £10,000 to the purchase price of £55,000. Burton also bought Tintoretto's *Origin of the Milky Way* and *Unfaithfulness* by Veronese. Vermeer's *Lady at a Spinet* (1383) and Hogarth's portraits of his servants (1374) were the outstanding purchases of 1892. Sir Frederick Burton retired in 1894 after having been Director for twenty years and with his retirement there passed the great era when masterpieces could still be acquired with comparative frequency. Germany had by now become a formidable competitor on the Continent and American buyers were beginning to make their presence felt in this country. Burton had continued the fine example set by Sir Charles

Eastlake and in spite of the shrinking market had bought 180 foreign pictures for the nation. Nearly three-quarters of his purchases still rank among the finest things in the Gallery.

Meanwhile the Trustees had been carrying on disheartening negotiations with the Government for the provision of a further extension to the Gallery. The St. George's Barracks still remained and to the vexation of the Trustees the Government had given part of the site to the National Portrait Gallery in 1889. The deadlock was eventually broken in 1900 by a fire which broke out in a shop situated between the Gallery and Hamptons. The appalling danger to which the national collection had been exposed aroused an immediate outcry in Parliament and the Press, which led to the final demolition of the barracks in 1901. Although the site was now cleared the Treasury still pursued a policy of masterly inactivity and it was not until the end of 1907 that a further set of five rooms was completed behind the West Wing of the Gallery.

On April 26th, 1894, Edward John Poynter, R.A., succeeded Sir Frederick Burton as Director. His powers were not so great as those of his predecessors, for by a Treasury Minute of the same date as his appointment the position of the Director was somewhat altered. Competition for available pictures was already keen, and criticism of the Gallery became extremely bitter when Rembrandt's *Preacher Ansloo* went straight from the Ashburnham collection to Berlin in 1894. There seemed to be no policy for retaining masterpieces in this country. In his first year Poynter bought Mantegna's *Agony in the Garden* (1417), Antonello's *S. Jerome* (1418) and the Flemish *Legend of St. Giles* (1419) but these admirable purchases were overshadowed by public anxiety as to the probable fate of many famous pictures in private collections.

In the same year two Rembrandts (Nos. 1674 and 1675) were bought from Lord de Saumarez. These were followed by Alfred Stevens' portrait of Mrs. Collmann (1775) in 1900. Sir Edward Poynter retired at the end of 1904 but before he left the Gallery he acquired Dürer's *Portrait of his Father* (1938), a picture which came in for a great deal of severe criticism, Titian's so-called *Ariosto* (1944) an early work, and Hogarth's portrait of *James Quin* (1935). The year 1905 was also interesting for the rediscovery at the Gallery of a beautiful group of unfinished oil sketches by Turner. In November 1905 the country was shocked to discover that the 'Rokeby' *Venus* (2057) (Pl. 10*b*) by Velasquez was already at a dealer's awaiting sale to the highest bidder. A wave of indignation fell upon the heads of the Trustees who were still without a Director. Fortunately assistance was at hand in the form of the National Art Collections Fund, which had been founded in 1903 for the specific purpose of rescuing important works of art for the nation. The Fund recognised at once that the 'Rokeby' *Venus* was a picture which must at all costs be secured for the country. By a great effort £45,000 was raised and this unique example of the work of Velasquez was saved for the nation.

In 1906 Sir Charles Holroyd was appointed Director of the National Gallery. He had made a reputation for himself as the first Keeper of the Tate Gallery, which had been opened in 1897. Much of his period of office was clouded by the ever-present threat of important pictures leaving the country. The Treasury grant for buying pictures amounted to £5,000 a year, a sum quite inadequate in view of the great increase which was taking place in the price of pictures. The Gallery received the magnificent Temple West bequest of £99,000 in 1907, which provided much-needed financial assistance. In 1909 another crisis arose. Holbein's *Christina Duchess of Milan* (2457) (Pl. 7*a*) was in imminent peril of being lost to the nation. Once more the National Art Collections Fund came forward to help, but on this occasion the public response was disappointing and for some months it seemed as if the picture could not be saved. The National Gallery was unable to help as in 1908 it had obtained a special grant and had pledged future income in order to buy the Frans Hals *Family Group* (2285). At the last moment Holbein's *Christina* was saved by a wonderful gift of £40,000 to the National Art Collections Fund by an anonymous lady. In 1910 Mr. George Salting bequeathed 192 pictures of all Schools to the Gallery and the Trustees purchased Crome's *Poringland Oak* (2684). Lord Carlisle, who had been a Trustee of the Gallery for thirty years, died in 1911 and the Gallery bought the Castle Howard Mabuse (2790) from the Dowager Countess for £40,000.

For some years the Board of Trustees had been subjected to severe criticism because they appeared to have no policy for stemming the drain of masterpieces from this country to the Continent. In the same year that the Board had bought the Castle Howard Mabuse, the Bowood *Mill* by Rembrandt came up for sale. It was generally accepted that there were in this country some 12 or 15 pictures of the highest importance which ought to be saved at all costs, as they could never be replaced. In this group were the Bridgwater Titians and the Bowood *Mill*. The price required to save the *Mill* was £95,000 and to everybody's consternation it was found that there was no provision of any kind to meet the emergency. The 'Rokeby' *Venus* (2057), the Hals portrait group (2285) and Holbein's *Christina* (2457) had been saved at the eleventh hour by private benefactions and special Government grants. This time the price was too high for the nation to subscribe and the *Mill* went to the United States. A committee of the National Gallery Trustees was thereupon set up to enquire into 'The Retention of Important Pictures in this Country and other matters connected with the National Collections'. The Committee under the chairmanship of Lord Curzon began its sittings in the winter of 1912 and sat for two years, covering a very wide field of enquiry. The finances of the Gallery, its administration, the drain of masterpieces from the country, export duties and taxes on art sales and the opinions of experts, were among the subjects discussed which affected particularly the National Gallery. In its report the Committee made a number of important recommendations for the retention of masterpieces in this country. The National Gallery Picture Purchase Grant was to be raised from £5,000 to £25,000 a year, and in cases of emergency the Treasury were to be asked for extraordinary grants.

Among other far-reaching recommendations were the formation of a Gallery of Modern Foreign Art, the conversion of the Tate Gallery into a Gallery of British Art analogous to the Luxembourg and the institution of a separate Board of Trustees for the Tate. Since its foundation the Gallery at Millbank had been administered by the National Gallery Trustees. Unfortunately the publication of the Committee's report took place at the beginning of the 1914–18 war and the recommendations had to await a more favourable moment.

In 1913 Lady Carlisle allowed the Trustees to make a choice of some of her finest pictures, and six masterpieces were acquired for the Gallery including Rubens' *Landscape with a Shepherd* (2924) and Barnaba da Modena's *Triptych* (2927). The Countess presented the *Portrait of Arundel* (2968) by Rubens in the following year. During the Gallery's existence the pictures had been subjected to many vicissitudes but they had not suffered deliberate physical violence. In March 1914, however, the 'Rokeby' *Venus* was attacked by Suffragettes and as a result the Gallery was closed for two weeks. In May of the same year the Suffragettes attacked five Bellinis: this time the damage was more serious and the Gallery was closed indefinitely. The advent of war caused the Suffragettes to abandon their campaign of violence and on August 20th the Gallery was once more re-opened to the public. In view of the possibility of air attacks arrangements were at once made with the Office of Works to disperse about 700 of the most important pictures in places of safety. Batches of pictures were removed to the tunnels of the Underground Railways in London, to Cheltenham Art Gallery and to Lady Wantage's house at Lockinge. Half of the National Gallery premises were then taken over by the Government for offices. In 1916 Sir Charles Holroyd, with the aid of the National Art Collections Fund, made his last great purchase for the Gallery. This was the majestic *Madonna and Child* (3046) by Masaccio, the central panel of an altarpiece painted by the master for the Church of the Carmine in Pisa in 1426. Sir Charles Holroyd resigned in June 1916 owing to ill health and was succeeded by Mr. Charles John Holmes, the Director of the National Portrait Gallery, an ex-Slade Professor at Oxford, and a member of the New English Art Club. The Florence bequest of £10,000 and a number of pictures took place in 1916 and Sir Henry Layard's bequest of 67 pictures in 1894 also matured. This resulted in examples of work by Gentile Bellini and Carpaccio being added to the national collection. Other events included the purchase of Rembrandt's early *Philosopher* (3214) and the much-disputed bequest of modern foreign pictures by Sir Hugh Lane which included Renoir's *Les Parapluies* (3268).

1918 was remarkable for the most courageous action ever taken by Parliament on behalf of the National Gallery. Although grappling with one of the greatest crises of the war the Government made a special grant for purchases at the Degas Sale in Paris. The result was that for the first time examples of work by Ingres, Delacroix and Manet were procured for the national collection. In 1919 H.M. the King graciously lent to the Gallery his panel of the Pesellino Altarpiece (727) to be re-united to the panels already in the Gallery, as well as a fine *Madonna and Child* by Gentile da Fabriano. Among the more sensational purchases of the year was El Greco's *Agony in the Garden* (3476), a picture which strengthened the Spanish collection. During the year a number of pictures of the British School were transferred to the Gallery at Millbank.

The purchase of Pieter Brueghel's *Adoration of the Kings* (3556) in 1921, an unusual example of the painter's work, did something to fill a serious gap in Flemish painting. In 1922 the incisive *Portrait of a Man* (3604) by Lucas van Leyden was presented in memory of the Rt. Hon. Lewis Fry and a *Madonna and Child* (3664) by Quentin Massys was given by Mr. Charles Clarke. The Trustees bought Van Dyck's *George and Francis Villiers* (3605) from Lady Lucas, a fine example of the artist's last phase.

The important bequest of Dr. Ludwig Mond was received in May 1923 on the death of Mrs. Mond. This included the early Raphael *Crucifixion* (3943), the very late Titian *Mother and Child* (3948), two Botticelli's of the *Life of St. Zenobius* (3918, 3919) and the Pietà by Giovanni Bellini (3912). Among interesting purchases in 1925 were the *Legends of St. Benedict* (4062) by Lorenzo Monaco, the *Nativity* (4081) by Geertgen Tot Sint Jans and the *Meeting of Joachim and Anna* (4092) by the Maître de Moulins. Bequests included *The Lesson* (4077) and *House of Cards* (4078) by Chardin, which added welcome strength to 18th-Century French painting.

In 1928 Sir Charles Holmes retired from the Directorship and was succeeded by Sir Augustus Daniel. In the next year two outstanding purchases were made. The first was the *Wilton Diptych* (4451), a lovely example of French or possibly English work of the late 14th Century, procured by a special grant-in-aid and by generous contributions from the National Art Collections Fund,

Lord Duveen, Mr. Samuel Courtauld, Lord Rothermere and Mr. C. F. Stoop. The second acquisition was the great *Vendramin Family* (4452) by Titian, purchased by a special grant-in-aid and by contributions by Lord Duveen, Mr. Samuel Courtauld and the Claude Phillips Bequest. An interesting event of 1930 was the reconstruction of the *Holy Trinity and Saints* by Pesellino. The four panels owned by the Gallery were joined to that lent by H.M. the King; the missing part was filled in by a reconstruction by Professor Tristram and the original predella was lent by Mr. Felix Warburg.

Sir Augustus Daniel retired in 1934 and Sir Kenneth Clark succeeded him as Director. The full-size oil sketch of *Hadleigh Castle* (4810), one of Constable's most impetuous works, was bought by the Gallery in 1935. There were two other notable purchases during the year; the *Crowning with Thorns* (4744) by Jerome Bosch which did something to fill another gap in the Flemish collection and scenes from the life of St. Francis (4737–4763) by the 15th-Century Sienese master Sassetta. A fine full-length Gainsborough of the 10th Viscount Kilmorey (4777) was also bought. The gifts included an attractive portrait group by Hogarth, *The Graham Children* (4756), a good example of the artist's technical qualities.

1936 was remarkable for a violent controversy which broke out over the cleaning of Velasquez' full-length portrait of Philip IV in brown and silver (1129). The correspondence began in the *Daily Telegraph* but was soon taken up in *The Times*. By March 1937 more than fifty letters and a dozen articles had been published on the subject. In 1936 Mr. Gulbenkian deposited on loan his fine collection of pictures, which included examples of many great European schools of painting from the 15th to the 19th centuries. Among the bequests of 1937 were two important works by Filippino Lippi, *Moses causes water to flow from the Rock* (4904) and *The Worship of the Golden Calf* given by Sir Henry Bernard Samuelson.

In the years immediately preceding 1939 the probability of international conflict grew ever more obvious and the safety of the national collection became a matter of first-rate importance. In the 1914–18 war it had been rightly considered prudent to evacuate the pictures. The danger of aerial bombardment in any future war was almost certainly going to be far greater and the damage caused would be on a much larger scale. Consequently a number of steps were taken to facilitate a rapid and complete evacuation of the 2,000 pictures in the Gallery. It was considered that partial evacuation of the most valuable works would not be satisfactory as it would entail an arbitrary selection among paintings which were nearly all masterpieces. Arrangements were made to move the whole collection to North and West Wales. Hospitality was offered and gratefully accepted at the National Library of Wales at Aberystwyth, at the University College of North Wales at Bangor, and at Penrhyn Castle; further dispersion was also carried out subsequently in country houses elsewhere.

The Munich crises in 1938 provided an opportunity to put into effect the arrangements which had been worked out for evacuating the Gallery; two loads of pictures were in fact despatched from London but were returned without being unpacked on the easing of the crisis. During the period between September 1938 and the outbreak of war in 1939 further improvements were made to the arrangements; in the closing days of August 1939 the plan for evacuation was once more translated into action. On August 23rd the first load of pictures left Trafalgar Square and by September 2nd the Gallery was clear. Routes and time-tables had been carefully prepared by the railway companies so that there should be no delay in getting clear of London. These were anxious days for the staff, because although war had not yet been declared there was always the possibility of sudden air attack to be reckoned with.

The temporary homes provided for the pictures in Wales presented a number of difficulties. The size of some of the pictures made not only transport a problem but also accommodation of a suitable nature. Two most important factors in the life of any picture, namely temperature and humidity, had to be given special attention in the temporary resting places provided for the collection: in 1940 the fall of France produced fresh problems. Air raids became widespread and enemy aircraft in considerable numbers passed over Bangor on their way to Merseyside. The danger that bombs might be dropped haphazard on or near the buildings where the pictures were stored became very real. After still further dispersal of the pictures the Trustees decided that if possible underground storage must be provided for the pictures. After considerable enquiry Manod Slate Quarry near Blaenau Festiniog was selected as providing the most suitable refuge. Not only did it provide sufficient accommodation but in addition the quarry had a road leading to it. The owners and manager readily agreed to let the National Gallery have the whole of one floor, but there were a number of physical difficulties to be overcome. It was necessary to enlarge the entrance to the quarry very considerably so that the lorries carrying the pictures could drive in and unload. Most of the floors of the quarry had to be levelled and this entailed blasting away many tons of rock; then buildings had to be erected in the caves inside the quarry so that suitable conditions of atmosphere could be provided for housing the pictures. The manager of the quarry and the Ministry of Works carried out all this work within the space of nine months and installed the necessary electrical equipment for power, lighting and air conditioning. Library accommodation was provided and a daylight studio was installed where a number of important pictures were cleaned. The whole of the National Gallery was moved from its dispersed places of refuge to Manod Quarry by the end of the summer of 1941 and remained there in security under excellent atmospheric conditions for four years.

Meanwhile the National Gallery building in Trafalgar Square which had been closed on the outbreak of war was reopened in October 1939 and the lunch-time concerts, which became such a feature of war-time London, were commenced. The concerts which were organised by Dame Myra Hess and Sir Kenneth Clark were held daily from Monday to Friday until April 1946. A canteen was also established and became such a popular feature that after the war a café was introduced as a permanent institution at the Gallery. In 1940 the first of a series of special exhibitions took place in the Gallery; some of them were organised in association with C.E.M.A. and the R.I.B.A. The Tate Gallery also held a number of exhibitions at the Gallery. The War Artists Advisory Committee held a continuous exhibition at the Gallery throughout the war years, the pictures being constantly changed as fresh examples of the work of war artists was produced. From March 1942 some of the famous pictures belonging to the national collection were brought to Trafalgar Square singly from Wales and were exhibited for three weeks at a time. 'The Picture of the Month' as it became known, was an immediate success, and the arrangement was continued until the first pictures returned to the Gallery after the war. Nine bombs fell within the precincts of the Gallery and the damage to glass and ceilings by shrapnel was heavy. The eastern half of the building escaped serious structural damage but a bomb which exploded in the foundations of the western half destroyed one gallery completely with the floors beneath it and put out of action almost all the Reference Section. Other parts of the Gallery also suffered considerable damage, especially to the roofs.

From 1938 onwards the Director and Trustees continued to acquire a number of important pictures and this activity continued throughout the war. In 1938 Rembrandt's *Flora* was purchased with the aid of the National Art Collections Fund and in 1941 *Margaretha Tripp* by the same artist was presented by the National Art Collections Fund. *A Bacchanalian Scene* by Dosso Dossi was bequeathed by Sir Lionel Faudel Phillips in 1941. *Pentecost*, attributed to the Studio of Giotto, was bequeathed to the nation by Mrs. G. E. Coningham and Titian's *Portrait of a Lady* was presented by Sir Francis Cook, through the National Art Collections Fund in 1942. *Four Scenes from the Life of S. John the Baptist* by Giovanni di Paolo were bought with the aid of the National Art Collections Fund in 1944. Nicholas Poussin's *Annunciation* was presented by Mr. E. C. Norris in the same year.

In 1944 plans were prepared for the return of the National Gallery to Trafalgar Square from Wales and during V.E. week the first two containers of pictures selected by Sir Kenneth Clark were despatched to London. By the Saturday following V.E. day some 50 pictures were once more on view to the public. By the first week in December 1945 everything had been safely returned to Trafalgar Square. The state of the Gallery was such that only a representative collection of pictures could be exhibited and in 1946 plans for the restoration of the building were agreed upon. It was decided that the Galleries in the East Wing should be restored as quickly as possible. Between December 1945 and October 1947 the Ministry of Works carried out the necessary repairs and reglazing of the eastern half of the building including the entrance vestibule and its dome. The more severely damaged West Wing presented a different problem, and it was decided to institute a long-term policy for the repair of this part of the building, which included a scheme for the reconstruction of the galleries and the installation of air conditioning. The Ministry of Works and the Department of Scientific and Industrial Research have prepared the necessary plans and have submitted a model of one gallery designed for air conditioning and relighting. The work of reconstructing this Gallery will, it is hoped, be undertaken shortly as an experiment. As more experience and plant become available the work of reconstruction will be carried out in the remaining galleries. Meanwhile, those rooms which could be temporarily repaired were fitted with racks for storage of those pictures which could not be shown.

At the end of 1945 Sir Kenneth Clark retired after a most exacting term of office. Not only had he been subjected to the cares and anxieties inseparable from the Directorship of the Gallery, but upon his shoulders had rested in large measure the responsibility for the complete removal of the nation's pictures, attended by all the hazards of war, to Wales and back again. He was succeeded by Sir Philip Hendy, whose vigorous direction has already proved itself in the service of the Gallery.

The acquisitions since 1945 included *The Adoration of the Golden Calf* by Nicholas Poussin (Pl. 11*b*), bought with the aid of the National Art Collections Fund in that year, and in 1947 the *Landscape with Snake* by the same artist was bought by the Trustees. A serious gap in the work of Nicholas Poussin represented in the National Collection was thus filled. *The Virgin with the Iris*, attributed to Dürer, was bought in 1945, again with the assistance of the National Art Collections Fund. Mantegna's *Imperator Mundi* was acquired in 1946 and in the same year Major C. E. W. Wood presented Zurbaran's powerful *S. Francis*. After the war the policy of holding special exhibitions was continued at the Gallery. The pictures from the Walker Art Gallery, Liverpool, and from Dulwich will be fresh in many people's minds. The acquisitions by the National Art Collections Fund, Spanish Paintings, Cleaned Pictures and the pictures from the Munich Gallery were other exhibitions which attracted wide attention in recent years.

The Exhibition of Cleaned Pictures which was opened to the public in October 1947 resulted largely from the heated controversy which broke out in the winter of 1946–47 over the pictures which had been recently cleaned in the Gallery. The controversy of 1846–53 and the second one of 1936–37 have already been referred to. In both these cases the great weight of the attack had been against cleaning of any kind; by 1946–47 the principle of cleaning had been generally recognised as correct and the attack was directed chiefly against the methods used. The Trustees decided that the best way of meeting the criticism which had been levelled against them was to place all available information before the public. The exhibition included, therefore, not only the 70 pictures cleaned since 1936 but 170 photographs and X-radiographs taken before, during and after cleaning. A number of pictures were exhibited partly cleaned and a series of photographs were included which showed the scientific instruments used. An International Committee under the chairmanship of Mr. J. R. H. Weaver, President of Trinity College, Oxford, was asked to report on the condition of those pictures which had been cleaned. A summary of the report was published in *The Times* of May 8th, 1948, and in it the Committee stated that 'none of the pictures examined was found to contain evidence of loss of original paint or other damage from recent treatment', while there was no indication that undue risks had been taken in cleaning. The Committee further reported that the use of expert restorers and the necessary scientific equipment would reduce the risks from cleaning to a minimum. The real danger lay in the large number of pictures which now required attention. The Committee recommended a long-term plan of maintenance, additional staff and equipment to deal with arrears, and the installation of a scheme of full air conditioning.

The visitor to the National Gallery today will have to make allowances for the damage done to the building by bombs and shrapnel. It is still only possible to exhibit rather less than half the number of pictures on show before the war and it must inevitably follow that at any given time there will be some masterpieces that

9.a LEONARDO DA VINCI
The Virgin of the Rocks

*National
Gallery*

9.b PIERO DELLA FRANCESCA
The Baptism of Christ

*National
Gallery*

10.*a* TITIAN Bacchus and Ariadne   *National Gallery*

10.*b* VELASQUEZ The Rokeby Venus   *National Gallery*

have to be relegated to the Reference Section of the Gallery. As far as possible a representative collection of pictures illustrating the major schools of painting in Europe is maintained on public exhibition, but it has not been found possible to illustrate the full breadth of the national collection, which is one of its outstanding qualities. A glance through the catalogue of the Gallery will reveal this clearly enough. In closing it may be convenient to summarise shortly the chief masterpieces of the various schools belonging to the Gallery.

In Italy the 14th-Century Sienese School is represented by four examples of the great master Duccio. Three of these panels, *The Annunciation* (1139), *Christ healing the Blind Man* (1140) and the *Transfiguration* (1330) were all originally part of the *Maestà*, the altarpiece painted in tempera for Siena Cathedral between 1308 and 1311. Fine in their formal pattern and lovely colouring, they represent the high-water mark of Sienese painting. The absence of an example of the work of Simone Martini is the only serious gap in the representation of this School. The 15th Century in Siena is represented by Sassetta, who combines Gothic grace with Sienese colour in his six panels from the St. Francis altarpiece painted for Borgo San Sepolcro. The four scenes from the life of St. John the Baptist painted by Giovanni di Paolo and the *Madonna of the Girdle* (1155) by Matteo di Giovanni are also among the Sienese treasures of this century.

The Florentine School of the 14th Century is represented by the remarkable *Pentecost* from the studio of Giotto, and by fine examples of the late Giottesques, such as the *Coronation of the Virgin* by Agnolo di Taddeo Gaddi (568) and Nardo di Cione (569). The Florentine version of the International Gothic style in the first years of the 15th Century is shown in Lorenzo Monaco's painting of the same subject (1847), while the North Italian equivalent appears in two exquisite panels by that rare painter, Pisanello; the *Vision of St. Eustace* (1436) and the *St. Anthony and St. George* (776).

The first impact of the new Humanism of the Florentine early Renaissance is seen in Masaccio's *Madonna* (3046) of 1426, and the exploitation of scientific method not always for humanist ends is shown at its clearest in Uccello's *Rout of San Romano* (583). The later phase of this development is exemplified in Antonio and Piero Pollaiuolo's *Martyrdom of St. Sebastian* (292), a textbook of scientific anatomy. The Florentine masters of the second generation are well represented: Castagno by the Crucifixion (1138), Domenico Veneziano by a damaged but noble Madonna (1215) and two heads of saints (766, 767), Filippo Lippi by a delicate *Annunciation* (666). The full range of Botticelli's powers is seen in a series of works, beginning with the early *Adoration of the Magi* (1033), continuing with one of his most poetical compositions, the *Mars and Venus* (915), and ending with one of the most deeply felt religious works of his last years, the *Nativity* (1034).

Umbrian painting can be seen in outstanding examples. The *Baptism of Christ* (665) (Pl. 9b) and the *Nativity* (908) are among Piero della Francesca's most magnificent easel paintings, and his pupil Signorelli is represented by three full-scale altarpieces which reveal at his best his heavy but powerful style. Finally Perugino's *Madonna adoring the Child* (288) can be classed among his most popular and attractive paintings, showing to the full his qualities as a painter of landscape.

Quattrocento painting of Northern Italy is also substantially represented, particularly by the group of Mantegnas, of which the *Agony in the Garden* (1417) is perhaps the most remarkable, and of works by the Bellini family. Two portraits by Gentile (1213, 3099) are typical of his more archaic manner, while the mellow beauty of Giovanni Bellini's style can be seen in the *St. Peter Martyr* (802) and in the celebrated portrait of the *Doge Leonardo Loredano* (189). His early *Agony in the Garden* (726) makes an interesting comparison with Mantegna's treatment of the same subject. A more conservative side of Venetian painting can be seen in the range of 9 works by Crivelli, which form a unique collection outside Italy.

The painting of the High Renaissance can be seen in typical works of its greatest masters. The Gallery is lucky in possessing one version of Leonardo's *Virgin of the Rocks* (1093), (Pl. 9a), and two paintings which, though they have often been challenged, are now once more generally accepted as originals by Michelangelo: the *Madonna and Child, St. John and Angels* (790) and the *Entombment* (809). Raphael's style can be seen developing from the exquisite early *Vision of a*

Knight (213) through the grander but tentative manner of the *Ansidei Madonna* (1171) to the maturity of the *Madonna of the Tower* (2069). The purely Florentine variant of the High Renaissance could hardly be seen to better advantage than in Andrea del Sarto's *Sculptor* (690).

The Gallery is particularly strong in Venetian painting of the 16th Century. The series opens with the works of Giovanni Bellini's two greatest pupils, Giorgione and Titian. Giorgione, a rare artist, is represented by a little painting of the *Adoration of the Magi* which has once more been attributed to him after cleaning. Among Titian's paintings in the Gallery the *Bacchus and Ariadne* (Pl. 10a) is world famous for its colour and dazzling technique. *Christ and the Magdalen* (270) and the late *Mother and Child* (3948) are other fine examples of his work. The great portrait group of the *Vendramin Family* is not only a splendid solution of a difficult problem but well illustrates Titian's development in technique during the 1540's. Aspects of Tintoretto's powers are illustrated by the superb portrait of Morosini (4004), and by the *St. George and the Dragon* (16) and the *Origin of the Milky Way* (1313). Among a number of works by Veronese *The Family of Darius before Alexander* (294) shows the painter's genius for combining wonderful decoration with portraiture. Faced with the difficulty of painting members of the Pisani family in a group, he uses the device of making his sitters take part in a tableau illustrating an episode of history which was popular in Venice at the time. North Italian portraiture is finely represented in works by Lorenzo Lotto, Moretto and Moroni, and the Mannerists of North and Central Italy by Parmigianino, Pontormo and Bronzino. Of Correggio's works *Venus, Mercury and Cupid* (10) is the best known, but the *Madonna of the Basket* (23) is particularly charming.

Eclectic painting of the 17th Century is illustrated by the work of Annibale Carracci, Guido Reni and Guercino. More in keeping with the taste of today, perhaps, is the splendidly naturalistic *Christ at Emmaus* (172) by Caravaggio. Good examples of the work of Domenichino and Salvator Rosa emphasise the development of landscape painting during the century.

The Gallery contains some fine examples of 18th-Century Venetian painting; two notable Canalettos being the *Scuola di San Rocco*

(937) and a *View in Venice* (127). Among a number of Guardi's paintings *Sta. Maria della Salute, Venice* (2098) is particularly fresh and sparkling, Tiepolo is well represented by the moving *Deposition* (1333).

Fifteenth-Century Flemish painting is represented by three notable portraits by Jan van Eyck, including the famous *Arnolfini group* (186) (Pl. 7*b*). Painted in 1434, this picture, the earliest known portrait group, is not only an early example of secular painting but, owing to its minute realism, is a social document of great interest. Robert Campin's *Madonna of the Firescreen* (2609) is another important example of early Flemish painting. This picture is a link in the chain of evidence which was established in the early years of the 20th Century attributing to Campin a number of works which had formerly been described as by the Master of Flémalle or the Master of the Mérode Altarpiece. The two small portraits by Campin (653A and B) form an interesting contrast to the work of Van Eyck. The *Portrait of a Man* (943) by Dirk Bouts is an exceptionally fine example of 15th-Century Flemish portraiture showing, among other things, the artist's grasp of natural lighting. The lovely triptych *The Virgin and Child with Angels* by Hans Memlinc lent by the Duke of Devonshire, not only has an exceptional pedigree but glows with that translucent colour which comes from the Flemish masters' precise technique in the use of transparent oil glazes. Lastly, there are at least two outstanding works by Gerard David, the *Marriage of St. Catherine* (1432), and *A Canon with his Patron Saints* (1045), the latter showing his great interest in landscape. The 16th Century is not so well represented. There is a small late Quentin Massys, the *Marriage of St. Catherine* (3664) painted in tempera on linen; two portraits and the glowing *Adoration of the Kings* (2790) by Mabuse and a characteristic landscape by Patinir (4826). The *Crowning with Thorns* (4744) by Jerome Bosch illustrates something of that artist's biting commentary. The *Adoration of the Magi* (3556) by Pieter Brueghel shows his satire but does nothing to illustrate his gift for landscape painting which at present remains unrepresented in the Gallery.

The final culmination of Flemish painting at the hand of Rubens in the 17th Century is splendidly represented by a number of works entirely from his own brush, not such a usual occurrence in view of the great output of his studio. The one exception is the *Triumph of Silenus* (853) painted 1625–27, which is now ascribed partly to his pupil Van Dyck. The large *Peace and War* (48), a fine example of Rubens' allegorical painting, was carried out in 1629 as a present to Charles I, after the artist's visit to England in that year. The children in this picture are portraits of his own family and the painting shows how much Rubens owed to Veronese as a decorator and his debt to Titian's breadth of handling. Among his portraits the *Chapeau de Paille* (852) (Pl. 8*b*) is the best known and is a painting of Suzanne Fourment, the sister of Rubens' second wife, Hélène. The brilliant colouring and fluent brushwork reveal Rubens' zest for the physical attractions of his subject. The *Rape of the Sabines* (38) is an example of his power in handling complicated baroque movement. His great landscape, the *Château de Steen* (66), a companion piece to the *Rainbow Landscape* in the Wallace collection (Pl. 24*b*), shows Rubens dealing with landscape in the 'grand manner': it was lent to the British Institution in 1815 and had great influence upon subsequent British landscape painting. Rubens' technique in the *Château de Steen* is clearly reflected in Constable's work after 1815.

Seventeenth-Century Dutch painting is very well represented in the Gallery, largely owing to the collection of Sir Robert Peel, many of whose pictures were procured for the nation. The excellent condition of the Dutch paintings in the Gallery is something to be especially noted. Several fine pictures of Dutch courtyard scenes and interiors show De Hooch's skill in balancing to a nicety every aspect of design and colour, under the most minute treatment of surface and detail. The *Lady standing at the Virginals* (1383) by the impeccable Jan Vermeer reaches the culminating point in Dutch genre. Perfect balance, meticulous selection and a delightfully cool scheme of colour are some of the qualities which emanate from this Dutch master.

The landscape of Holland is faithfully handled by Van Goyen, Philips Koninck and Jacob Ruisdael. Hobbema's *Avenue at Middelharnis* (830) (Pl. 11*a*) is known to most people through reproduction and is the best picture he ever painted. Good examples of Cuyp, Van de Velde and Van Huysum, representing other aspects of Dutch taste in the 17th Century, can also be found, together with a number of works by lesser men. The greatest master of them all, Rembrandt, is worthily represented by a series of magnificent portraits which the Gallery has steadily acquired throughout its existence through purchase and gift. These range from the early portrait of Philips Lucasz (850) and the self-portrait of 1640 (672) to the late paintings of Margarethe Trip (1675) and the self-portrait of 1663 (221) (Pl.8a) in which the full intensity of his psychological insight and expressive power are visible. His earlier religious painting is illustrated by *Christ before Pilate* (1400), painted in 1634, and the *Adoration of the Shepherds* (47) of ten years later. Here the handling is more decisive than in the previous picture, the colouring more austere, the lights and shadows more subtle in their relationship. Of the lesser Dutch portrait painters, *A Man in a Fur Cap* (4042) by Karel Fabritius, a pupil of Rembrandt, is a distinguished experiment. Here, contrary to current practice, the artist silhouettes a dark figure against a light background.

The *Wilton Diptych* represents the style of French painting in the last years of the 14th Century, though it is maintained by some critics that it was actually painted by an English artist imitating the French manner. It shows Richard II presented to the Virgin and Child by his three patron saints, St. John the Baptist, St. Edward the Confessor and St. Edmund, King and Martyr. The date of the picture is probably about 1395. The next important French picture in the Gallery dates from the late 15th Century, the *Meeting of Joachim and Anna* (4092) by the Maître de Moulins, which seems to be the left-hand panel of an altarpiece. There is then a gap until the 17th Century which is well represented by Nicolas Poussin and Claude Lorraine. The *Bacchanalian Dance* (62) reveals Poussin's love of order in his compositions. The breadth of light and shade and the simplification of masses and modelling are characteristic of the artist. Only in the little putti to the left of the picture do we find a lingering memory of Titian, whom Poussin admired so much in his earlier days. His love of order and logical explanation is also reflected in the noble *Landscape with a Snake*. Claude is splendidly represented by 10 pictures mostly early in date; all of them show Claude's masterly handling of light and are examples of his poetic dissertation on nature. The full-length portrait of Richelieu (1449) by Philippe de Champaigne is a first-rate example of French portraiture during the 17th Century. A more homely note, somewhat akin to the subjects chosen by Dutch artists, is struck by the works of Antoine and Louis Le Nain.

French 18th-Century painting is only modestly represented in the National Gallery, one little painting by Antoine Watteau, *La Gamme d'Amour* (2897), shows the artist's exquisite taste in colour and selection; the little figures, perfectly drawn, are essentially part of that dream-like world distilled by Watteau from the society of his time. Chardin, the painter of the middle classes in France, is represented by two good examples, the *Young Schoolmistress* (4077) and the *House of Cards* (4078), both examples of a polite genre inspired by Dutch painting. His treatment though realistic and objective is broad and atmospheric. The 19th-Century group of pictures can only be regarded as a token collection, many of the great painters being only represented at the Tate Gallery. Ingres is represented by two portraits including *Mme. Moitessier* (4821) and by two classical subjects; a full-length portrait of Baron Schwiter (3286) by Delacroix is an excellent example of Romantic portraiture. Both paintings by Degas in the Gallery are unfinished.

Spanish painting of the 15th Century is represented by Bartolomé Bermejo's *St. Michael overcoming Satan*, where the influence of Flemish painting is particularly strong; in its treatment of realistic detail the picture is unmistakably Spanish. The next great figure is El Greco, who was working in Toledo from 1577 until his death in 1614. Born in Crete, he retained a strong interest in formalism throughout his life and remains an isolated figure in Spanish art. Technically he is close to the great Venetian painters, notably Tintoretto. His intense mysticism found the religious atmosphere of Toledo congenial. He is represented by a magnificent late religious composition *Christ driving the Traders from the Temple* (1457) and by one portrait possibly of Luigi Cornaro (1122). Zurbaran's finest work and one more typically Spanish in its detailed realism and sombre ecstasy is *The Franciscan* (230).

The greatest Spanish painter of all, Velasquez, is very well represented in the Gallery. His early 'bodegones' or kitchen pieces, which are nearly all in English collections, are illustrated by *Christ in the House of Martha* (1375), sound in technique and realistic in the extreme. His progress through some uneasy experiments is represented by *Christ after the Flagellation* (1148), painted in 1633 with its debt to Guido Reni. His appointment as court painter to Philip IV in 1623 had enabled him to study Italian painting for the first time, notably the work of Titian, Tintoretto and Veronese. His outlook and technique changed miraculously after his first visit to Italy in 1629 and *Philip IV as a Young Man* (1129) is the first complete expression of his new outlook. His second visit to Italy in 1649 prepared the way to his last great phase illustrated by the bust portrait of Philip IV as an ageing king (745), and the *Venus and Cupid* (2057) (Pl. 10b). This, which is popularly known as the 'Rokeby' *Venus,* is the only painting of a female nude by Velasquez which is left to us. His realism has by now turned from realism of detail to realism of overall vision. The colour is cool and the modelling of the figure of Venus almost shadowless. In Goya's incisive portraiture in the Gallery can be seen his admiration for Velasquez. The nightmare mood which animated the Caprichos is illustrated in *A Scene from a Play* (1472). The German School is the least well represented in the whole Gallery but it contains one supreme masterpiece, Holbein's *Christina, Duchess of Milan* (2475) (Pl. 7a), as well as his important group *The Ambassadors* (1314) and two paintings attributed to Dürer, a Madonna and a portrait of his father (1938).

As one would expect, British painting is strongly represented in the national collection. The earliest picture is a portrait of *Edmund Butts* (1496) by John Bettes, who appears to have been a very competent follower of Holbein. The 17th Century is overshadowed by the genius of Van Dyck, whose equestrian portrait of Charles I (1172) is a noble example of his style in England. *George and Francis Villiers* (3605) is another fine example of the graceful and aristocratic painting of Van Dyck. William Dobson is represented by his portrait of *Endymion Porter* (1249). In the 18th Century Hogarth revives the native genius and he is represented by a number of typical works. *Calais Gate* (1464), the somewhat colourless title now given to a picture originally known as *O the Roast Beef of Old*

England, is an example of his biting commentary on a scene which he witnessed in 1748 at Calais. The *Heads of Six of his Servants* (1374) shows his grasp of character when he was really interested in his sitters, and the fresh and lively sketch of the *Shrimp Girl* (1162) (Pl. 12*b*) is perhaps his most popular work. Reynolds is represented in most aspects of his portraiture ranging from the early *Self Portrait* (889) painted in the 1750's to the *Lord Heathfield* (111) of 1787. His great rival Gainsborough is exemplified by the two portraits of *The Painter's Daughters chasing a Butterfly* (1811) and *The Painter's Daughters teasing a Cat* (3812) (unfinished). Both paintings were apparently carried out while Gainsborough was in Ipswich about 1759 and show his freedom of brushwork allied to great delicacy of tone and colour. *John, 10th Viscount Kilmorey* (4777), painted in 1768 when the painter was in Bath, and *Dr. Ralph Schomberg* (684) are good examples of his later portraiture. As a landscape painter he is an important figure in the British School. His early work illustrated by *View of Dedham?* (1283) is strongly under the influence of 17th-Century Dutch painting but after his removal to Bath the influence of Rubens, Van Dyck and Watteau brought about a change to a more classical type of landscape well represented by *The Market Cart* finished in 1786.

Romney and the unhappy Richard Wilson, who often nearly starved because of his devotion to landscape which nobody would buy, are represented at their best. Lawrence's portrait of *Queen Charlotte* (4257) painted about 1790 shows how good he could be on occasions. A brilliant draughtsman, he all too often fell a victim to his own facility and love of glitter. Owing to his great bequest of pictures to the nation, Turner is represented in all his phases from the dark *Calais Pier* (472) of 1803, through his period of admiration for Claude, illustrated by *Crossing the Brook* (497) (Pl. 12*a*) to the *Rain, Steam and Speed* (538) of 1844, where light and colour are the most important elements in the picture. Constable's work includes a number of his sketches both calm and impetuous and his finished work is illustrated by *The Hay Wain*, which was exhibited in the Paris Salon in 1824 and influenced Delacroix, and the Barbizon painters in France. *The Cornfield* painted in 1826 is a fine solution of Constable's problem of combining the freedom of his sketches with sufficient finish to suit the requirements of public exhibition. Of the later painters a portrait of *Mrs. Leonard Collmann* (1775) by Alfred Stevens is notable and the Pre-Raphaelites are represented by the well-known *Ophelia* by Millais, while Frith's *Derby Day* (615) is the masterpiece of the Victorian narrative style.

There are many galleries in Europe which are greater in extent than the National Gallery or which can illustrate one particular school far more brilliantly, but it may reasonably be claimed that few, if any, can produce such a balanced and representative series of masterpieces according to the standards of today. This is the advantage which it gains over older institutions of the same kind most of which were built up when taste was different and by individuals whose own views were often idiosyncratic. The National Gallery may lack the personal stamp of ancient accumulations such as the Prado or the Vienna Gallery, but in compensation it has the advantage of having been formed on wider and more historical principles.

The Gallery is open free 10 a.m. to 6 p.m. on weekdays; 2 p.m. to 6 p.m. on Sundays.

CHARLES CLARE,
Lecturer

THE TATE GALLERY

THE Tate Gallery, Millbank, which was opened in 1887, contains the national collection of British Painting of Modern Foreign Painting and of Modern Sculpture.

Looking back at the Victorian cultural scene, one cannot fail to notice the extraordinary interest in art which developed in England after 1850. For this the spread of education, the development of engraving, the Great Exhibition and the enthusiasm of the Prince Consort for everything pertaining to art were all partly responsible. Though the interest in art was widespread it was not notably critical or enlightened, and the Royal Academy was then, as now, the home of the more popular modes of painting and sculpture. The following extract from a contemporary diary provides an interesting comment:

> I left my carpet-bag at the Paddington Cloak Room and went straight to the Academy exhibition at Burlington House which I reached shortly before 4 o'clock. There was a great press of people, one hundred or more, round Miss Thompson's famous picture 'Calling the Roll after the battle of Inkerman'. A policeman stands on duty all day by this picture from 10 o'clock till 6.0 in the evening saying, 'Move on, ladies. Ladies please move on.' [1]

All this may seem to us now merely a fragment of period history, but it has its relevance. These 'pictures-of-the-year', and the innumerable reproductions of them which found their way into the houses of rich and poor alike, were an influential factor in persuading people that contemporary art was as good as anything the past had to offer. And the irony of it was that they were in a sense right, though the evidence for such a belief was not to be found on the walls of the Royal Academy or of the Paris Salon, but in the studios of certain obscure painters mostly active in France and England. Though the public in its enthusiasm mistook too frequently the spurious for the genuine, there was a body of responsible opinion

[1] *Kilvert's Diary*. Edited by William Plomer. Cape.

that recognised the need for a permanent exhibition of modern British art which would serve as a record of contemporary achievement and also as a means of encouraging living artists. This idea had first received tangible support in the will of Sir Francis Chantrey, a successful sculptor, who died in 1841, bequeathing a large sum of money for the purchase of painting and sculpture 'executed (as the will stipulated) within the shore of Great Britain'. The will also stipulated that no part of his bequest should be spent on the housing of the collection. So British art, though duly honoured and encouraged, remained without a permanent or a worthy home. Those people who fondly imagined that the government of the day would come forward with proposals for building a gallery worthy of the British school were sadly disappointed. Victorian Governments, like those of other times, believed that art was an admirable thing so long as it did not become a departmental nuisance. In the case of the Turner Bequest, when the painter bequeathed his paintings to the nation on condition that a gallery was provided to house the whole collection, the gift was accepted, but the question of a gallery was adroitly shelved. In 1847, nine years before the Turner Bequest became effective, Robert Vernon had presented 157 works by British artists to the nation and in 1857 John Sheepshanks gave his extensive collection of 233 British paintings to the South Kensington Museum. These events kept the question of a Gallery of British Art very much in the public eye. As *The Times* put it: 'This generation has rightly made up its mind that in certain departments of art the English school is not only great, but supreme: and it is but fair to demand that, if this is so, it should be represented as completely in the National Gallery collection as the art of Italy or Holland.'

England was then in a particularly unfortunate position; not only was she without a specific collection of British art, but her own painters were poorly represented, in comparison with the painters of other countries, on the walls of the National Gallery in Trafalgar Square. This question was brought to a head by James Orrock, a landscape painter, who, in a paper read before the Society of Arts, severely criticised the National Gallery for its policy towards British art. He pointed out that the British paintings shown at the National Gallery were mostly second-rate and that the great collection of

Turner drawings and water-colours had been ignominiously relegated to the cellars.

These complaints were made by Orrock in the spring of 1890, and it happened that about this time some indiscreet person disclosed the contents of a letter written in the previous October by Mr. (afterwards Sir Henry) Tate, to the Trustees of the National Gallery, offering his collection of English painting to the nation. News of this communication appeared in the press on March 10th, and three days later *The Times* printed a leading article setting out the whole position. A brief extract from it has already been quoted, but as this article provoked a long and bitter but ultimately fruitful controversy, it is worth recalling certain of its salient points. Relating Orrock's strictures with the announcement of Tate's offer, the writer criticised the authorities for their persistent neglect of British art. Of the National Gallery he said:

> The collection falls short of even a reasonable standard of excellence in many important ways, while on the other hand there have been from time to time so many redundant examples of inferior British painters that the Trustees were a few years ago compelled to come to Parliament to ask for powers to weed out this portion of the Gallery by means of the ingenious device of a National Loan Act. . . . For the first thirty or forty years of its existence—that is to say from 1824 to about 1860—scarcely any British pictures were purchased at all.

And later:

> A wealthy country like ours, which possesses so fine a national school as we do—a school of landscape and a school of portraiture containing so many of the elements of greatness—ought to be able to stop the mouths of foreign critics by showing them a really representative and choice collection of our art gathered together in some great central gallery. . . . Why cannot we have in London, started partly by voluntary effort and afterwards subsidised and directed by the Government, a gallery that shall do for English art what the Luxembourg does for French?

By drawing attention to the official neglect of the British school and by advocating a new gallery for housing 'a really representative and choice collection', the writer of the article was merely defining what, in the opinion of many, was the error and its remedy. In Tate's offer of 65 paintings to the National Gallery, the public saw a long-overdue opportunity of securing the proper representation of British art in the national collection, and the offer was warmly welcomed by the press. Tate made it a condition that all the pictures must be accepted, and not a selection only, and that they should be hung in the National Gallery without unnecessary delay. The National Gallery, however, pressed for space and, chary of admitting so many newcomers to its walls, declined the gift.

On June 23rd *The Times* published a letter which Tate had addressed to the Chancellor of the Exchequer, in which he again raised the question of these proffered pictures. In this letter Tate referred to the various suggestions that had been made 'respecting the establishment of a national gallery exclusively confined to works by British artists', and he appended a draft proposal for the establishment of such a gallery. First, he insisted that a gallery should be established 'on lines similar to those of the Luxembourg, Paris'; that it should be maintained by means of annual grants from the Treasury and be devoted to works produced since 1750 or thereabouts by British artists. On the question of administration, he stipulated that the gallery should be administered by a new body of trustees, quite independent from the National Gallery or any other art institution.

> Upon these conditions [he wrote] I am prepared to present to the nation a selection of pictures out of my collection . . . numbering fifty-seven, and further to allow the committee of selection to take any of the others which I possess, and which they may think it desirable to have included in my gift.

On June 27th *The Times* published the Treasury's cautious and evasive reply in which it intimated

> that the Eastern and Western galleries at South Kensington, now temporarily assigned to other purposes, might be devoted to the establishment of a representative collection of modern British pictures in which the works that are at present scattered in various institutions might be brought together.

But on the question of an independent administration and the granting of financial aid, the Treasury, with true British prudence, dug in its heels and refused to commit itself to a specific answer.

In the press, meanwhile, the merits and demerits of possible sites for the new gallery were hotly discussed. Kensington Palace had been proposed and subsequently St. James's. When these sites proved impracticable and the Government came forward with its offer of the Eastern and Western Galleries at the South Kensington Museum, opinion became distinctly critical. *The Pall Mall Gazette*, for instance, uttered a note of warning:

> The Government, it will be remembered, favours the South Kensing-
> ton site, on the ground that accommodation already exists there in the
> Galleries which are shortly to be vacated by some of the Science collec-
> tions. As a stop-gap this suggestion is by no means a bad one; but it is a
> stop-gap only, and if the money for building a New Gallery outright can
> be obtained, there would be no advantage whatever in adopting the
> stop-gap. On the contrary, there would be decided disadvantages in so
> doing. There is a wide-spread dislike of the mere name 'South Kensing-
> ton'. The galleries are poor places. There is already far too great a con-
> centration of exhibitions and institutions at the South Kensington site.
> To start the New National Gallery as a twopenny-halfpenny affair, to be
> packed away in the lumber-galleries of South Kensington, would be to
> start it under a cloud. . . .

And *The British Architect* was no less critical:

> Truly our Government is a delighter in make-shifts; of that we have
> had abundant proof in other than art matters. In spite of expert evidence
> as to the wonderful qualities of the galleries in question for the purpose
> proposed, we cannot think, having regard to the future, that the scheme
> is a wise one.

Henry Tate himself was apparently of the same opinion, for shortly afterwards he made it known that he found the Government's offer unacceptable. Thus ended the first phase of what might be called the battle for a Gallery of British Art. But before the dust of this preliminary skirmish had died down, Tate was already deploying on a wider front. On March 21st, 1891, *The Times* published a letter written by Mr. Humphry Ward to the Chancellor of the Exchequer, giving reasons for the rejection of the Government's scheme and announcing a much bolder proposal. On this occasion Humphry Ward was acting as a mouthpiece for Tate—

the anonymous friend referred to in the letter. First the writer enumerated the objections to the original offer of the Eastern and Western Galleries at South Kensington.

It is felt [he wrote], that those galleries, though fairly lighted for the display of pictures, are inconvenient in shape, wanting in that compactness which is so desirable, and without any external attractiveness whatever. In fact, no one has ever pretended that the scheme could be regarded as a final solution of the question.

Holding this view, a friend of mine (whose name I have given you in confidence, his earnest wish being that it should not be made public) authorises me to make the following proposal:—He offers to build at his own expense and at a cost not exceeding £80,000, a gallery for British Art. . . .

The principal condition of Tate's offer was that the Government should give, as a site for the new gallery, a plot of land at South Kensington, at the south-eastern corner of Imperial Institute road, and that a piece of land adjoining should be reserved for a future extension of the building.

Everything seemed at last set fair for the realisation of Tate's great project: the Government had agreed that the Gallery should be independently administered and they were now willing to provide a site. Yet once again the question of a site proved a contentious issue and once again the dust of controversy disturbed the tranquil atmosphere of South Kensington. This time it was Art versus Science—the point at issue being whether the Royal College of Science had a prior claim to the land set aside for the erection of the new gallery. According to the scientists, this land was needed for extending their laboratories, and they were outraged at the prospect of having a building devoted to pictures sandwiched between two sections of a science school. To avoid this indignity they immediately started a campaign of active opposition: deputations were sent to the Chancellor of the Exchequer, and questions were asked in Parliament on their behalf. As was to be expected, science won the day, and the Government withdrew the offer it had made to Tate.

There then followed an attempt to negotiate for a site on the Embankment; but the price asked by the City Corporation proved too high, and the negotiations came to nothing. The crisis foretold

11.*a*   HOBBEMA   The Avenue, Middelharnis   *National Gallery*

11.*b*   POUSSIN   The Worship of the Golden Calf   *National Gallery*

12.a TURNER Crossing the Brook *National Gallery*

12.b HOGARTH The Shrimp Girl *National Gallery*

by the press had now been reached. Shortly afterwards it was learned that Tate had withdrawn his offer of the pictures and the money.

It is perhaps appropriate here to say a word about the man who was the victim of so much maladroitness and obstruction. Born at Chorley, Lancashire, on March 11th, 1819, the eldest son of a Unitarian Minister, and beginning in a humble way, Henry Tate amassed a great fortune in the sugar industry, and his name was associated with numerous and munificent philanthropic gifts. Among other institutions Liverpool University, Bedford College, London, and Manchester College, Oxford, owed much to his enlightened generosity. He died on December 5th, 1899. As a selfmade man, he had acquired qualities of patience and persistence which proved indispensable in his dealings with Ministers of State. Yet dignified and patient though he was, a note of forgivable exasperation crept in at the end of the abortive negotiations. Writing to the Chancellor of the Exchequer on March 3rd, 1892, he said (referring again to the proposal to house a collection of British art in the Eastern and Western Galleries at South Kensington):

> So strong was my feeling on this subject that, to save British art from the humiliation of being housed in those tunnel-like edifices, I determined to offer a new and modern gallery. I must, therefore, decline to entertain either the Eastern or Western galleries or the site at present occupied by the Art Needlework Society, with the possible extension to the aforesaid galleries. The Embankment site being unattainable, and you having considered it wise to withdraw the offer made to me of the site in Imperial Institute and Exhibition roads, and as no other suitable site appears likely to be available, and moreover taking in consideration the difficulties, delays, and in some respects uncalled-for opposition which the proposed Gallery of British Art has met with, I really feel there is no course open to me but to withdraw my offer to the Government of the pictures and the erection of a suitable gallery, which for the sake of the art-loving public, and in the interests of British art, I do with extreme reluctance. . . .

So the project for a Gallery of British Art ended in what seemed an unresolvable deadlock. During the prolonged and fruitless negotiations the scheme was the subject of strong criticism in the press and elsewhere. 'There probably never was', said *The Graphic*, 'a public benefaction more criticised, scorned and rejected.' Much of the criticism was malicious or ill-informed, but a certain section of opinion expressed legitimate misgivings lest the new gallery should merely endorse the questionable standards of the Royal Academy. Certainly Tate's choice of pictures gave some grounds for apprehension. Sickert and George Moore attacked the paintings in *The Times*, and were rebuked by Millais as 'insolent disturbers'. Yet in spite of these criticisms, the general feeling was that a great and splendid opportunity had been missed.

In November 1892 came the surprising announcement that Henry Tate had renewed his offer to the new Chancellor of the Exchequer, Sir William Harcourt, and that the site of Jeremy Bentham's 'model' Penitentiary at Millbank had been offered on behalf of the Government and accepted by Tate. The work of demolition began almost at once, and on July 21st, 1897, the Tate Gallery was formally opened by King Edward VII, then Prince of Wales.

What, one may ask, had brought about this astonishing transformation? Sir William Harcourt in his speech at the opening ceremony supplied the answer.

> It so happened [said Sir William], that some three or four years ago I had the pleasure of making the acquaintance of Mr. Tate; he was then in rather an unfortunate position. He was in the hands of a concert of institutions—artistic, scientific, and official—all quarrelling as to where should be his site, what should be his building, and what should be its management. Well, that Concert proceeded deliberately, we were not getting on, and I ventured to say to Mr. Tate, 'Don't you think that we had better have done with all the institutions and that you and I should settle this matter in half-an-hour?'

The invitation was accepted, and in that profitable half-hour the future of the gallery was finally settled. For an almost Proustian description of the opening scene we are indebted to *The Daily Graphic*:

> Here a gay throng of that portion of London Society which is seeing out the season to its bitter end was gathered, and welcomed the Royal party with a vigour undiminished by the warmth of a very crowded

assemblage in a gallery where ventilators had apparently been hermetically sealed. The party of Royalties and trustees; benefactors and beneficiaries ranged themselves on a little platform at one end of the room immediately beneath the incongruous background of Lord Leighton's depressing 'The sea shall give up its dead'—against which the bonnets of the ladies stood out with gay irrelevance. When the spectators had got down from their chairs and the cheering had ceased, Mr. Tate came forward and delivered a dedicatory address to the Prince, candidly reading it from the roll of paper which he carried. It was a short speech, simply worded, and holding out a generous promise of additional buildings, should the necessity arise for them: and at its close Mr. Tate, bowing, handed the deeds of gift of the gallery to the Prince. The Prince, with a word or two and a smile, took them and delivered them into the charge of the First Commissioner of Works, Mr. Akers-Douglas: and from that moment the gallery became irrevocably the property of the nation.

The 65 pictures and the 3 pieces of sculpture which Tate had presented to the nation formed, as he intended, the nucleus of a representative collection of British art. Additional paintings were transferred to the new Gallery from other sources: a selection from the Vernon collection and certain other appropriate works from the National Gallery; the Watts Gift, being eighteen pictures by G. F. Watts, recently presented to the nation by the artist, and the Chantrey collection, from the South Kensington Museum.

Ever since its opening the history of the Tate has been one of continuous expansion both of the Gallery itself and of the collections, due to private munificence and to the constant generosity of the Contemporary Art Society (founded in 1910) and of the National Art-Collections Fund (founded in 1903). In 1899, to the existing seven galleries and central hall, the founder added eight galleries and a sculpture hall, thereby more than doubling the original exhibition space.

In 1908, through the generosity of Sir Joseph Duveen, the elder, work upon nine new galleries was begun for the exhibition of the Turner Bequest, previously housed, but mostly not shown, at the National Gallery. These were opened informally—owing to the death of King Edward VII—by King George V on July 18th, 1910. In 1919, as a result of the recommendation of a committee presided over by Lord Curzon that the Tate should be a National Gallery of British Art of all periods, more than 200 pictures were transferred from Trafalgar Square.

In 1916 Sir Joseph Duveen, the younger (afterwards Lord Duveen of Millbank), undertook to provide four additional galleries on the main and two on the ground floor for modern foreign art—for which no provision existed in the national collection—in connection with the bequest in 1915 of 39 modern foreign pictures, mostly French, by Sir Hugh Lane.

The Modern Foreign collection underwent a brilliant enrichment in 1923, when Mr. Samuel Courtauld placed a sum of £50,000 at the disposal of the Trustees for the acquisition in particular of French painting of the latter part of the 19th Century. The magnificent works thus acquired by Manet, Monet, Degas, Renoir and others were placed in the new galleries. Lord Duveen later added a gallery for the work of Sargent. These further extensions and a vast new sculpture hall, also the gift of Lord Duveen, were opened on June 28th, 1926, and June 29th, 1937, by King George V.

The Gallery's collection of British paintings now numbers over 3,000 works, of modern foreign paintings and sculpture more than 500. It is not, however, for the scale—impressive as this is—on which the Tate has grown in the first half-century of its existence so much as the values for which it has come to stand that it is chiefly remarkable. At the time of its foundation it was entirely subordinate to the National Gallery, and it was not until 1917 that the appointment of a separate Board and Directorship enabled a fully independent policy to be adopted. During his term of office Sir Charles Holroyd, the first Keeper, was chiefly occupied with problems of organisation, but as Director of the National Gallery from 1906 he lent his support to the independent policy with which the Tate developed and which, with varying degrees of tenacity, it has consistently pursued. The apprehension which actuated many of those opposed to its establishment, that it would become a mausoleum of popular official art, was swiftly allayed.

A new tradition, audaciously begun by the second Keeper (1906–11), Mr. D. S. MacColl, manifest in the acquisition of work, by Rossetti, Alfred Stevens and Steer, assumed, with his successors, a still more positive and impressive form. Under the courageous and enlightened guidance of Charles Aitken (Keeper 1911–17; Director 1917–30) the Tate took its place among the great art galleries of the world; and its progress has been maintained ever since, so that today, as the National Gallery of British Painting and of Modern Foreign Art, it possesses unique collections of not only Turner, but of Blake, the Pre-Raphaelites, Stevens and contemporary British painting, while its collection of late 19th- and early 20th-Century French paintings is among the most representative in Europe.

Shortly before the outbreak of the second world war in 1939, the contents of the Gallery were removed to places of safety, in accordance with a pre-arranged plan. As a result of this precaution the collections remained unharmed, though the Gallery itself suffered extensive damage from bomb blast and incendiaries. The war years, however, coincided both with a period of notable enrichment from the point of view of the collections and with the initiation of a new and more liberal exhibition policy.

The 422 works of art acquired between 1939 and 1945 included important collections of works by Blake and the Pre-Raphaelites, and a group of French paintings by Renoir, Sisley, Cézanne, Toulouse-Lautrec, Modigliani, Rouault and Vuillard. These and other examples were the gifts of generous donors. During the same period the Trustees pursued an active purchasing policy to the full extent of their small resources, and their ideal of establishing complete representation of what is finest in contemporary British art, including, it may be said, its last-minute developments, became for the first time a realisable aim. Works were bought by Sickert, Steer, John, Spencer and Matthew Smith, and also by artists whose talent is of more recent growth—such as Sutherland, Moore, Piper, Burra, Ravilious, Pasmore and David Jones, none of whom had previously been represented. Continental paintings acquired by purchase included the first examples in the collection of Paul Klee, Max Ernst and Marc Chagall. After the war a selection of 73 pictures by official war artists was transferred to the Tate, and thus a full representation of this phase of British painting was secured.

The exhibitions which the Tate has organised or sponsored frequently in association with the Arts Council since 1939 can only be mentioned briefly, though these features of its activity have become national and even international in scope. During the war, while the Gallery remained closed, the Trustees and Director of the National Gallery generously allowed space for these exhibitions, which since the re-opening of the Tate on April 15th, 1946, have been held at Millbank. These include two separate exhibitions of the Tate's war-time acquisitions, exhibitions of the work of Wilson Steer, Paul Klee, James Ensor, Braque, Rouault, Alexander Cozens, Blake, Turner, Constable, Hogarth, Marc Chagall, Van Gogh, Jack Yeats, J.-L. David, Richard Wilson, James Pryde, Paul Nash and William Rothenstein; the Samuel Courtauld Memorial Exhibition, a retro-spective exhibition of British painting of the past fifty years, and exhibitions of Cézanne's water-colours, of American painting from the earliest times, of South African art, and of art treasures from Vienna. In addition to housing these exhibitions, the Tate has lent paintings from its own collection for numerous exhibitions of British art held abroad.

In spite of the splendour of its possessions and the illustrious char-acter of its special collections, the Tate suffers, like other national art collections, but to a marked degree, from various anomalies and defects. Its functions have never been very precisely defined; its collections have consequently grown in a rather haphazard fashion, since the Trustees and Director have never possessed, until the allocation of a Government Grant of £2,000, in 1946, 1947, 1948 and 1949, an income over which they exercised complete control.

Reference has already been made to the Chantrey Bequest, but since its history is so closely connected with that of the Tate, some more detailed discussion of the matter is required. Although the terms of Chantrey's will were published in 1841, the request did not become operative until after the death of Chantrey's widow in 1875. As the will made no provision for the housing of the pur-chases, the Treasury arranged that the pictures bought out of the Chantrey funds should be sent to the Tate. Thus from its foundation the Tate was condemned to be the repository for any example of inferior art which the Council of the Royal Academy cared to choose from the heterogeneous exhibitions at Burlington House. In 1903 D. S. MacColl brought matters to a head by an article in *The*

Saturday Review entitled 'The Maladministration of the Chantrey Trust'. In this article he challenged any fair-minded person to read the will, then go to the Tate

> where the purchases made are arranged as a separate collection and ask themselves soberly whether the clearly expressed and admirable intentions of the testator have been carried out: whether there is evidence of any attempt to carry them out, or whether it is not clear that the provisions of the will have been ignored, its intentions perverted and the funds at the disposal of the Trustees grossly maladministered.

In his will Chantrey had stated emphatically that he wished the Trustees to purchase 'works of fine art of the highest merit in painting and sculpture'. And he also insisted that in the purchase of such works preference should on all occasions be given 'to the works of the highest merit that can be obtained'.

Yet from the outset the Council of the Academy ignored Chantrey's explicit instructions and their choice of paintings was more often governed by considerations of popular appeal than of intrinsic merit. MacColl was therefore amply justified in his attacks which resulted in the appointment of a Select Committee of Enquiry in 1904, under the chairmanship of Lord Crewe. This committee heard the evidence of thirty-one witnesses, thirteen of them from the Royal Academy. Though the evidence was, on balance, against the Academy's methods of selection and its interpretation of the will, the committee produced only a timid report. It did, however, decide that too many pictures with a merely popular appeal had been bought and it recommended that the Academy should cease purchasing exclusively from its own exhibitions. In spite of these recommendations, nothing of importance was achieved, except that the Royal Academy reduced the size of its selection committee.

In 1912 a Committee of Trustees of the National Gallery under the Chairmanship of Lord Curzon was appointed to examine the organisation of the national galleries and museums. Its report on the administration of the Chantrey Bequest was damaging in the extreme. In one paragraph of its report the suggestion was made that the Tate, as a means of enforcing reform, 'should decline to accept further Chantrey purchases, in which case a deadlock would straightway ensue'.

Again no appreciable reform was effected, but in 1918 the Tate was allowed to voice its opinion, and in 1922 it was permitted to appoint two members out of five to the committees which select paintings and sculpture for the Royal Academy Council's final decision. As the voting on these committees has to be unanimous, the business of preliminary selection was generally limited by the necessity for the tamest compromise.

Another committee, appointed in 1944 by the Chancellor of the Exchequer and the Minister of Education, under the chairmanship of the Right Hon. Vincent Massey, was set up to examine questions relating to the 'Functions of the National Gallery and the Tate Gallery, and in respect of Paintings, of the Victoria and Albert Museum'. The Massey Report, published in 1946, recommended that the Chantrey money should be transferred to the Trustees of the Tate Gallery by legislation. The Standing Commission on Museums and Galleries, however, reported in favour of the maintenance of the 1922 agreement.

Happily recent efforts to settle the vexed question of the Chantrey Bequest have had a more satisfactory outcome. Under an arrangement with the Treasury and the Royal Academy in 1949 the Tate should now be in a position to ensure that future Chantrey purchases will be unobjectionable to the Trustees. By this arrangement it has been agreed:

1. That no recommendation for purchase shall go forward to the Academy Council until an assurance has been given to the Secretary of the Recommending Committees for Painting and Sculpture by the Director of the Tate Gallery that his Trustees are willing to accept the work in question.
2. That in order to reduce to a minimum the cases in which the full Board of Tate Trustees have to be consulted for this assurance, the Tate Trustees shall have, equally with the Academy, three representatives on each of the Recommending Committees, it being understood that in cases requiring prompt action these three representatives may be able to give the necessary assurance on behalf of their Board.

By this commonsense arrangement the Tate is freed from the

13.*a* REYNOLDS
Catherine, Lady Bamfylde
Tate Gallery

13.*b* WHISTLER
Miss Cicely Alexander
Tate Gallery

14.a GAINSBOROUGH The Watering Place   *Tate Gallery*

14.b CONSTABLE Dedham Mill   *Tate Gallery*

15.a CEZANNE Aix-en-Provence, Paysage Rocheux *Tate Gallery*

15.b DEGAS La Plage *Tate Gallery*

16.b BLAKE Inscription over Hell Gate

16.a TURNER Music Party, Petworth

necessity of having to receive works of art which it is unwilling to exhibit. This may result in fewer Chantrey purchases being made, but it will also go some way towards ensuring that the works selected possess the intrinsic merit upon which Chantrey himself insisted. If any doubt existed as to the wisdom of the Tate's policy in regard to the Chantrey purchases, such doubt must surely have been dispelled by the exhibition of the whole Chantrey collection held at Burlington House in 1949. Almost without exception the critics condemned the Academy's choice of works and they were equally unanimous in lamenting the splendid opportunities that had been missed.

It may, on the other hand, be claimed that the Tate, with its limited financial resources, has consistently attempted to pursue a policy designed to ensure the assembly of a collection of art representative of the finest plastic vision of our time. Such a policy necessarily involves an element of risk, since a large proportion of the works purchased are by young artists with unestablished reputations. An artist may die before attaining the status of a master, in which case his work is merely evidence of unrealised potentialities; or he may belie his first promise and achieve no more than mediocrity. These are the obvious risks, yet to take them boldly is surely the most profitable way of encouraging British art. For to play for safety, to accept only the 'placed' and the established is, in these days of limited patronage, a disservice to the public and the artist. To buy the work of a painter when he has reached the Old Master stage is a costly business for a gallery with limited means, and obviously from the painter's point of view it is better to bestow official encouragement at the beginning of a career rather than at the end.

It is therefore the policy of the Tate to show preference for the work of the younger artists and to buy as far as possible directly from the artists themselves. Particular stress has been laid on the acquisition of works with imaginative or intellectual, as opposed to the 'popular' qualities. (An example of such a choice is the purchase by the Trustees of six works by Edward Burra.) The original decision to include in the Gallery's collection only British pictures painted after about the middle of the 18th Century has been revised by the Trustees, and examples of British art from the earliest period are now included. As a result of this new policy, still-life paintings by the Anglo-Dutch artist Edward Collier (born in the middle of the 17th Century) have been purchased; and the Gallery's collection has been further enriched by a number of early paintings, mostly Elizabethan, generously lent by Group-Captain Loel Guinness and Mr. Francis Howard. Among the paintings in this group are the interesting portraits by Gheeraets and a small but charming portrait of Lady Ann Pope by an unknown artist.

Though the Gallery possess some good examples of Stuart painting, the recent transfer of a fine portrait by Kneller from the National Gallery to the Tate gives the 17th-Century collection a more representative character. Of the many 18th-Century masterpieces in the Tate's possession, mention must be made of Hogarth's brilliant painting *The Staymaker* (another work transferred from the National Gallery); and also his famous series of six satirical paintings, *Marriage à la Mode*. Besides paintings by Stubbs, Samuel Scott and Richard Wilson, the Tate also possesses two very early portraits by Sir Joshua Reynolds of Francis and Susannah Beckford—as well as his later portrait of Lady Bamfylde (Pl. 13*a*) and numerous portraits by Gainsborough and other contemporary artists. Among the finest works by Gainsborough are the beautifully sensitive *Musidora bathing her Feet*, the *Watering Place* (Pl. 14*a*) and the masterly *Landscape, Sunset* which anticipates the luminous painting of Turner and Constable. The romantic element in the art of the 18th Century is well exemplified by two characteristic paintings by Joseph Wright, *An Experiment with the Air Pump* and *The Lighthouse*. In English paintings of the 19th Century the Tate is particularly rich. Beginning with the landscape painters, mention must be made of three paintings by Constable—a version of his favourite subject, *Dedham Mill* (Pl. 14*b*), the *Dell at Helmingham Park* and the lovely early sketch, *View at Epsom*. The Norwich School is excellently represented by such paintings as Crome's noble *Slate Quarries* and Cotman's little masterpiece *The Drop Gate*. On the grand scale, James Ward's *Gordale Scar, Yorkshire* stands out as one of the most imposing achievements of the English School and his *Harlech Castle*, formerly in the National Gallery, makes an impressive addition to the Tate's permanent collection. Bonington is well represented by a powerful sketch, *Mountain Landscape*, and also by a characteristic French view, *Scene in Normandy*.

The illustrious name of Turner is honoured by a comprehensive collection of work which covers every aspect of his achievement (Pl. 16*a*). The paintings range from his first exhibited picture (now on permanent loan to the Tate) *Fisherman at Sea off the Needles* —a masterly study of phosphorescence—to examples of his last phases, such as *Yachts approaching the Coast* or *Sunrise with a Sea Monster*.

Another artist uniquely represented at the Tate is William Blake (Pl. 16*b*), whose visionary genius is splendidly recorded in a series of paintings and drawings, many of which came from the famous Graham Robertson collection. With Blake must be mentioned his disciple Samuel Palmer who is represented by some drawings in monochrome and also by two small landscape paintings of the Shoreham period, *Coming from Evening Church* and *Hilly Landscape*.

Thanks mainly to the enthusiasm and foresight of the late D. S. MacColl, the Tate has built up an important collection of works of Alfred Stevens which are housed together in a special room. These works comprise not only drawings and sculptures, but also a number of superb portrait paintings, notably *Mrs. Mary Ann Collmann*, *John Morris Moore* and the Degas-like painting of a man seated by a stove, *Portrait of an Artist*.

Paintings by Stevens' contemporaries include Millais' *Ophelia* and *Christ in the House of His Parents*; Rossetti's *The Beloved* and *Monna Vanna*; Ford Madox Brown's *The Last of England*; Arthur Hughes' *April Love*; William Holman-Hunt's *Claudio and Isabella*; Henry Wallis' *Death of Chatterton*. In addition to these there is a large collection of paintings by G. F. Watts.

The Tate also possesses an unrivalled collection of portraits by J. S. Sargent which occupy a special gallery. Among these late Victorian and early 20th-Century portraits are such notable works as *The Misses Hunter*, the elegant *Mr. Graham Robertson*; and on a smaller scale, the daringly original *Miss Priestley* and the vividly personal *Vernon Lee*. Sargent's compatriot, James McNeill Whistler, is represented by such characteristic works as *Portrait of Miss Cicely*

Alexander (Pl. 13*b*), *Old Battersea Bridge* and *Valparaiso*, and *Nocturne —Black and Gold*.

The importance of Wilson Steer and Walter Sickert in modern English painting is duly emphasised by a number of outstanding examples of their work. Of particular interest are the early Steer paintings—*Beach at Walberswick, Southwold, Portrait of Mrs. Cyprian Williams and Children* and *The Music Room*. In the case of Sickert the essential quality of his art is admirably conveyed by such paintings as the *Café des Tribunaux, Dieppe, Interior of St. Mark's, Le Tose*; and by such genre pieces as *Off to the Pub* and *Ennui*.

Of other contemporary painters represented, besides those previously mentioned, the names of Gwen John, Harold Gilman, Paul Nash, Duncan Grant, Wyndham Lewis, Frances Hodgkins and Christopher Wood will indicate the scope of the Tate collection of modern British painting.

No mere enumeration of masterpieces, however, can do justice to the Tate's superb collection of French painting which ranges from the beginning of the 19th Century to the present day. Of this great period, beginning with the classicism of Ingres and culminating in the experiments of Picasso and Braque, the Tate possesses or has on loan many masterpieces which have acquired a cardinal importance in the history of modern art.

Among the smaller works, mention must be made of the exceptionally fine sea piece of Boudin *A Squall from the West*; and the subtle *Self-portrait* by Fantin-Latour. In the category of naturalistic landscape, Courbet's *The Pool*, Daubigny's *Willows* and Corot's magnificent early *Palace of the Popes, Avignon* are all outstanding examples of their period.

Yet, lovely as these things are, it is in another group of paintings at the Tate that the supreme expression of French pictorial genius is to be found. This group includes such masterpieces as Manet's *La Serveuse de Bocks, La Musique aux Tuileries, The Firing Party* ; Monet's *Le Bassin aux Nymphéas, Vétheuil: Sunshine and Snow*; Camille Pissarro's *Portrait of the Artist, Le Louvre: Matin Neige, Boulevard des Italiens*; Degas' *Danseuses, Femme Assise, Miss Lola at the Cirque Fernando* and *La Plage* (Pl. 15*b*); Renoir's *La Première Sortie*; Cézanne's *Aix*: *Paysage Rocheux* (Pl. 15*a*), *The Gardener,*

Cézanne Chauve, *Man with a Pipe* (Courtauld Institute loan); Gauguin's *Flowers*, *Nevermore* (Courtauld Institute loan); Sisley's *L'Abreuvoir*; Seurat's *Une Baignade*, *La Poudreuse* (Courtauld Institute loan); Henri Rousseau's *Flowers*; Toulouse-Lautrec's *Private Room at the Rat Mort* (Courtauld Institute loan).

The great Dutch painter Vincent Van Gogh is represented by such well-known pictures as *The Yellow Chair*, *View at Auvers*, *Sunflowers*, *Landscape with Cypress Trees*. Important examples of Modigliani's work include *Le Petit Paysan* and *Portrait of a Girl*.

Among contemporary French paintings at the Tate are characteristic works by Braque, Utrillo, Rouault, Matisse and Léger. Picasso is represented by a collection of paintings typifying the most important phases of his art: *Femme à la Chemise*, *Flowers*, *Femme Assise*, *Femme Nue Assise* and *Buste*.

Finally mention must be made of a significant group of paintings by non-French artists—works by Paul Klee, Max Ernst, Marc Chagall, Edward Munch, Oskar Kokoschka and Giorgio Morandi.

The Tate has also established its own Publications Department responsible for printing and selling catalogues and reproductions for the use of schools, the press and the general public. It has also published several books on art dealing with the various aspects of the Gallery's own collection.

Thus since its opening at the end of the last century the Tate has shown a record of continuous progress. One of the largest galleries in the world devoted solely to the exhibition of pictures and sculpture, the Tate attracts every year a greater number of British and foreign visitors, and its contribution to the artistic life of the nation becomes increasingly important. This is what Henry Tate himself would have wished. And surely no art gallery ever had a more generous or far-seeing founder.

Open free weekdays 10 a.m. to 6 p.m.; Sundays 2 p.m. to 6 p.m. Closed Christmas Eve, Christmas Day and Good Friday.

JOHN ROTHENSTEIN,
Director and Keeper
CARLOS PEACOCK.

THE NATIONAL PORTRAIT GALLERY

THE National Portrait Gallery was founded in the year 1856. It was then the only collection of its kind in the world. Even now there are only two other galleries of a nearly similar nature, the Scottish and Irish National Portrait Galleries, and neither of these is an entirely independent body, being in each case under the same body of Trustees as their respective National Galleries.

Portraits began to accumulate in this country in such places as Guild and College Halls in the 16th Century when they ceased to be great rarities. Indeed some wealthy men went to a deal of trouble to form collections of portraits of celebrities. Two large private collections formed in the latter part of that century are known from surviving inventories. They were those of Robert Dudley, Earl of Leicester, and of John, Lord Lumley. In the Earl of Leicester's collection there were 127 portraits and 168 in the collection of Lord Lumley.

Neither of these men confined themselves to English portraits. In Lord Leicester's collection portraits of the crowned heads and nobility of Europe predominated. Lord Lumley was more catholic in his taste.

It was Edward Hyde, Earl of Clarendon, who, a century later, made the first collection confined almost entirely to portraits of famous Englishmen. His collection included portraits of some of his contemporaries who were still living and modern copies of portraits of persons of an earlier date. Samuel Pepys, on the advice of John Evelyn, collected portrait engravings and not paintings. Evelyn pointed out to him that greater wealth than he possessed was required to collect and house a large collection of portrait paintings, whereas a great many persons could be represented in a collection of portrait engravings at a fraction of the cost.

By the middle of the 18th Century the universities, colleges, Inns of Court, City Guilds, hospitals and other institutions had accumulated large numbers of portraits of their benefactors (often persons of fame) and of their more famous members or alumni. These collections had all grown in a haphazard way by gifts and bequests; rarely by purchases by the institutions themselves. Soon after 1763 the collections at Cambridge were of such a size that a bookseller thought it worth his while to publish a list of the pictures (mainly portraits) there as a companion to a Guide to Cambridge of that date. In it more than 450 portraits are mentioned, including 94 at Trinity College and 74 at St. John's College.

In the course of the 18th Century, portraits of the famous that had been sold by descendants of their original owners found a home first with one collector and then another, for the best collections formed in that century, such as those of Robert Harley, Earl of Oxford, Sir Richard Meade, and James West, F.R.S., were each dispersed soon after the collectors' deaths. Exceptionally that of Horace Walpole remained intact at Strawberry Hill for nearly fifty years until 1842. A few men gave or bequeathed portraits to institutions in which they were interested. Among these were Dr. Richard Rawlinson, benefactor of the Bodleian, and Dr. Andrew Gifford, assistant librarian of the British Museum.

In the second half of that century the collecting of portrait engravings became a fashionable hobby. The Rev. James Granger, a dutiful parish priest and a collector of portrait-engravings, compiled his *Biographical History of England*, in which are catalogued the known portrait engravings of British persons living up to the end of the reign of James II. This publication which was first issued in two volumes in 1769 was added to and ran to five editions in fifty-five years. The hobby continued unabated throughout the first half of the 19th Century, during which period many reprints of rare engravings and new engravings from old or original paintings were published. The finest compilation of the latter type known as *Lodge's Portraits* comprised 240 portraits accompanied by biographies by Edmund Lodge. It was published in fascicules over a period of twenty years (1814–34) at cost stated to have been £40,000. The only living person included was the Duke of Wellington.

Whilst this latter work was in progress one of the annual exhibitions of paintings held at the British Institution, that of 1820, was devoted to portraits of persons of fame in British history.

Meantime, Lord Mahon, later 5th Earl Stanhope, whose *History of England from the Peace of Utrecht* was published in 1836, was becoming interested in the idea of the formation of a national gallery of portraits of the nation's most famous sons and daughters. Like Macaulay, Mahon also took a part in politics, but on the opposite benches. He was first elected to Parliament in 1832. It was in 1845 that he brought the subject forward in the House of Commons. When he raised the question a second time in 1852 it found favour with Disraeli, who was Chancellor of the Exchequer. Mahon succeeded his father as Earl Stanhope in 1855 and on March 4th, 1856, he proposed a motion in the House of Lords that such a collection should be formed. He had informed the Prince Consort of his intention and had received a favourable reply which is now in the Gallery archives.

In the course of his address, Lord Stanhope showed why such collections as were housed at Hampton Court, Holyroodhouse and the British Museum did not answer the purpose and could not be the nucleus or model of the kind of collection that he had in mind. The Hampton Court portraits should remain undisturbed as part of the furnishings of a royal palace. The earlier part of the series of portraits of Kings of Scotland at Holyrood was imaginary, whereas the collection to be formed should consist only of authentic portraits. Those accumulated at the British Museum were a mixed collection only some of which were of persons of historic importance.

Following a debate the motion was agreed to that 'an humble Address be presented to Her Majesty, praying that Her Majesty will be graciously pleased to take into Her Royal Consideration the Expediency of forming a Gallery of the Portraits of the most eminent Persons in British History'.

When the matter came up for debate in the House of Commons on June 6th, 1856, the motion 'That a sum not exceeding £2,000 be granted to Her Majesty towards carrying out measures for the formation of a Gallery of the Portraits of the Most Eminent Persons in British History in the year ending the 31st day of March 1857' was carried by 98 votes to 28.

Five months later, on December 2nd, 1856, the first Trustees were appointed by the Lords Commissioners of Her Majesty's

17.b ANON Queen Elizabeth

17.a ROBERT WALKER Oliver Cromwell

18.b KNELLER Sir Christopher Wren

18.a HON. JOHN COLLIER Charles Darwin

Treasury. As this minute may be described as the Trustees' terms of reference it is here quoted in full:

My Lords have under their consideration the subject of the grant of Parliament, made last Session, of 2,000 l., towards carrying into effect the measures contemplated in the address to the Crown, agreed to in the House of Lords on 14th March last for the formation of a gallery of the Portraits of the most eminent persons in British History. Viscount Palmerston and the Chancellor of the Exchequer suggest to the Board that, as the best mode of carrying into effect the intentions of Parliament, the sum in question should be placed at the disposal of Trustees, who will be responsible to the public for its application to the purposes of the grant; and they suggest to their Lordships the Names of the following noblemen and gentlemen, who, they have reason to believe, will be willing to undertake the duty, viz.:—

The Lord President of the Council (for the time being)
The Marquess of Lansdowne
The Earl Stanhope
The Earl of Ellesmere
The Lord Elcho, M.P.
The Right Hon. Sydney Herbert, M.P.
The Right Hon. Benjamin Disraeli, M.P.
The Lord Robert Cecil, M.P.
The Right Hon. Thomas Babington Macaulay
Sir Francis Palgrave
Sir Charles Eastlake, P.R.A.
William Smith, Esq.
W. H. Carpenter, Esq.

Thomas Carlyle was added to the Board a few weeks later in place of Lord Ellesmere who had died. Thus the first Board, which was appointed by a Whig Prime Minister, was composed of 2 Whig leaders (Granville and Lansdowne); 1 Peelite (Herbert); 2 Conservative leaders (Disraeli and Cecil); 1 Independent (Elcho); 4 historians and men of letters, of whom one (Stanhope) was a Conservative and one (Macaulay) a Whig; 3 concerned chiefly with the Arts (Smith, Carpenter, Eastlake).

The board was subsequently slightly increased in size; its number has never been fixed. The Lord President of the Council and the President of the Royal Academy are now Trustees *ex officio*.

The first meeting was held on February 9th, 1857, when Lord Stanhope submitted in draft rules for the guidance of the Trustees on the admission of portraits. These were amended and adopted at their second meeting. They have undergone little change since. In their present form they are as follows:

1. The rule which the Trustees desire to lay down to themselves in either making purchases or receiving presents, is to look to the celebrity of the person represented rather than to the merit of the artist. They will attempt to estimate that celebrity without any bias to any political or religious party. Nor will they consider great faults and errors, even though admitted on all sides, as any sufficient ground for excluding any portrait which may be valuable as illustrating the history of the country.
2. No portrait of any person still living, except only of the reigning sovereign, and of his or her consort, shall be admitted. But this rule is not to be considered as applying to portraits of persons, some living and some deceased, in a group or series comprised in the same picture, and combined for one common object.
3. No portrait of any person deceased less than ten years shall be admitted, if so many as three of the Trustees shall personally, if present at the meeting, or within one fortnight by letter, state their dissent.
4. No portrait shall be admitted by donation, unless three-fourths, at least, of the Trustees present at a meeting shall approve it.
5. No modern copy of an original portrait shall be admitted.

Immediately there began to pour in a fair number of offers of gifts and bequests and of portraits for sale. These offers were sifted for the Trustees by Sir George Scharf the first Director. During his period of office of nearly forty years some 900 portraits were acquired. The collection was, however, without a permanent home of its own. The building in which it is now housed was opened in 1896. Its cost was almost entirely defrayed by William Henry Alexander. An extension, the gift of Lord Duveen, was opened in 1933.

There are now in the collection portraits of some 2,700 people of fame, but about 850 of these appear only in groups or collections of drawings. Some 1,900 persons are represented by one portrait or in one group only and 800 by more than one portrait.

There are approximately 1,500 paintings in oils, 1,500 drawings of which 1,100 are in collections, not acquired individually, 230 busts and large-scale reliefs, 100 miniatures and a smaller number of medallions. There are 44 groups in which 1,060 persons of some fame are represented. Almost exactly 1,000 named artists are represented. Only one photograph, that of Mrs. Beeton, is exhibited. About half the collection has been acquired by gift or bequest, and half by purchase.

As is the case with most Museums and Galleries, it is not possible to exhibit all the portraits that have been acquired. In fact, about one-third of the collection is on view. Everything is in the catalogue and can be seen within a few minutes on request. With very few exceptions a photograph of any portrait can be supplied on request.

The Gallery is an admirable 'book of illustrations' for students of British Political History or Literature of the last 400 years. It is also, incidentally, the only public gallery where a student of the history of portrait painting in this country can find an adequate amount of material to study.

The exhibition galleries are on several different floor levels. There is a lift and the visitor is advised to take it to the top floor where the earliest portraits are hung, for the collection is arranged chronologically.

The earliest contemporary original portrait in the collection is a small portrait of King Henry VII painted by a Flemish artist for a German merchant. This is in Room 7, the first room entered on leaving the lift. On the top flight of stairs close to the lift are electrotypes from effigies on Royal tombs. These include Edward III, Queen Philippa and the Black Prince. Every monarch from the reign of Edward III, excepting only Edward V and Lady Jane Grey, is represented at the Gallery. The paintings of those before Edward IV are not on exhibition.

Room 7 is devoted to 16th-Century portraits. Near Henry VII are Henry VIII, the first two of his Queens and his two principal statesmen Cardinal Wolsey and Thomas Cromwell Earl of Essex. Then there are the churchmen of the Reformation including Tyndale (translator of the Bible) and Cranmer, and a large composite painting of Sir Thomas More, his family and descendants.

Queen Elizabeth is represented by two paintings, a lovely three-quarter length of about 1572 from Cobham Hall (Pl. 17b) and a whole length of 1592 from Ditchley in which she is shown standing on a map of England.

Assembled round Elizabeth are her Secretaries of State Sir Francis Walsingham, Lord Burghley and his son Robert Cecil Earl of Salisbury, her favourites, Leicester and Essex, and other men of action and learning, Sir Philip Sidney, Sir Walter Raleigh and Sir Richard Grenville, hero of *The Revenge*. Sir Francis Drake is represented by a print from a contemporary engraved plate commemorating his circumnavigation of the globe. Of Shakespeare there is the posthumous engraved portrait by Martin Droeshout which was prefixed to the *First Folio* of 1623. Few engravings are exhibited as usually they are not directly from life, and paintings, drawings and sculpture generally convey more to the spectator. However, of some persons no better representation exists than a contemporary or near contemporary engraving. Of some such as Christopher Marlowe and Edmund Spenser of this period no certain contemporary portrait is known. Often such as do exist have not come to this Gallery.

The 17th Century is represented in Rooms 8 to 11. In Room 8 James I is seen seated in robes on his throne with his favourite motto *Beati pacifici* inscribed above him. Near him are Inigo Jones, Ben Jonson and John Donne; Sir Francis Bacon is at full length at the other end of the wall; opposite James I is his unpopular favourite Buckingham with his family.

Charles I and Henrietta Maria are at one end of this room and Oliver Cromwell (Pl. 17a) at the other end; of other major figures of the reign of Charles I Strafford and Laud are either side of a group of five children of Charles I and Prince Rupert is alongside a painting of Charles I dictating orders in the field.

Room 9 contains Thomas Hobbes and Isaak Walton, Isaac Newton and William Dampier, Christopher Wren (Pl. 18b), John Dryden, John Locke, John Bunyan, Samuel Pepys and Purcell. In the doorway are engravings of John Milton by William Faithorne and John Evelyn by Robert Nanteuil, both from drawings done from life.

In Room 10 are Charles II and Catherine of Braganza in Portuguese costume opposite William III and Mary II; James II and his two wives and an endearing painting by Largillierre of his two children, a poor portrait of his sister Minette, the Duke of Monmouth and a Mignard portrait of Louise de Querouaille, Duchess of Portsmouth; members of the Cabal ministry; Monck, restorer of Charles II; and William Bentinck Earl of Portland, general and companion through life of William III.

Judge Jeffreys, whose 'bloody assizes' embittered the general populace against James II, is in Room 11. Other occupants of the room who came to fame in Queen Anne's reign include John Churchill Duke of Marlborough, and his wife Sarah, Sir George Rooke to whom we owe Gibraltar, Tory statesman Robert Harley Earl of Oxford and Sidney Godolphin, and the financier John Law of Lauriston.

From this period onwards politics are separated from the arts and science. The Kit-Cat Club portraits (1700–20) are in Room 29 and are more conveniently viewed later. The visitor should walk through Rooms 3, 4 and 5 to Room 6.

In Room 6 are portraits of Queen Anne and the first three Georges with the most famous men of action and statesmen of the middle of the century, among them Sir Robert Walpole, William Pitt the elder and Admiral Lord Anson. The '45 rebellion is recalled by portraits of the Young Pretender Prince Charles Edward Stuart, his brother Cardinal York and the Duke of Cumberland.

Late 18th-Century statesmen are in Room 5, among them the younger Pitt and his gifted opponent Charles James Fox, Edmund Burke, John Wilkes, George Washington, Benjamin Franklin and Lord North.

In Room 4 are men of action and Empire-builders: Clive, Warren Hastings, Stringer Lawrence of India, Arthur Philip, founder of Australia, Sir Stamford Raffles, founder of Singapore, Nelson, and among other famous Admirals Rodney, Duncan, Hood and Howe.

In Room 3 and on the landing outside are a number of busts. The series of paintings continues in the West Wing. In Room 12 are three large groups, Pitt addressing the House of Commons in 1793, the first House of Commons elected after the Reform Bill of

1832, and the House of Lords in 1820 during the discussion of the Bill to dissolve the marriage of George IV and Queen Caroline. In the same room are George IV, Princess Charlotte and William IV, a fine portrait of the Duke of York by Sir David Wilkie and portraits of the political reformers, Jeremy Bentham, the 2nd Earl Grey and Sir Francis Burdett.

In the next room are the Duke of Wellington and other generals distinguished in the Peninsula and at Waterloo. On other walls are the principal statesmen of the early 19th Century, Castlereagh, Canning, Liverpool, Huskisson and Brougham. With them is an unfinished portrait by Sir Thomas Lawrence of Wilberforce.

Room 14 is devoted to statesmen of Empire, explorers, churchmen, and social and political reformers. India is represented by Warren Hastings, Sir Thomas Munro, Outram, Dalhousie, Lord Lawrence and Lord Hardinge. Opposite is Sir George Grey, wise colonial governor, Sir Bartle Frere of South African fame and the explorers John Franklin and David Livingstone, with their contemporaries at home Sir Robert Peel, Lord Macaulay, Cardinal Newman and Octavia Hill.

Room 15 contains our leading statesmen of the last hundred years, Lord Durham, Lord Melbourne, Palmerston, Gladstone, Disraeli; Cobden and Bright, Lord Salisbury, Joseph Chamberlain and John Burns. Here also are the South African leader, Cecil Rhodes, 'General' Booth, founder of the Salvation Army, the 7th Earl of Shaftesbury, philanthropist and founder of the 'ragged' schools. The two sovereigns, Queen Victoria by Sir George Hayter and Edward VII by Sir Luke Fildes, are at one end of the room and at the other is a large group by Sir James Guthrie of Statesmen of the 1914–18 war, an imagined group of the leading British and Empire Statesmen assembled under the shadow of The Winged Victory.

The visitor must go back from here to the landing outside Room 12. Here are bronze busts of Florence Nightingale made a few years after her return from the Crimea; Lord Lister, whose discoveries, notably in the use of antiseptics, revolutionised surgical practice. Here too is a bust by Jacob Epstein of Ramsay MacDonald, Britain's first Socialist Prime Minister.

On descending to the first floor by the staircase adjacent to

Room 12 the visitor should turn to the left. In Room 24 are some fine busts, notably a terra-cotta of William Hogarth by Louis François Roubiliac and an amusing coloured plaster bust with glass eyes also by him of Colley Cibber, comedian and poet-laureate.

In Room 25, Dean Swift, author of *Gulliver's Travels*, by his friend Charles Jervas is seen, seated, pen in hand. There is a small self-portrait of Hogarth seated at his easel; Alexander Pope, and small portraits of Samuel Richardson the father of the English novel and Laurence Sterne; a head and shoulders portrait of Handel; portraits of Isaac Watts, the saintly nonconformist preacher and hymn writer, of John Wesley preaching in the open air, and of George Whitefield preaching from a pulpit to an attentive congregation; William Cowper and Arkwright, inventor of the spinning jenny.

One wall in Room 26 shows us Dr. Johnson and his circle. Below Dr. Johnson, who is in the centre, is a fine early self-portrait of Sir Joshua Reynolds. To the right are Boswell, Oliver Goldsmith and John Hunter the great surgeon. The theatre is represented by Garrick, Sheridan and Mrs. Siddons, architecture by Robert Adam. There is a fine unfinished self-portrait of George Romney. A small portrait of Thomas Gray is one side of the door and on the other side is James Cook the explorer.

Robert Burns is in Room 27 with writers of the late 18th and early 19th Century, Wordsworth, Coleridge, Lamb, Byron, Shelley, Scott and Dickens, whose names, if not their works, are known to all. Scott is seen in his study with the many historical relics which he collected around him. The Shelley is the only authentic portrait of him from life: Byron is in a costume he brought to England from Albania: Dickens is seen in the day of his earlier successes. Nearby are the engineers James Watt and George Stephenson, with Sir John Soane, architect of the Bank of England, Bonington and Girtin, talented landscape painters, who both died young.

In Room 28, the last and largest of the octagon rooms, we come to recent days. Here are Humphry Davy and the great Faraday who began as his assistant, Charles Darwin (Pl. 18a) and Thomas Huxley; a head of the young Tennyson, Robert Browning and his wife Elizabeth Barrett Browning painted in Florence, Matthew Arnold,

Thackeray, Trollope, Henry James, Rudyard Kipling and Thomas Hardy. For the stage, music and painting are Henry Irving and Ellen Terry (Pl. 19b), Gilbert and Sullivan, Millais and Watts, many of whose portraits are in the collection, notably in this room and in Room 15.

The drawings on this floor fill some of the gaps and show many of the lesser lights of the learned and artistic professions.

In the little corridor by the octagon rooms are William Bragg, Ernest Rutherford and J. J. Thomson, famous names in modern physics, Joseph Priestley their predecessor of the 18th Century, Dalton and Clerk Maxwell. There is also a drawing by Bartolozzi done from a self-portrait by Gainsborough, a coloured etching of Dr. Arne and Allan Ramsay's self-portrait in red chalk done late in life.

In Room 18 (the near end of the large corridor) are musicians and actors, including the brothers Grossmith and Dame Ethel Smyth, and a water-colour portrait by Downman of Elizabeth Farren who later became Countess of Derby, 'Perdita' Robinson, Mistress of the Prince Regent, and the 18th-Century composer and historian of music, Dr. Burney.

Opposite are sportsmen: the Marquess of Queensberry who gave his name to the rules of boxing, and the Guardsman-balloonist Colonel Burnaby by the French painter J. G. Tissot.

In the small cross gallery (Room 19) are connoisseurs, scholars and patrons of the arts, with a large oil painting of the Private View of the Old Masters' Exhibition at the Royal Academy in 1888 in which the leading figures of the day are assembled around the President, Sir Frederick Leighton.

Opposite, in Room 22, are some of the 19th-Century religious leaders. Paintings of Cardinal Manning in his robes, by G. F. Watts, and of Charles Kingsley with his fishing rods are on opposite walls, around them are drawings of Pusey and Keble, Newman as a young man, Trench, bishop and philologist, and Stubbs, bishop and historian.

On the south wall of Room 18 (the farther end of the corridor) is a series of writers: Keats (Pl. 19a), Barham, author of The Ingoldsby Legends, young Hazlitt, 'George Eliot' as a girl, Charlotte

M. Yonge by George Richmond, and the tiny sketch of Jane Austen by her sister Cassandra. Among the writers of more recent times are Rupert Brooke, Robert Bridges, W. H. Davies, A. E. Housman, Lawrence of Arabia, James Barrie and Arnold Bennett, and a pastel study of George Moore by Henry Tonks.

On the north wall facing the writers are their contemporaries among the artists : Ben Marshall, Rowlandson, George Morland, Cotman and Turner in the earlier time and following them the black and white draughtsmen of the middle of the century, Leach, Tenniel and Keene, Whistler in caricature by 'Spy' and finally Ricketts, Shannon, Tonks, and McEvoy by Augustus John.

Other rooms on this floor are used for temporary exhibitions and lectures.

A flight of stairs leads to the Royal Landing with portraits of Queen Victoria and Prince Albert, Edward VII and Queen Alexandra, and a large group of King George V and Queen Mary with their two eldest children painted in 1913 by John Lavery.

Next to the Royal Landing, in Room 29, are the portraits of the members of the Kit-Cat Club painted by Sir Godfrey Kneller in the first twenty years of the 18th Century. These tell the story of the Whig Party then coming into the ascendant. Among the members were Sir Robert Walpole, Congreve, Steele, Addison, Vanbrugh and the Duke of Newcastle the great 18th-Century political manager.

On the ground floor are the naval and military commanders of the 1914–18 war, with Captain Scott, the Antarctic explorer, and busts of Generals Wolseley and Gordon.

Open free 10 a.m. to 5 p.m. Mondays to Fridays, 10 a.m. to 6 p.m. Saturdays, 2 p.m. to 6 p.m. Sundays. Closed Christmas Eve, Christmas Day and Good Friday.

C. K. ADAMS,
Assistant Keeper

THE VICTORIA AND ALBERT
MUSEUM

THE Victoria and Albert Museum houses the national collection of English water-colours and the national collection of miniatures. It also houses a large collection of oil paintings, mainly British, though some masterpieces by foreign painters have become absorbed into the collections from various sources; the most important was, in past years, the 'Ionides' Bequest. But quite recently the munificent gift of the Duke of Wellington, among other paintings, has vested in the Museum's administration five paintings by Velasquez, Correggio's *The Agony in the Garden*, a magnificent Rubens, two superb Jan Steens, the interesting life-size portrait of the 'Iron Duke' on horseback by Goya and the equally interesting and brilliant portrait of him by Lawrence. These will be exhibited in due course at Apsley House in a museum devoted to the Great Duke, his life and his possessions; equally at Ham House, which is administered as a branch of the Victoria and Albert Museum, an interesting range of 17th-Century English portraits by Lely, Kneller and others are among the contents that have recently been bought for the nation.

The collection of oil-paintings at the Victoria and Albert Museum first came into being through the bequest of John Sheepshanks, a wealthy Victorian business man from the North, who wished to found a gallery of British art in connection with the Department of Science and Art and the Schools of Art. His will, which is unusually liberal and unrestrictive, provided for temporary loans to suitable places inside and outside London, but it is doubtful whether the recommendations made by the Massey Report that the collections should be transferred to the Tate Gallery *in toto* could possibly be implemented, short of legislation, which would have to move contrarily to the expressed wish of the benefactors; the same is equally true of the gifts and bequests of Miss Isobel Constable and Mr. Henry Vaughan.

The Sheepshanks Bequest comprises one of the most important collections of British oil-paintings of the 19th Century in any public gallery. It contains six Constables, including the first version of *Salisbury Cathedral*, exhibited at the Royal Academy in 1823, *Dedham Mill* signed and dated 1820 and *Hampstead Heath*, exhibited at the Royal Academy in 1830; three fine paintings by the Romantic artist Francis Danby, representative Ettys and Friths, sixteen Landseers including the celebrated *Old Shepherd's Chief Mourner*, twenty-three Leslies comprising among others *My Uncle Toby and the Widow Wadman*, the enchanting painting of *Trissotin reading his sonnet to Les Femmes Savantes* and a delightful sketch of Queen Victoria in her Coronation robes. Among other very important 19th-Century English paintings are the group of canvases by Mulready; these include *The Seven Ages of Man* (R.A. 1838), *The Fight Interrupted* (R.A. 1816), *Choosing the Wedding Gown* (R.A. 1846) and *Shooting a Cherry* (R.A. 1848). The Stothards include *John Gilpin*; the Turners *Line-fishing off Hastings* (R.A. 1835) and *East Cowes Regatta* (R.A. 1828). While the Wards are not as good as the *Bulls Fighting* given to the Museum by Mr. C. T. Maud, the Websters and Wilkies are of considerable interest. Other lesser-known 19th-Century painters are represented by one or more paintings and it would be difficult to get together again a collection so characteristic of English 19th-Century art of the representational kind.

To this generous bequest must be added, as far as English oil-paintings are concerned, the superb gift by Miss Isobel Constable of 95 oil sketches by John Constable, the finished painting *The Cottage in the Cornfield*, and the two magnificent, full-size sketches for *The Leaping Horse* (Pl. 20b) in the Diploma Gallery and *The Hay Wain* in the National Gallery, bequeathed by Mr. Vaughan. These two sketches alone, considered by many people to surpass the finished paintings, would necessitate a pilgrimage to the Victoria and Albert Museum. Since, however, they are combined with the long series of exquisite sketches, the notes of a scale which plays on the whole range of Constable's limpid observation of nature, the visit is imperative for anyone who is interested in the greatest of all English painters.

Other extremely interesting English paintings are to be seen in the Dyce and Forster Bequests, the Townshend Bequest and those of other benefactors. In the Forster Bequest is the well-known painting of St. Michael's Mount by Bonington and Gainsborough's portrait of his two daughters as children; in the Dyce, Kneller's self-portrait, the portrait of John Donne attributed to Janssen; in the Townshend Bequest are two fine Morlands, in the Jones a particularly fine Reynolds of an unknown man, the well-known Morland called *Johnny going to the Fair*, the series of theatrical scenes by Frith and the interesting version of Charles I's equestrian portrait by 'Old' Stone after the Van Dyck at Buckingham Palace. Purchases at various times from Museum funds have included the beautiful painting of Mousehold Heath by 'Old' Crome, Gainsborough's fine portrait of Queen Charlotte and the superb portrait of Mrs. Thomas Whetham by Sir Joshua Reynolds.

The paintings bequeathed by Constantine Alexander Ionides form a small but important group. The Louis Le Nain is a beautiful example of that rare master (Pl. 21*b*). A superb Adrian Brouwer, the small Rembrandt of 1640 of *Abraham dismissing Hagar and Ishmael*, a fine De Koninck and the interesting Botticellesque portrait of Smeralda Bandinelli are all paintings of considerable importance. Among the modern section, however, are things of equal importance; the Ingres *Odalisque*, the Degas of the ballet from *Robert le Diable* (Pl. 21*a*), Millet's *Woodcutters* and examples of Delacroix, Courbet, Corot and members of the Barbizon group form a group of distinction, while the long series of Daumier drawings is outstanding. There are fine paintings by Rossetti and Burne-Jones and a whole series of portraits of the family by G. F. Watts.

A few other foreign paintings are to be found throughout the Museum and include, apart from some good Cassoni, the large and important 15th-Century Spanish altarpiece of the life of St. George by Jorges Martial de Saz, a large altarpiece by Meister Bertram of Hamburg and perhaps the most important early Italian tempera painting in England, *Christ on the Cross* by a North Italian painter of about 1200.

The national collection of water-colours also forms part of the

Victoria and Albert Museum. While in some directions, Turner and Blake for instance, the collection cannot compete with the British Museum and the Tate Gallery respectively, in others, notably in the work of Constable, its range is unrivalled. Over 300 water-colours and pencil drawings illustrate his work in different parts of the country, while three important sketch-books in which he drew during the years 1813, 1814, and 1835 are of the greatest interest. The splendid water-colour of Stonehenge (exhibited R.A. 1836) is a typical example of the quality of his water-colour painting, while the large pencil drawing of *Trees at Old Hall Park, East Bergholt* (Exhibited R.A. 1818) is a sketch of incredible virtuosity. Of the other principal exponents of this characteristic English art interesting and important examples are in the collections of the works of Alexander Cozens, Francis Towne, J. R. Cozens, Rowlandson, Girtin, Paul Sandby, Dayes, Downman, the two Varleys, De Wint, David Cox, Cotman, Bonington, Blake, Palmer, etc.

The Rowlandsons include the superb *Scene in the Mall*, the original drawings for the illustrations to *Dr. Syntax's Tour in Search of the Picturesque* and the exceptionally large drawing of *George III Launching Ships at Deptford*; the Girtins the magnificent *Kirkstall Abbey—Evening* (Pl. 20a) and the enchanting *Scene on the Wharfe*, the De Wints (an artist particularly well represented) *Old Houses on the High Bridge, Lincoln* and the well-known *Cottage and Harvesters*. The Cotmans are fine and numerous, particularly good being the *Landscape with River and Cattle* with its wonderful tones of blue and brown, *The Road to Capel Curig* and *The Lincolnshire Windmill*; the Coxs include *Windsor Castle* and *The Cornfield*; the Boningtons *The Street in Verona* and *The Quay*. Blake, while not nearly so well represented at the Victoria and Albert Museum as at the Tate Gallery, is shown to advantage in the superb *Satan among the Rebel Angels*, the *Finding of Moses* and the *Third Temptation*; his successor, Samuel Palmer, by the *Farmyard at Shoreham* and the opulent *Shoreham Garden*.

The 19th-Century water-colour painters, Birket Foster, Hunt, Callow, Lewis, Shotter Boys, etc., are all well represented and a selection of 20th-Century water-colours also is included in the collection. A series of about 150 selected examples are always shown in Room 41 and are changed once a year. The remainder of the collection is always available on application to the Students' Room, the Department of Engraving, Illustration and Design and Paintings on the first floor. The Museum also houses a large number of interesting sketch-books of all periods.

The collection of miniatures is the only extensive one in a national collection and may therefore fitly be termed the National Collection of Miniatures. When the fine examples in the Salting and Jones Bequests are added to the main collection the result is a formidable repertory of the art. The English group covers all dates and starts with the superb portrait of Anne of Cleves by Holbein, who for this purpose may be termed English, in the Salting collection and the equally fine portrait of Mrs. Pemberton from the Murray Bequest. The unrivalled series by Nicholas Hilliard, a painter who has only recently come into his own, includes the portraits of himself, his wife and his father; the Jones *Queen Elizabeth* and the romantic full-length of a euphuistic young man standing behind rose-bushes from the Salting Bequest. The Isaac Olivers include the magnificent costume-piece of Richard Sackville, Earl of Dorset, and the touching portrait of a man against a background of flames. The 17th Century is dominated by the group of miniatures by Samuel Cooper and John Hoskins, but the interesting portrait of Charles I as prince by Sir Balthasar Gerbier, dated 1616, and the fine portraits of Charles II and James II by the artist W. P. are outstanding works. An interesting group of late 17th-Century plumbago portraits includes David Loggan's sensitive portrait of the Duke of Ormonde and Faber's Admiral Sir George Rooke.

To single out all the outstanding examples of the 18th Century would be a long task, but in the earlier part may be mentioned Bernard Lens' portrait of the Duchess of Marlborough dating from 1720, in the latter half the fine self-portrait of Richard Crosse, whose miniature-painter's box is also in the collection, the enchanting portrait of a girl in a feather bonnet by Samuel Shelley, Richard Cosway's unnamed gentleman in the Salting Bequest and Andrew Plimer's portrait of James Daniell. Examples by the Engleheart family are numerous and range from the good early portrait of

Mrs. Gillespie by George to the characteristic portrait of an unknown man by J. C. D. Engleheart, dated 1812.

In foreign miniatures the collection is also strong, particularly in the Jones collection, where the long range of 17th-Century enamel portraits by Petitot is particularly outstanding. The superb large portrait of Louis XIV and Sevin's equestrian portrait of Marshal Turenne are both masterpieces, as is the interesting early 18th-Century portrait of Peter the Great. A recent addition to the collection of the utmost importance is the large portrait of the Duc de Reichstadt as a boy by Isabey, bequeathed by Sir Bernard Eckstein.

The miniature collection is now exhibited in two sections; the early group up to about 1720 in Room 55, the later miniatures in Room 57.

In addition to the contents of the permanent collection, mention must be made of one series of paintings which are on semi-permanent loan. This is the set of seven cartoons for tapestry by Raphael which have been lent from the Royal Collection since 1865. These cartoons were acquired by Charles I when Prince of Wales, probably in Genoa, and were used as models in the tapestry factory at Mortlake. By good luck they survived the sale of the King's collection by the Commonwealth and were later hung at Hampton Court and Windsor until, as a kind of memorial to the Prince Consort's deep interest in Raphael they were deposited in the Victoria and Albert Museum where they could be more easily seen by the public. They form the most important series of High Renaissance paintings in this country, and were used by generations of English artists as a source of inspiration. They were executed for Pope Leo X in the years 1515 to 1516, and were handed over to craftsmen in Brussels, who wove from them tapestries which are still hung on certain feasts in the Sistine Chapel. Though much of the execution is from the hands of pupils the cartoons embody Raphael's principles of composition and draughtsmanship at the highest point in his artistic development.

Open free 10 a.m. to 6 p.m. weekdays and Bank Holidays; 2.30 p.m. to 6 p.m. Sundays.

LEIGH ASHTON,
Director

THE WALLACE COLLECTION

THE collection of paintings at Hertford House is only a part of the famous assembly of works of art bequeathed to the nation by Lady Wallace, widow of Sir Richard Wallace, Bt., in 1897. Nevertheless, by reason of its range and quality, it ranks high among the great picture galleries of the world.

The curious story of how it came into existence is bound up with the fortunes and tastes of successive generations of the family of Seymour-Conway, Marquesses of Hertford. The line descends from Sir Edward Seymour, 4th Baronet, who was Speaker in the Long Parliament from 1672, and whose second son was created Baron Conway of Ragley, Warwickshire, in 1702. The latter's elder son by his third wife was created Viscount Beauchamp and Earl of Hertford in 1750, and filled several high offices of state, being Lord Lieutenent of Ireland, Master of the Horse and Lord Chamberlain to King George III. He was created Earl of Yarmouth and Marquess of Hertford in 1793. His elder son, who succeeded to the family honours in 1794, married as his second wife, Isabella Ingram-Shepherd, daughter of the 9th Viscount Irvine, and by her had, in 1777, an only son, Francis Charles, who in 1822 became the 3rd Marquess of Hertford. In 1798 the latter had married the beautiful Maria, daughter of the Marchesa Fagnani, who began her career as an Italian dancer. She is important to the story because she herself was able to bring a very considerable fortune to her husband. She had inherited large sums of money and considerable property from the 4th Duke of Queensberry, as well as from the Duke's great friend, George Selwyn, the celebrated wit, who himself took an almost paternal interest in her when she was a child, although the Duke was almost certainly her real father. The 3rd Marquess and his mother were both intimate friends of George IV, both as Regent and King, and the latter's visits to the 2nd Marchioness in Manchester Square were sufficiently frequent to excite comment. The Marquess himself lived apart at Dorchester House in Park Lane.

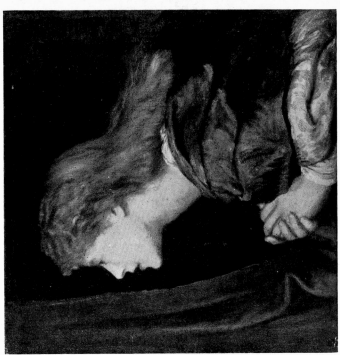

19.a CHARLES ARMITAGE John Keats

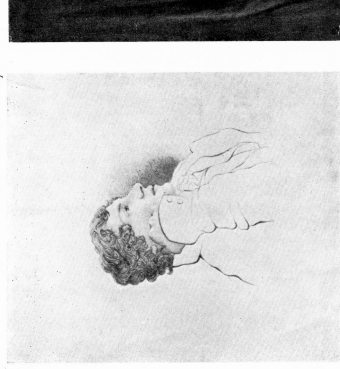

19.b GEORGE FREDERICK WATTS Ellen Terry

20.a GIRTIN Kirkstall Abbey, Evening *Victoria and Albert Museum*

20.b CONSTABLE Study for 'The Leaping Horse' *Victoria and Albert Museum*

The 3rd Marquess was a brilliant figure in Court and political circles during the Regency and reign of George IV. His lavish mode of living combined with his great wealth, wit and dissipation made him a legendary figure in society. He built the villa of St. Dunstan's and his sumptuous entertainments there earned him the title of the *Caliph of Regent's Park*, and when he went on special mission to St. Petersburg the splendour of his retinue astonished even the Court of the Czar. Thackeray later portrayed him under the name of Lord Steyne in the novel *Vanity Fair*, and Disraeli took Lord Hertford as his model for the wicked Lord Monmouth in *Coningsby*. He was a man of great intelligence and taste, and as will be made clear later, he was the real originator of the collection.

The 3rd Marquess and his wife lived a great deal in Paris. After the rupture of the Treaty of Amiens in 1803, he was interned by the French and on his release three years later was employed on abortive negotiations with the French Government for a renewal of peace terms. It was in Paris also that their sons were brought up. The elder son, Richard, was born in 1800 and succeeded his father as 4th Marquess in 1842. As a very young man he held a commission in the 10th Hussars and made a brilliant *début* in politics, when Peel made him a Knight of the Garter. His mother's great fortune passed on her death in 1856 to her younger son, Lord Henry Seymour, who himself died three years later leaving his brother as his sole heir, with the result that the entire Hertford-Queensberry-Selwyn possessions and estates devolved upon Lord Hertford and he thus became one of the richest men of his day. But after the death of his mother, Lord Hertford, who was a bachelor, chose to live in Paris, deserting his houses in London (Manchester House of the Hertfords, St. Dunstan's which his father had built and Old Q's house in Berkeley Square). In addition to these houses he possessed three residences in Paris: his main town apartment at No. 2 rue Laffitte, where he lived with his mother, No. 1, rue Taitbout which had been occupied by his brother up to the time of the latter's death, and the charming little château of Bagatelle on the edge of the Bois de Boulogne, which had been built in 1777 by Bellanger for King Louis XVI's younger brother, the Comte d'Artois, later King Charles X, and which Lord Hertford had acquired in 1835 while he was still Lord Yarmouth. It was in the first and last of these houses, that he kept a large proportion of his collection. A certain melancholy combined with continual bad health compelled him to become almost a recluse and his life centred largely round his collections. He moved little in society and saw few people other than his immediate circle of relations and friends, among whom was the Emperor Napoleon III. A secretary, Richard Wallace, who had been brought up from a boy by his mother, lived with him and assisted him in his business affairs and his collecting activities. There is little doubt, though it has never been conclusively proved, that Wallace was in fact his son. As early as 1850, Lord Hertford made Richard Wallace his heir, although the latter appears to have been entirely unaware of the fact until the 4th Marquess's death. When this took place in August 1870 and the title and entailed Hertford properties passed to his second cousin, Wallace inherited all the unentailed fortune and property, including the lease of the house in Manchester Square, 105, Piccadilly, the income from the Queensberry estates, the Paris properties and the great collection of works of art which the 3rd and 4th Marquesses had formed during their lifetimes.

Lord Hertford's death took place on the eve of the Franco-Prussian war, and Wallace remained in Paris throughout the remainder of 1870 and the siege of the following year, during which time his philanthropic services to the distressed in the French capital and his founding and endowing of the Hertford British Hospital there, earned him a Baronetcy which was gazetted on December 24th, 1871. After the Commune Wallace decided to resume an English domicile (he spoke with a slight French accent to the end of his life) and transferred a large and most important part of his collections to London. He also re-opened the house in Manchester Square. While the house was being adapted to his purposes, Sir Richard lived at 105, Piccadilly and lent a large part of the collection for the opening exhibition of the Bethnal Green Museum, where it is said to have been visited by 5,000,000 people. Another part was stored in the Pantechnicon warehouse in Motcomb Street, where it perished in the fire of 1874. He still maintained the apartment in the rue Laffitte and also Bagatelle. During his early life in Paris Wallace moved in artistic circles and was the friend of a number of painters of the period including Meissonier. He also frequented the salon of Mme. Sabatier.

In February 1871, Wallace had married Mlle Amélie Julie Charlotte Castelnau, and thenceforward he and his wife spent a large part of the year in England, either in London or at Sudbourne Hall (a Queensberry property) in Suffolk, which he purchased from the 5th Marquess of Hertford. He represented in Parliament the borough of Lisburne, in Northern Ireland, where he owned a large Hertford property, from 1873 to 1885. His only son, Captain Edmond Wallace, who had distinguished himself in the war, predeceased his father in 1887. Like Lord Hertford, therefore, Wallace was left without a male heir.

Persistent statements that Wallace intended leaving his collection to the French nation on his death appear to be entirely without foundation, and his removal of the most important part of it to London after the Commune seems to point to his ultimate intention of leaving at any rate part of it to the country of his birth. Towards the end of his life he envisaged presenting his collection to the nation. Some time in 1888 he is known to have called a meeting of friends to discuss the matter, but on learning that the Government of the day was unlikely to agree to a scheme involving large building and endowment expenses, he adjourned the meeting and the project was temporarily abandoned. His indifferent health probably prevented him from pursuing the matter any further. He left London in 1888 for the last time and when he died in Paris two years later, he left everything unconditionally to his wife by an old will made twenty years before. At her death in 1897, Lady Wallace fulfilled her husband's wishes by leaving to the nation the works of art on the ground and first floors of Hertford House, which included the principal part of the collections inherited by her from her husband. It was a condition of the bequest that the nation should provide for the housing and upkeep of the collection, which was to remain a closed one. The Government of the day after considering the possibility of building accommodation adjacent to the site of the National Gallery, decided to acquire the freehold of Hertford House from the Portman Estate.

This, the principal London residence of the Marquesses of Hertford, was formerly known as Manchester House, and was built by the 4th Duke of Manchester between 1776 and 1778. It had passed, however, into the occupation of the Seymour-Conway family by the time of the 2nd Marquess. For thirty-four years it remained virtually unoccupied, being used mainly for storing the purchases which Lord Hertford made in England. Sir Richard Wallace made considerable alterations to it, putting on a new frontage and it was he who renamed it Hertford House in memory of the family to whom he owed so much. After Lady Wallace's death certain other alterations were carried out to make it more suitable to the requirements of a national museum, and it was formally opened to the public by the Prince of Wales, afterwards King Edward VII, on June 22nd, 1900.

The collection of pictures derives from a nucleus of Hertford family possessions inherited and augmented by the 2nd Marquess. The tastes of the first two holders of the title are, however difficult to determine, as little definite information survives about their contributions to the family collections. Understandably, both appear to have patronised Sir Joshua Reynolds. The 1st Marquess was painted by Reynolds in 1785 and it was undoubtedly he who commissioned from the painter in 1781 and 1784 respectively, the portraits of two of his daughters, Lady Elizabeth Seymour-Conway and Frances, Countess of Lincoln, which are still in the collection. The 1st Marquess is also known to have bought some Dutch pictures at sales in the late 1750's. The 2nd Marquess was painted as a young man by Reynolds and also by Tilly Kettle and his wife three times by Reynolds. He further purchased in 1810 the latter painter's now famous portrait of *Nelly O'Brien*, and also Romney's portrait of *Mrs. Robinson* which are still to be seen at Hertford House.

With the 3rd Marquess we are on safer ground. While still Lord Yarmouth, he was the close friend of the Prince Regent, of whose Household he was Vice-Chamberlain and frequently advised him about the acquisition of works of art. His name, moreover, appears on sale lists as a purchaser on behalf of the Prince; it is not surprising, therefore, to find among his known purchases, pictures and objects similar to those bought by the Regent, and now in the Royal

Collections. Among these should be mentioned Dutch pictures of the 17th Century, French furniture and Sèvres porcelain of the 18th Century. Amongst the most important pictures purchased by the 3rd Marquess are Titian's *Perseus and Andromeda*, painted for Philip II of Spain and later in the Orleans collection; Van Dyck's portraits of an Italian nobleman and of himself as the Shepherd Paris; the two large views of the *Bacino di San Marco, Venice* by Canaletto; Rembrandt's *Landscape with a Coach*; and works by Metsu, Steen, Cuyp, Wouverman, Van Ostade, Van Mieris and Berchem. He also received in 1818 as a gift from the Regent, Gainsborough's portrait of *Mrs. Robinson* (Pl. 23a) which is one of the outstanding works of the collection. Lord Hertford himself was painted by Lawrence.

It was upon this foundation that his son, Richard, 4th Marquess, built up his inheritance and transformed it into one of the greatest collections in existence. He not only increased the range and quality of the picture gallery, but also completely transformed the collections of furniture, sculpture and porcelain, as important in their kind as the paintings, and which contribute so much to the atmosphere of the Wallace Collection.

His most important contribution to the collection of pictures must always remain his acquisitions of so many masterpieces of French painting of the 18th Century. In this he was something of a pioneer, for French painting of the rococo period, and particularly the works of its most famous exponents, Watteau, Boucher, Fragonard and Greuze, suffered an almost total eclipse in public taste for nearly half a century following the French Revolution. The credit for its reinstatement in favour during the second half of the 19th Century is usually attributed to the critics Edmond and Jules de Goncourt, whose series of monographs on the principal painters of the *ancien régime* in France were published in 1856. It is therefore significant to find Lord Hertford purchasing for his collection during the 1840's and early 1850's such works as Watteau's *Les Charmes de la Vie* (Pl. 24a), *Les Champs Elysées*, *The Music Lesson*; Lancret's *Italian Comedians*; Fragonard's *The School Mistress*; Greuze's *L'Offrande à l'Amour*; Boucher's two large pastorals from the collection of the Duc de Stacpoole, his *Rape of Europa*, and

Mercury confiding the Infant Bacchus to the Nymphs, and even more important, his four panels painted for Mme de Pompadour's boudoir in the *Hôtel de l'Arsenal*, Paris, and the two great designs for Gobelins tapestry, *The Rising and Setting of the Sun*, also once in the possession of Mme de Pompadour, and regarded by Boucher as his most important work. Lord Hertford secured these two great works in 1855 at the sale of the Baron de Commaille's collection for the small sum of 2,200 francs. These remarkable purchases were augmented later by Boucher's portrait of *Mme de Pompadour* herself (Pl. 23*b*); Fragonard's masterpiece, *The Swing*; Watteau's *Le Rendez-vous de Chasse* and works by Le Moyne, Lancret, Pater, Nattier, Oudry and Mme Vigée le Brun.

It will be seen, therefore, that Lord Hertford's acquisition of these works provided him with a unique collection of them at least twenty years before fashion veered again towards 18th-Century art and is in itself a remarkable example of his connoisseurship, particularly as his purchases at the same time of French 18th-Century furniture, sculpture and porcelain were of the same high quality. Contemporary taste may find reasons to regret the absence of any work by Chardin from the collection, but in spite of the De Goncourts' sympathetic essay, Chardin never obtained anything like public esteem until the very end of the 19th Century.

Lord Hertford's love of pictures, however, was not confined to 18th-Century France. His wide range of interests and catholicity of taste, as well as his remarkable judgment, appears in his purchases of paintings of other schools. Before his death in 1870 he had enriched his collections with nine works by Rubens, including the great *Rainbow Landscape* (Pl. 24*b*); three outstanding portraits by Van Dyck; Velasquez's portraits of *Don Balthasar Carlos* and the *Lady with a Fan* (Pl. 22*b*); eight works by Murillo; five works by Rembrandt, including the beautiful portrait of his son, *Titus* (Pl. 22*a*); Frans Hals' celebrated *Laughing Cavalier*; four landscapes by Hobbema; two interiors of the highest quality by Pieter de Hooch, and many works by other Dutch genre painters of the 17th Century such as Jan Steen, Metsu, Terborch and Gerard Dou. He also bought a large number of works by the Dutch still-life and flower painters, Weenix, Hondecoeter, Fyt and Van Huysum.

His interest in the Italian school was mainly confined to the 16th and 17th centuries and led him to purchase two Madonnas by Luini and another by Andrea del Sarto, an important altar-piece by Sassoferrato, and a fine landscape by Salvator Rosa. He did, however, acquire at Lord Northwick's sale in 1859, the *St. Catherine of Alexandria* by Cima, the centre panel of that artist's altar-piece painted for the church of San Rocco at Mestre. His most outstanding Italian acquisitions were, however, the magnificent set of four Venetian views by Francesco Guardi, which are some of the finest in existence.

He also acquired some important paintings of the French school of the 17th Century, including works by Poussin, Claude and Philippe de Champaigne, and he added to his inherited collection of English portraits by his purchase of such works as *Miss Bowles*, *The Strawberry Girl* and *Mrs. Carnac* by Reynolds, *Miss Haverfield* by Gainsborough, *Miss Siddons* by Lawrence, and he re-purchased Hoppner's portrait of George IV as Prince of Wales, which had formerly belonged to his father, the 3rd Marquess, to whom it had been presented by the Prince. It is to Lord Hertford also (and to a lesser extent to his brother, Lord Henry Seymour) that the collection owes the remarkable number of works both in oil and water-colours, by Bonington, which were purchased during the 1840's and form the largest single collection of this artist's work.

Lord Hertford's interests, however, did not cease with the art of the past, for in addition to the formation of a collection of old masters of the calibre indicated above, he also found the time and the money to buy a large number of works by French 19th-Century painters such as Prud'hon, Delacroix, Géricault, Corot, Isabey, Meissonier, Couture, Delaroche, Decamps and Horace Vernet, the possession of which carries the representation of French painting in the collection up to the birth of the Impressionist movement. He also bought pictures by his English contemporaries, such as Wilkie, and Landseer whose works he is known to have been particularly anxious to add to his collection, and others by William Hilton, Richard Westall, David Roberts and Clarkson Stanfield.

The majority of the works already mentioned were bought in the English and continental salerooms. Lord Hertford's almost continuous bad health prevented him from travelling far from Paris, and he consequently entrusted a large part of his purchasing activities in the London saleroom to S. M. Mawson, an agent in whose judgment and ability he appears to have placed great confidence, and with whom he corresponded on almost intimate terms. A series of his letters to Mawson written between the years 1848 and 1861, when Lord Hertford's collecting activities were at their height, have survived, which show that communication with Mawson in London in his own handwriting took place almost daily, and Lord Hertford is at pains throughout to tell Mawson how much he trusts his judgment, how anxious he is to remain anonymous in the saleroom and to thank him for all his advice and help. Mawson, on the other hand, does not seem to have made a single purchase without previously consulting his patron and the letters are valuable in revealing Lord Hertford's predilections in the matter of painting, and also the determination and definition of his tastes. They contain such revealing statements made by Lord Hertford as:

> . . . I do not at all remember the Velasquez you allude to. By your account of it, it must be very good and on the strength of your judgement you may purchase it for me if it does *not* go to an extravagant price and not much beyond what you think I might get for it in the improbable event of my not liking it. You know fancy has a great deal to do with pictures as well as with everything else. I hope I shall get some good news tomorrow as I should be extremely annoyed not to have the Lancret . . . I depend upon your not mentioning my name. . . . [May 26th, 1853.]

Again on June 23rd, 1853, Lord Hertford writes:

> . . . I saw the famous Murillo when it was here a few months ago, and tho' a very fine picture I do not much like it. I think it dry and it has not the rich, mellow quality I so much admire in that Master, so I will have nothing to do with it . . .

On July 12th of the same year in another letter, he says:

> . . . I do not much like buying pictures that I do not know by sight, but I have the greatest confidence in your taste and judgement and I must say I should like to have the Wilkie as you say it is good. I am anxious to have a Landseer and your account of the Dead Game No. 774

21.*a* DEGAS Ballet to Robert le Diable *Victoria and Albert Museum*

21.*b* LOUIS LE NAIN Peasants *Victoria and Albert Museum*

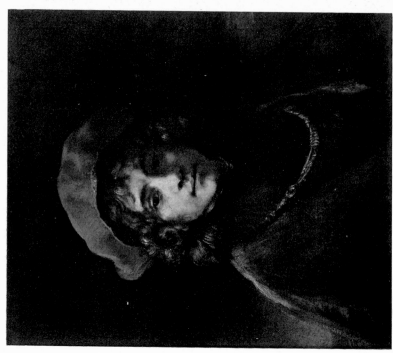

22.*a* REMBRANDT Titus

22.*b* VELASQUEZ Lady with a Fan

23.a GAINSBOROUGH Mrs. Robinson as Perdita   23.b BOUCHER Mme. de Pompadour

24.*a* WATTEAU Les Charmes de la Vie *Wallace Collection*

24.*b* RUBENS Rainbow Landscape *Wallace Collection*

is very satisfactory. The Bonnington [*sic*] I think I should also like to have. . . .

Another indication of Lord Hertford's tastes is given in a letter dated July 31st, 1854:

. . . By the list you were good enough to send me I do not perceive any pictures likely to suit us—Primitive masters that I have not yet adopted and that I don't think I ever will. . . .

Of the pictures in the Rogers sale of 1856, Lord Hertford writes:

. . . The Garofalo I have no immense fancy for, but if it could be had a *sort* of bargain we might throw this Virgin into our collection. There I stop as I do not much like Rubens' landscapes and besides I have a good one. The same observation applies to Poussin. . . .

A little later he writes again:

. . . Only think of the Raffaelle drawing selling for 462—enormous. I am very glad I don't dabble in drawings as well as in other Articles that sell rather dear. . . .

And on June 28th, 1860:

. . . Now comes the Rubens. I do not well understand the Article concerning this Picture in the Catalogue. It would appear that at one time, when Horace Walpole wrote the *Anecdotes of Painting* it was *not* considered *certain* that the picture was by *Rubens*. Even *now* it seems, by what you say, that there is a doubt about its authenticity. If there was the *very slightest doubt about* its origin I wd. have nothing to say to it. . . .

Later probably in 1861, he writes:

. . . You know my taste (good or bad) perfectly well and your observation about the Landseer is quite correct. You mention 'blood on all the animals' and *that* I do not admire—I have no doubt by your description that it is a very fine picture, but I do not regret it and then it is rather expensive, especially at my age and in my bad state of health, to wait eighteen months for it. . . .

And again on July 4th of the same year:

. . . I am certain, by your account, that it is a very fine picture, but it is almost impossible to give such large sums without having *even had a sight* of the *Article*. You know there is a great deal of fancy in Works of Art. A Picture may be magnificent and yet not please. This observation may not apply to the Rubens in question but still it might. If the price was not so very great I daresay I should be tempted to run the risk—but £4,000 is terrible—how very few pictures sell for that price unless purchased by *Nations* when money is often of little or no consequence— . . . I have bought a great deal this year and nothing but a bargain can tempt me. . . .

Lord Hertford also entrusted to Mawson the supervision of such of his pictures as were stored in London, either at Manchester House or at 33, Berkeley Square, his usual residence during his rare visits to London. Mawson was also instrumental in persuading his patron to lend a number of the latter's more important pictures to the Manchester Art Treasures Exhibition of 1857, and undertook responsibility for their transport. He appears to have been an exemplary agent possessed of genuine acumen as to the quality of works of art, and also in the knowledge of how to act firmly and intelligently in the saleroom. He acted for Lord Hertford at such important sales as those of the Duke of Buckingham in 1848, King William II of Holland in 1850, King Louis Philippe in 1853, Samuel Rogers and the Earl of Orford in 1856 and the Hon. Edmund Phipps in 1859.

Sir Richard Wallace's additions to his father's collection of pictures are not very numerous, and do not depart to any great extent from the canons of taste established by Lord Hertford. Wallace's main concern appears to have been to redress to a certain extent the representational balance of the collection which on his inheritance was almost entirely 17th or 18th Century in character. To this end he purchased intact the Comte de Nieuwerkerke's collection of Mediæval and Renaissance ceramics, goldsmiths' work, bronzes and armour, to the last section of which he was able to add part of Sir Samuel Meyrick's remarkable collection of European armour. His principal additions to his picture gallery appear to have been Foppa's fresco of *A Boy Reading*; Jordaens' *Riches of Autumn*; Teniers' *Boors Carousing*; Hobbema's *The Outskirts of a Wood*; Terborch's *A Lady at her Toilet*; De Troy's *A Hunt Breakfast* and *The Death of a Stag*; Fragonard's *A Boy as Pierrot*; Nattier's *Mlle de*

Clermont at the Bath; Prud'hon's *Venus and Adonis*, and Landseer's
The Arab Tent, thus following almost exactly Lord Hertford's
tastes. It seems that Wallace, probably because there was no wall-
space left at Hertford House, was content to fill the gaps in this
great collection with objects of art rather than pictures, and to
consolidate his inheritance on British soil.

In her will, Lady Wallace left as the residuary legatee to her estate
Mr., later Sir John Murray Scott, who had been Sir Richard
Wallace's secretary and companion during the Siege of Paris and the
Commune, and who after her husband's death became Lady Wallace's confidential adviser. He received possession of the Lisburne
estate, the remainder of the lease of Hertford House, and of everything there except the works of art on its ground and first floors, the
apartment in the rue Laffitte, the *Château de Bagatelle*, and all the
works of art contained in these last two places. In 1904, he sold
Bagatelle to the French Government, and after his death in 1912,
the works of art in his own London house, No. 5, Connaught
Square, all of which derived from Sir Richard Wallace's collection,
were sold at Christie's in June 1913. He bequeathed the apartment
in the rue Laffitte and all it contained to Victoria, Lady Sackville,
wife of the 3rd Baron Sackville of Knole, a bequest which was
unsuccessfully contested at law by his two sisters. In 1914, Lady
Sackville disposed of the greater part of her legacy to Messrs.
Jacques Seligmann of Paris, and thus a large amount of sculpture,
furniture, porcelain, tapestries, books and prints of the highest
quality, together with some pictures, became dispersed throughout
the world. Many of these works of art have found their way into
collections in the United States.

For his services in connection with the opening of the collection
to the public, John Murray Scott was created a baronet, and one
of the original Trustees of the Collection, which is administered by
a Board of seven Trustees, appointed by the Prime Minister, and a
Director and two assistants.

The French Revolution and the wars of Napoleon played a great
part in shaping the general character of the collection, while the
Franco-Prussian war and its aftermath, the Commune, were the
causes of the removal of the collection from Paris to London. In the

first world war it sought refuge from air raids in the Post Office tube and, in September 1939, war once again drove it from its home to seek safety, this time in the countryside. The exhibition galleries at Hertford House suffered some superficial damage during the air raids of 1940 and 1944, but this has now to a great extent been repaired, and the collection, which returned unscathed from the country in 1945, is now fully open for exhibition to the public in Manchester Square.

The hours of opening are from 10 a.m. to 5 p.m. on weekdays and from 2 p.m. to 5 p.m. on Sundays; admission is free. The collection is closed on Christmas Eve, Christmas Day and Good Friday.

ROBERT CECIL,
Assistant to the Director

THE NATIONAL MARITIME
MUSEUM, GREENWICH

THE National Maritime Museum at Greenwich was founded by
Act of Parliament in 1934, and occupies the buildings vacated by
the Royal Hospital School when the school was moved to Holbrook
in Suffolk. The old school buildings have been carefully restored
and converted into exhibition galleries, and the necessary museum
offices, by H.M. Ministry of Works through the generosity of Sir
James Caird, Bart.

The central feature of the Museum is the Queen's House, completed in 1635 for Henrietta Maria, the Queen of Charles I.

Samuel Pepys, who became Secretary of the Admiralty in 1673,
collected ship-models, those exquisite scale models produced in
advance by the shipwright before he built a new man-of-war.
James, Duke of York, the Lord High Admiral, commissioned Peter
Lely to paint, in 1665, portraits of the 'Flaggmen,' those distinguished officers who had supported him at the victory he won over
the Dutch at the battle of Lowestoft; and some time after 1670
James invited the famous Dutch marine artists, the Willem Van de
Veldes, father and son, to visit England; and, further, he provided
them with a studio, in which to paint pictures of British ships, in
the Queen's House, Inigo Jones' little palace at Greenwich. Seventeenth-century ship-models of the kind Pepys admired so much,
the Lely 'Flaggmen' and paintings by the Van de Veldes can be
admired by visitors today in this same Queen's House.

The story of the foundation of the National Maritime Museum
at Greenwich can be said to commence when a Captain William
Locker, Royal Navy, who had been Nelson's captain in the
Lowestoffe, became Lieutenant-Governor of Greenwich Hospital
and collected manuscript material for a naval history; his son,
Edward Hawke Locker, who became a Civil Commissioner of
Greenwich Hospital, was instrumental in starting a naval picture
gallery in the Painted Hall of the Hospital in 1823. This scheme

enjoyed royal patronage and both George IV and William IV presented pictures and models from the royal palaces. The fame of Nelson, whose body had lain in state in the Painted Hall after Trafalgar, inspired the project, and his relics were collected here, the Prince Consort buying and presenting to the hospital in 1845 the very uniform coat worn at Trafalgar with its four glittering orders and the bullet hole in the left shoulder. When the naval pensioners had been dispersed and the Admiralty turned the buildings into a Royal Naval College, a Royal Naval Museum was placed within the College containing the Admiralty collection of ship-models which had once been at Somerset House and then at South Kensington. Thus, at the beginning of the 19th Century, Greenwich was already a Mecca for the student of naval history, where could be seen naval portraits, battle-pieces and relics, as well as scale models of the old wooden walls and early ironclads.

With the formation of The Society for Nautical Research in 1910, the desire arose for a more scientific exhibition, a national museum where picture could be compared with model, portrait be shown close to the manuscripts of the sitter, the pictures of the battles in which he fought and of the ships in which he served, as well as the instruments he used and the charts he pored over. The Technical Sub-Committee of the Society, which sought out the historic records by means of which H.M.S. *Victory* at Portsmouth was restored to her condition as at the battle of Trafalgar, showed that the will and the material were there; but the difficulty experienced in raising a fund by public appeal for the *Victory's* restoration, showed one immense obstacle to the founding of such a museum. The princely munificence of Sir James Caird, and the opportune vacating of the buildings of the Royal Hospital School, together with the co-operation of the Admiralty in offering to the proposed Museum the Greenwich Hospital collection and Royal Naval Museum collection on permanent loan, solved these problems. The National Maritime Museum Act was passed in 1934 and in 1937 Their Majesties came by river to Greenwich and opened the Museum in the presence of a distinguished gathering.

Many factors brought the Museum into being, but to Sir James Caird, who paid for the conversion of the Caird Galleries and formed and presented a priceless collection of pictures, books, models and instruments (including the famous Macpherson collection of maritime prints), and to Sir Geoffrey Callender, the Museum's first Director and himself a well-known naval historian who taught naval history to generations of naval officers, to the steady infectious enthusiasm and organising ability of these two men, the National Maritime Museum principally owes its being.

It is not easy in a few words to define the scope and aims of the Museum. The collections are designed to illustrate the whole maritime story of the growth of the British Empire in all its aspects, covering the duties and histories of the Royal and Merchant Navies and Fishing Fleets, both in peace and war, and also the biographies of the sea officers and men who have built and manned our ships and administered our trade and promoted the formation of our Empire through the use of sea transport.

As a picture gallery, the National Maritime Museum must surprise the casual unprepared visitor, especially when it is remembered that pictures are primarily exhibited because of their subject matter, and historic importance, as apart from their artistic excellence. The galleries are arranged chronologically, and the Queen's House covers the 16th and 17th Centuries.

Contemporary portraits of Henry VII and Henry VIII, and of Queen Elizabeth, are displayed to remind us of the part the Tudor monarchy played in the creation of the Royal Navy and the encouragement of the projects of exploration and colonisation which formed such a healthy background to the more colourful expeditions which had the plunder of the Spanish treasure fleets as their chief incentives.

Portraits of Drake, Frobisher and Essex remind the visitors of the circumnavigation of the world, the search for the North-West Passage, and the capture of Cadiz in 1596. Perhaps the finest of the early portraits is the full length in the Great Hall of the Queen's House of Lord Howard of Effingham, the Lord Admiral and the Commander-in-Chief of the English Fleet in the Armada campaign of 1588. This canvas is by Daniel Mytens and was presented by George IV to Greenwich Hospital in 1825.

Exciting almost contemporary paintings of the Armada campaign show the fireships off Calais, and also, on a panel, a curious representation of the opposing fleets, perhaps a design for a tapestry, and including pictures of a Spanish galleass and the English flagship, the *Ark Royal*.

The 17th-Century marine paintings, of which a large number are exhibited in the Queen's House, are nearly all the work of the Dutch artists, and include examples of the work of Van Ertvelt, Van Antum, Willarts, Vroom, De Vlieger, Zeeman, Van Diest, Verschuier, Backhuizen; to mention some of the better known. These Dutch marines enable the modern sailor to visualise the common sea scenes of the 17th Century with almost photographic exactitude: whether it be the English and Dutch men-of-war locked in combat, the great convoys being taken up-channel with the riches of the East, or the smaller merchant ships and coasting vessels sailing in or out of harbour. All the many phases of seamanship are shown.

As has already been mentioned, the Van de Veldes are known to have used a room in the Queen's House as a studio, and here produced those excellent records of the sea fights of the Dutch Wars, for the artists cruised with the fleet in their yacht, and so painted the actions at close quarters.

Round the walls of the gallery which surround the Great Hall of the Queen's House, and on to which open the Queen's Bedchamber and Presence Chamber (with their fine painted and carved ceilings), hang the six paintings by Van de Velde the Elder of the battle of the Texel, fought in 1673.

As well as numerous examples of their paintings in oils, a large collection of Van de Velde drawings is kept in the Print Room of the Museum, and a selection is always on public exhibition.

Many fine portraits of 17th-Century seamen are exhibited in the Queen's House, including a magnificent example by Ferdinand Bol of Miguel de Ruyter, painted in 1667, the year he brought the victorious Dutch Fleet to the Medway. Portraits by Sir Godfrey Kneller of both Will Hewer and Samuel Pepys remind us of distinguished Englishmen who served our Navy so well as Civil Servants.

The most famous series of portraits are the twelve 'Flaggmen,' painted by Sir Peter Lely to the order of James, Duke of York, the

25.*a* TURNER Battle of Trafalgar   *Greenwich*

25.*b* SERRES Quiberon Bay   *Greenwich*

26.a LELY Sir Jeremy Smith   Greenwich

26.b ABBOTT Nelson   Greenwich

Lord High Admiral, in 1665. These were the officers who served under James at his victory over the Dutch known as the battle of Lowestoft and include the Earl of Sandwich, Pepys' kinsman and patron, as well as the Duke of Albemarle, Sir Jeremy Smith (Pl. 26a) and Sir William Penn, the father of the founder of Pennsylvania, and the man whose name was commemorated in the naming of the Colony.

The 'Flaggmen' series of portraits was presented to Greenwich Hospital by George IV. The portraits are hung together in the West Bridge Room of the Queen's House and are much admired by visitors.

It is interesting to note that in the Royal Naval College visitors can see the series of Admirals of the 1939–45 war painted for the Admiralty by Sir Oswald Birley.

As well as pictures of ships, seascapes, monarchs and seamen, there are in the Queen's House some interesting old views of Greenwich, showing the little palace as it stood in relation to the old Tudor Palace, and also after the Tudor Palace was pulled down and the buildings of Wren's Greenwich Hospital were erected on the site, to be a home for worn-out sailors, the Greenwich Pensioners, whom Dibden wrote his songs about, and Marryat introduced into his sea novels.

Having walked through the rooms of the Queen's House, admiring the architecture, the views from the windows, either towards the river, between Wren's twin domes, or up the grassy slopes of Greenwich Park to the buildings of the Royal Observatory, of which the Octagon Room was designed by Wren and built in 1675, the visitor makes his way to the Caird Galleries. Here the story of British maritime achievement is carried on by picture, relic and model, through the 18th and 19th Centuries. It is possible to refer to only a few of the fine pictures shown in these galleries.

The visitor proceeds up the staircase made of the teak from old wooden men-of-war into Caird Gallery No. 3. The galleries are arranged chronologically and the attractions of Gallery 3 are the fine portraits of naval officers, many from the Greenwich Hospital collection, and painted by Sir Godfrey Kneller and Michael Dahl. Here we find portraits of Jennings, Rooke, Byng, Wager, Leake,

Shovell and Benbow; Admirals clad in coats of many colours, rusty browns, bright blues, scarlet slashed with gold, and all with gold buttons. Mostly they carry batons: Rooke an antique telescope: Benbow a drawn sword. Byng and Benbow wear breastplates. All these men have rubicund complexions, and stern looks accentuated by their big wigs. It is difficult today to recognise the hard fighter and strict disciplinarian in this seemingly fancy costume. There is much else to detain us on the walls of this gallery but only space here to mention Van de Velde's ship-portrait of the *Royal Sovereign*, a majestic picture and a worthy companion to the same artist's famous *Cannon Shot* in the Rijks Museum at Amsterdam.

In Gallery 4 are several paintings of men-of-war and merchant ships under sail by Charles Brooking, perhaps the first British marine artist of real power. Brooking studied the Van de Veldes, but his pictures have a quality all their own. William Hogarth is represented by a most amusing character study of Lord George Graham, as the Captain of a man-of-war, at ease in his cabin with his retinue about him. The portrait of Admiral Sir William Rowley is interesting because it shows the first British naval uniform introduced for officers in 1748. The blue, white and gold of course survives in the full-dress naval uniform of today.

In Gallery 5 commences the long line of naval portraits by Sir Joshua Reynolds. Augustus Viscount Keppel took Reynolds with him to the Mediterranean and a magnificent full-length shows Keppel when a Captain stepping ashore from a wreck on the French coast; immaculately clad, Keppel appears to be in the act of walking up the beach and there is every appearance of movement. Sir Joshua painted a number of famous sea officers and the Museum is lucky to have so many examples of his work. Here are also hung paintings of actions in the Seven Years' War, such as the *Battle of Quiberon Bay* (1759) by Dominic Serres (Pl. 25*b*).

The best-known portrait of Captain James Cook by Nathaniel Dance hangs in Gallery 6, alongside a striking reconstruction of the scene of his death at Hawaii by John Zoffany; there are also pictures by William Hodges, the official artist who accompanied Cook on his second voyage, and who gives us surprisingly beautiful and entrancing peepshows of the islands of the South Seas visited by the *Resolution* and *Adventure*.

A full-length portrait of the 4th Earl of Sandwich by Thomas Gainsborough, another of Admiral Kempenfelt by Tilly Kettle, naval officers painted by Romney and Reynolds all attract attention in Gallery 7. Gallery 8 is dominated by De Loutherbourg's vast canvas of the battle of the Glorious First of June fought in 1794. A most entertaining companion picture by Henry Briggs shows King George III presenting Lord Howe with a Sword of Honour in gracious recognition of his splendid victory. The portrait of Lord Howe in the same gallery is a very pleasing work by John Singleton Copley. Fine portraits of Duncan, St. Vincent and the Hoods and other officers are also here. It is interesting to compare Romney's romantic and melting portrait of Lady Hamilton as Ariadne with the same artist's manly interpretations of Sir Charles Hardy and the Honourable John Forbes.

The favourite portrait of Nelson is by Lemuel Abbott (Pl. 26*b*). The artist sketched Nelson during a sitting in Captain Locker's residence in Greenwich Hospital in 1797 or 1798. From this sketch a finished picture was prepared for Nelson's friend and prize agent, Alexander Davison. Later Abbott painted a companion portrait from the same sketch showing the Admiral wearing in his cocked hat the diamond ornament, the Chelengk, presented to him by the Sultan of Turkey. A delightfully naïve series by Richard Westall illustrate Nelson's life; here we have the popular version of young Horatio and the polar bear, Lieutenant Nelson boarding the prize in a gale of wind, and the other well-beloved stories. There are portraits of the famous 'Band of Brothers', as Nelson called those British captains who accompanied him on the Nile campaign, when the enemy's fleet was all but annihilated in a night action. It is fitting these men should be gathered round their chief. Turner's great picture of the battle of Trafalgar (Pl. 25*a*) was commissioned by King George IV as a companion picture to De Loutherbourg's Glorious First of June and they were both hung in the Council Chamber at St. James' Palace before being presented to Greenwich Hospital. Although much admired by Ruskin, sailors immediately objected that the picture had not one line of truth. No doubt the artist intended a symbolic rather than an historically true picture of the battle.

It is difficult in a short space to do justice to a large collection. At Greenwich pictures are exhibited because of their historical importance and because they enable the person interested in our maritime history to visualise the scene described by the naval historian or by the shipmaster on the uneasy ocean writing up his log in crabbed script. The fine portraits by Lely, Kneller, Reynolds, Gainsborough, or Romney, the seascapes by the Van de Veldes, Charles Brooking, Samuel Scott, the Cleveleys, the Serres or Turner, pictures such as these entice to Greenwich the art historian or connoisseur; indeed, the student of marine art must come to Greenwich. The man or woman who loves the sea and ships, as we British are all supposed to do, will find here at Greenwich a treat and a feast which can be nibbled at again and again. For the National Maritime Museum at Greenwich has been founded as a tribute to our sailors who have through the centuries made our maritime greatness.

The Museum is open free 10 a.m. to 6 p.m. weekdays; 2.30 to 6 p.m. Sundays. Closed Good Friday, Christmas Eve and Christmas Day.

GEORGE NAISH,
Assistant Director

THE COURTAULD INSTITUTE

THE Courtauld Institute of Art, 20, Portman Square, London, W.1, houses a collection of 19th- and 20th-Century French pictures which, though comparatively small in size, is in quality unrivalled in England. It is moreover unusual in that it was formed not by a Board of Trustees advised by a Director, or a series of Directors (as has been the case with many of the galleries dealt with in this book), but by an individual who devoted a large part of his great wealth to a serious and high-minded pursuit of beauty. Mr. Samuel Courtauld, who died in 1947, was of French Huguenot descent, his family having come to England in the late 17th Century, after the Revocation of the Edict of Nantes. They were craftsmen of a high order, silversmiths and silk-weavers, and their sense of quality, together with their seriousness of purpose, was still present in their descendant. Mr. Courtauld was for twenty-five years Chairman of Courtaulds Limited, a man of many interests and of considerable wealth. His determination to use that wealth in ways which would help towards a wider appreciation of art is seen in his gift in 1923 of £50,000 as a trust fund to enable the Tate Gallery to acquire Impressionist and Post-Impressionist pictures, and by the foundation in 1932 of the Institute which bears his name. Here, for the first time in England, students were to be trained in a thorough knowledge of the history of art, while public lectures were provided to reach a wider audience. Shortly after the first inception of the Institute by Mr. Courtauld and his friend Viscount Lee of Fareham, Mrs. Courtauld died and her husband decided to hand over to the University the lease of the splendid Adam house in which they had lived, and which had been a great centre for lovers of painting and music. This house, built in 1773 and known as Home House from its first owner, the Countess of Home, will contain the Institute and the collection of pictures (properly known as the Home House collection) until a new building, which will include a picture gallery, is erected on the University site near the

British Museum. It is probably the best medium-sized Adam house still in existence, and is remarkable for its skilful planning and the elegance of its decoration, which includes ceilings by Angelica Kauffmann and Zucchi, and an overmantel by the latter.

At present, partly owing to lack of space at 20, Portman Square, but partly in deference to Mr. Courtauld's known desire that the largest possible number of people should enjoy his pictures, some of the masterpieces of the collection are loaned to the National or Tate Galleries. These loans are not 'permanent' and are in fact changed from time to time, so that it is not possible to say with certainty which pictures will be at any given moment in the Institute. Some of the finest will, however, always be there, and can be seen on Saturdays and occasionally at other times on application to the Secretary of the Courtauld Institute. Every effort is made to admit visitors who have only a short time in London and are unable to come on Saturdays, but the pictures are hung in rooms which are in daily use by the students and staff of the Institute, and it is not therefore possible to make them permanently available to the public.

Mr. Courtauld began to make his collection about 1923, soon after he moved to Home House. It is entirely personal in character and reflects his own choice, and his own supreme sense of quality. At that time, Impressionist paintings were not much sought after by English collectors, and the appreciation of Cézanne, whose work had, after all, only become known in England shortly before the first world war, was confined to a very few individuals. Mr. Courtauld did not, however, rely on the judgment of others, but decided on his purchases himself.

The larger part of the collection was formed during the 1920's. One of the earliest to be acquired, and also one of the earliest French pictures in the collection was Daumier's *Don Quixote and Sancho Panza*. Few important works by this master can be seen in England and though it is not at first sight a typical Daumier, the treatment, at once ironic and pathetic, and the low-toned handling, are completely characteristic of the master. A second, much smaller Daumier water-colour, *Le Malade Imaginaire*, was bought in 1929.

Daumier is not the only artist of his generation represented in the collection, for there are a number of interesting small studies by

Constantin Guys, but its richness lies mainly in works painted after 1870, that is to say when the realism of the most advanced artists of the mid-century had been transmuted into Impressionism. There is, however, one important work by Manet painted before he was touched by Impressionism, namely the large oil sketch for the *Déjeuner sur l'Herbe*. The final version, now in the Musée de l'Impressionisme, was of course one of the outstanding exhibits in the Salon des Refusés of 1863. The other Manet in the collection, the large *Bar aux Folies-Bergère*, is the artist's last important work, painted in 1882. In it, having passed through the phase in which he used the brilliant colours of the Impressionists, he reverts to his own favourite scheme of emphasis on black, foiled by the pink of the roses and the orange of the fruit, though the influence of Impressionism can be seen in the treatment of the whole interior of the theatre, with its sparkling lights, reflected in the mirror.

The strong attraction which the theatre had for painters of the day is also reflected in works by Degas and Renoir. The *Two Dancers on the Stage* by the former, probably painted about 1877, and *La Loge* by the latter (1874) are among the best-known pictures in the collection, and are both characteristic examples of these masters in one phase of their activities. The *Two Dancers* displays the keen interest in movement, the search for an unexpected asymmetrical design, based on an unusual angle of vision, the sense that life goes on outside the frame, and the refusal to sentimentalise so typical of Degas. The same characteristics can be seen in the two superb pastels of the *Woman drying Herself* and the *Woman before a Mirror*, both of the 1880's, while another aspect of Degas, his penetration of character, is revealed in the *Woman at a Window*. The Renoir *La Loge*, on the other hand, suggests the links between this artist and the great masters of the past. In its fullness of life it is the heir of Rubens; in its insistence on feminine charm of Boucher and still more of Fragonard. A more powerful, and much later example of Renoir's work is the *Woman tying her Shoe*. This, probably painted in 1918, the year before the artist's death, was one of the first French pictures bought by Mr. Courtauld. In it, the easy charm of the earlier work is replaced by a great monumentality of form and design, while the

fullness of life is now expressed by a greater richness of colour. The
third Renoir, the *Portrait of Ambroise Vollard*, is also a late work,
dated 1908. The subject is of special interest since Vollard the dealer
was the friend of many of the artists represented in the collection and was one of the first to recognise the quality of their
work.

The Impressionists proper are perhaps slightly less in evidence
than their friends. Monet is represented by *The Seine at Vétheuil*
painted in 1873, the year before the first Impressionist exhibition,
and the *Vase of Flowers*. Camille Pissarro's *Penge Station, Upper Nor-
wood*, was painted during his stay in England in 1871, when both
he and Monet were much impressed by English landscape painting.
The small *Quay at Rouen* is rather later (1883) and is masterly in its
handling of tone. The third member of the group, Sisley, is shown
by two contrasting pictures, the gay *Boats on the Seine* and the more
sombre, but more subtle *Snow at Louveciennes*.

Almost all the pictures so far described are of high quality, typical
of important phases of French art. Even so, they are overshadowed
by the works of the Post-Impressionist movement. Seven oil
paintings and 3 water-colours by Cézanne, 3 paintings by Gauguin,
two paintings and a drawing by Van Gogh, 5 paintings by Seurat,
a painting and several drawings and lithographs by Toulouse-
Lautrec, a Marchand, a Modigliani, an Henri Rousseau, an Utrillo,
a Bonnard and a Vuillard—these are in some respects unparalleled
in England. The Cézannes are a series of the greatest importance,
showing as they do almost the whole range of the master's mature
activity. *The Card Players* (very close to the smaller version in the
Louvre) and *L'Homme á la Pipe* display his search for essentials
applied to the human figure. The still-life paintings *L'Amour en
Plâtre* (Pl. 28a) and *Flowers and Fruit* and the superb water-colour of
fruit and bottles show the same spirit combined with a greater
brilliance of colour, while in the three landscapes, *L'Etang des Sœurs*
(1877), *La Montagne Ste. Victoire* (c. 1885–87) and *Lac d'Annecy*
(1896) the struggle for an ever-increasing unity of form and colour
can be traced till it emerges triumphant in the surpassing grandeur
of the last work.

The two Van Gogh's, the *Peach Trees in Blossom near Arles* and the

Self-Portrait (Pl. 28*b*), were both painted in 1889, and are therefore works of his most mature phase. Of the Gauguin's, one, *Harvesting in Britanny* (1889), is early, and rather tentative, while the two Tahitian paintings, *Nevermore* and *Te Rerioa*, were both painted in 1897. The former, with its sombre and poetical atmosphere, its haunting colour scheme, and its splendid controlled design, is among his grandest works.

Mr. Courtauld had a special love for the work of Seurat, and among the pictures by this master in his possession the Home House Trustees now own the *Pont de Courbevoie* and *La Poudreuse*. Both are painted in his fully developed *pointilliste* technique, but in both his reaction against the looseness of Impressionist methods may be seen. In the former, a very carefully balanced design of horizontals and verticals is apparent, and in the latter form is emphasised with stark geometrical simplicity. The two small Seurats, a sketch for *Le Chahut* and the 'nature note' of *Gravelines* are preparatory studies for larger pictures.

Of the other paintings of the end of the 19th Century, Toulouse-Lautrec's *Jane Avril leaving the Moulin Rouge* (1892) is probably the most important, though all repay careful study. A number of French drawings, which cannot be mentioned individually, are also to be seen in the house.

Finally there are two pictures which stand apart from the rest of the collection and prove that the founder's interests were by no means confined to French painting. A Rubens sketch in grisaille was one of his favourite possessions, and Gainsborough's *Portrait of the Artist's Wife*, with its wonderful fluency of handling, is proof of the high standard of English painting, at the precise moment when Home House was built.

The Courtauld Institute owns certain other pictures. Roger Fry's collection of paintings, pottery, etc., was bequeathed on his death in 1934, and is shown in a room on the second floor which bears his name. It includes a fine early figure painting by Bonnard, three water-colours by Rouault dating from the Fauve period, pictures by Sickert, Duncan Grant and three paintings by Fry himself. Other works have been given to the Institute from various sources, the most interesting being an unfinished 16th Century Italian *Holy*

Family, formerly attributed to Fra Bartolommeo, but more probably by Pierino del Vaga, presented by the National Art Collections Fund on the opening of the Institute in 1932.

MARGARET WHINNEY,
Lecturer and Assistant to the Director

THE DULWICH GALLERY

UNTIL the war of 1939 the collection of paintings belonging to Alleyn's College of God's Gift, Dulwich, was housed in the gallery built for it near the College by Sir John Soane. In 1944 the building was seriously damaged by a flying bomb, and, although plans for reconstruction were prepared immediately after the end of hostilities, conditions have delayed their execution and at the time of writing it is impossible to predict when the pictures will again be housed in their proper setting. As an interim measure a number of the paintings belonging to the Gallery were lent in 1947 to the Leeds Municipal Gallery, with the idea that they should remain there till the Dulwich Gallery was once again ready to receive them.

The nucleus of the collection was formed when the College was founded by the will of the actor, Edward Alleyn, who died in 1626. In addition to the sum of money left to found the College Alleyn bequeathed some 28 pictures, most of which survive. From a strictly artistic point of view they are not of much importance, but they have a certain historical interest as representing the taste of the period, for they consist of portraits of the Kings of England, mostly imaginary, heads of notable protestant theologians, and a series of panels depicting the sibyls. The bills for some of these purchases are extant, from which we learn, for instance, that Alleyn bought the set of royal portraits in the years 1618–20 for the sum of £8 13s. 4d.

This initial bequest was followed by another in 1688 from the bookseller and actor, William Cartwright. His collection, as shown in his autograph inventory, originally contained 239 items but of these only about 80 are now traceable in the College collection. Many were given away by Cartwright during his lifetime, others were stolen by his servants after his death, and yet others have disappeared in the course of time. Those that survive have, like Alleyn's pictures, little artistic merit. They consist for the most part of still-lifes, landscapes and emblematic paintings by anonymous and minor Flemish and Dutch artists. A few mediocre portraits by English painters of the 17th Century mark the highest level of his collection.

The Dulwich collection took on a wholly different character with the bequest of Sir Peter Francis Bourgeois' pictures in 1811. This bequest consisted of some 370 paintings, which had been brought together in rather singular circumstances.

The last years of the 18th Century were a golden age for collectors and dealers, since political and financial upheavals had thrown many of the great private collections of Europe on the market. One of the most successful dealers of the time was a friend of Bourgeois, Noël Desenfans (1745–1807). He was born in France but spent the greater part of his life in England, where he became a friend of most of the leading artists, including Reynolds and Gainsborough, and exasperated his rival dealers by his successful pose as a gentleman who only sold pictures out of consideration for his friends and not for profit. He had been a schoolfellow of Calonne, the French finance minister and collector, who settled in England a few years before the Revolution, and it was largely through his help that Desenfans was able to establish his business. He also managed to become Polish Consul-General, and through his connections in this capacity he obtained what should have been his most important commission. At the suggestion of Prince Michael Poniatowski, brother of King Stanislas of Poland, Desenfans was commissioned to form a gallery of pictures for the King. When, however, in 1795 Stanislas was forced to abdicate, Desenfans was left with a number of pictures collected for the King but never paid for. He at first attempted to persuade the British Government to buy the collection as the nucleus of a National Gallery, but this project failed, and in 1802 Desenfans offered the pictures for sale. Many, however, remained unsold and were still in Desenfans' possession at his death in 1807. In his will he bequeathed all his collections to his widow and to his friend, Sir Francis Bourgeois. Bourgeois (1756–1811) was a painter and pupil of Loutherbourg. In 1793 he was elected a Royal Academician and in 1794 was appointed landscape painter to George III. He was also an enthusiastic collector of pictures and before receiving the bequest from Desenfans had already acquired many works of importance. On his death in 1811 he bequeathed, after the decease of Mrs. Desenfans, all his paintings and other objects of art to Dulwich College. In fact, however, owing to the generosity of the latter the pictures were transferred to the College during her lifetime, and a gallery was built for them by Sir John Soane. The gallery was completed in 1815, when the bodies of Mr. and Mrs. Desenfans and of Bourgeois were transferred to the Mausoleum built for them as an addition to the main building.

In order to estimate the importance of the Dulwich Gallery in its early years we must remember that it was by far the most important collection of paintings on public display in London, since the National Gallery, for the foundation of which both Bourgeois and Desenfans had made pleas, was not in fact founded till 1824. The enthusiastic account of the pictures published by Hazlitt in 1823 in the *New Monthly Magazine* (and later reprinted in volume form) is good evidence of the position held by the Gallery and contains, incidentally, some of the most penetrating comments ever written on the paintings which it contains.

Since the Bourgeois Bequest the collection has been increased by several additions. The most important was the group of portraits by Gainsborough given at various dates before 1835 by members of the Linley family who were connected with the College. The portraits are of Thomas Linley and his children with whom Gainsborough was on terms of intimate friendship. In 1911 the Gallery received a further gift from Charles Fairfax Murray of some 40 paintings consisting of 17th- and 18th-Century English portraits of excellent quality.

As is to be expected from the manner of its formation, the Dulwich Gallery is not representative of all the various Schools of European painting. Naturally it is weakest in Italian painting before the 17th Century, for in the time of Desenfans and Bourgeois this school was not the main objective of collectors. There are, however, a few very remarkable specimens of the period. A portrait of a young man, bought by Desenfans as a Leonardo, is in reality a fine work of Piero di Cosimo. The Gallery is proud in the possession of two small panels of St. Francis and St. Anthony of Padua by Raphael which form part of the altar-piece painted for S. Antonio at Perugia in the years 1503–05. The main panel is in the Pierpont Morgan collection and the central part of the predella, which, like the Dulwich pictures, came from the Orleans collection, is in the National Gallery. The other Italian painting of the 16th Century worthy of notice is also a fragment of a large altar-piece, though in this case the central picture itself has been cut up. This is the *Saint blessing a donor* by Paolo Veronese, of which two other fragments are in Edinburgh and Ottawa. The recent cleaning of the Dulwich picture has revealed the fact that a former owner had painted out those passages which called attention to the fragmentary nature of the composition. Mention must also be made here of a single German picture of importance in the collection, the *Susanna* by Adam Elsheimer, probably painted in Rome about 1600.

On the whole the representation of Italian painting of the 17th Century is weaker than might be expected, but the generation of Desenfans and Bourgeois was beginning to turn from Italy to Holland as their main source of inspiration. The eclectic school of the Carracci is, however, represented by paintings of Domenichino (*The Nativity*), Guido Reni (a *St. John* and a version of the often-repeated *Death of Lucretia*), Guercino (*The Woman taken in Adultery*). The more picturesque tendency in Roman painting of the time can be seen in compositions by Salvator Rosa and Pier Francesco Mola.

Franco-Italian painting of the same period provides one of the most spectacular parts of the whole collection. The five canvases by Nicolas Poussin reveal the full range of his talent in his earlier and more obviously attractive period. The *Triumph of David* is a somewhat experimental painting of about 1627, but in the *Rinaldo and Armida* and the *Nurture of Jupiter* (Pl. 30*b*) of the 1630's his mastery of colour and of clear logical composition is apparent. The charming little panel of the *Assumption* is one of his earliest experiments in landscape; but in this field he is naturally overshadowed by his great contemporary Claude. The late *Jacob and Laban* is one of the latter's most subtle and restful inventions, remarkable also for its admirable state of preservation. French painting of the age of Louis XIV can be seen in two interesting early works by Charles Lebrun, painted when he was still a close imitator of Poussin, and in a small canvas by Sébastien Bourdon in an unusual vein, exploiting the manner of Teniers in the depiction of tavern scenes.

The art of the rococo is brilliantly shown in paintings by Watteau, whose *Bal Champêtre* (Pl. 30a) is among his most mature works, and Lancret to whom the *Fête Champêtre* is now attributed. Venetian rococo is represented in a sketch by Sebastiano Ricci for the decoration of the chapel in Chelsea Hospital, and by three virtuoso sketches for ceilings by G. B. Tiepolo.

The few Spanish pictures include the characteristic *Flower Girl* by Murillo and a portrait of Philip IV, formerly ascribed to Velasquez but now thought to be an exceptionally fine studio version of the picture in the Frick collection.

Desenfans specialised above all in the 17th-Century painting of the Netherlands. In quantity the Flemish group does not equal the Dutch, but its quality is exceptional. The eight paintings by Rubens include five brilliant sketches, of which one is for the Jesuit church at Antwerp and two others for the side panels of the Antwerp altarpiece of the *Elevation of the Cross*. The *Hagar in the Wilderness*, painted about 1630–32, is a larger composition but preserves the freshness of the sketches, while the *Venus, Mars and Cupid* (Pl. 29a) is a magnificent example of the artist's late style in full-dress classical compositions, and the *Duchess of Buckingham* shows his powers as a portrait painter. Van Dyck's development can be traced in examples ranging from the early *Samson and Delilah*, painted when he was still dominated by Rubens, to the late English portrait probably representing the Earl of Bristol.

Salient among the Dutch pictures are the two Rembrandts, the small portrait of the artist Jacob de Gheyn, dated 1632, and the *Girl at a Window* (Pl. 29b) of 1645. The latter had been greatly disfigured by alterations, which included the addition of a green curtain in the upper part of the composition, but the recent cleaning has restored the painting to its original state. A small picture of *Jacob's Dream* was in the 19th Century widely admired as one of Rembrandt's most poetical compositions, Hazlitt and Robert Browning being amongst those who wrote enthusiastically about it. Later critics, however, challenged its authenticity, and their doubts were finally confirmed when cleaning revealed, scratched with the wrong end of the brush, the full signature of one of Rembrandt's ablest pupils, Aert de Gelder. Dutch genre painting is represented by works of Gerard Dou and the two Ostades, but it is above all in the field of landscape that the Dulwich collection is remarkable. The most important group is that of works by Albert Cuyp, including a delicate painting in his early manner as well as examples of his cool and luminous later style. The classical painters of the middle of the century are represented by a typical Hobbema and two paintings by Jacob van Ruisdael, one painted while he was still under the influence of Rembrandt, the other when he had established his own independent method. Dutch painting of towns can be seen at its best in a view by Jan van der Heyden, and seascape in characteristic works by Backhuisen and William van de Velde the younger. The great Dutch tradition is carried on to its end in fine specimens by Wouverman and the Italianising group, such as Berchem, Carel Dujardin and Pynacker.

English painting was not widely represented in the collections of Desenfans or Bourgeois, but later gifts have made up for this deficiency. From the hand of Lely are two pictures, both presented by Fairfax Murray: the typical portrait of a young man, formerly identified as Abraham Cowley, and the *Nymphs at a Fountain*, one of his rare classical compositions. Other English portraits of the 17th Century are by Dobson and Cornelius Johnson.

The 18th Century is much more richly represented. Two sides of Hogarth's art are displayed in his portrait of a man and the charming little conversation piece, *A Fishing Party*. Reynolds is seen at his grandest in *Mrs. Siddons as the tragic Muse*, a replica mainly from the hand of the master himself of the famous portrait in the Huntingdon collection, California. A less familiar aspect of his work appears in *The Death of Cardinal Beaufort*, a sketch for the picture at Petworth painted for Boydell's Shakespeare Gallery.

With two exceptions the Gainsboroughs are portraits of the Linley family painted in Bath. The two exceptions are an enchanting early double portrait in a landscape, executed while the artist was still working at Ipswich, in which his naturalistic conception of landscape based on the study of Dutch painting is evident; and the portrait of Bourgeois' master in painting, Philip de Loutherbourg. The Linley

27.a REYNOLDS Master Philip Yorke

Kenwood

27.b VERMEER The Guitar Player

Kenwood

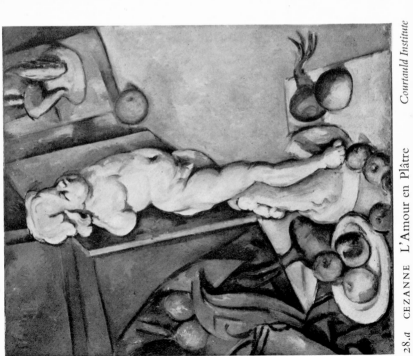

28.a CEZANNE L'Amour en Plâtre   Courtauld Institute

28.b VAN GOGH Self-portrait   Courtauld Institute

portraits display to the full on the one side Gainsborough's skill in rendering the charms of a really pretty sitter, and on the other the directness of his vision when depicting a less obviously appealing subject.

The cycle of English portraiture is brought to a close in its last great representative, Lawrence, whose three portraits of younger members of the Linley family are not unworthy to hang beside the Gainsboroughs of the previous generation. In this way the Linley gift rounds off the collection of Desenfans and Bourgeois, adding to it examples of the English masters of portraiture whom, though they were their contemporaries and even their friends, they themselves seem never to have patronised.

ANTHONY BLUNT

LONDON GUILDHALL ART GALLERY

THE Guildhall Gallery is maintained by the Corporation of London and was opened in 1886. It owes its existence to the enthusiasm of professional and amateur artists in the City during the late 19th Century and their ready support by the Corporation. Its rapid growth necessitated enlargement in 1890 and again in 1901. It was destroyed by enemy action in 1941 but a small temporary building has been erected on the site.

Within recent years it has been decided to restrict the acquisition of works of art to those of London interest or of outstanding artistic value. The policy of the Corporation today is to use the gallery for periodic exhibitions of selections from the permanent collection, for loan exhibitions and for the display of works by societies of approved standing.

The pictures in the permanent collection fall into four main groups. The first of these consists of works of London interest. These include pictures by Scott and Marlow and also works concerned with civic ceremonial, of which Miller's *Swearing in of Alderman Newnham*, 1782, is a good example.

Another group consists of English portraits, and includes the work of representative English portrait painters from the 16th Century to the present day. Notable examples in this group are *The Hales Family* by Lely, *Lord Camden* by Reynolds and *Lady Lavery* by Sir John Lavery.

A third group, consisting of landscapes and seascapes, includes a fine Constable, *Fording the River*, a number of works by Nasmyth and Linnell, *Echoes of a Far-off Storm* by John Brett.

The fourth group can be called narrative pictures and includes biblical, historical, and domestic subjects by 19th-Century painters. The most outstanding of these is probably Poynter's *Israel in Egypt*. Collins, Armitage, Maclise, Gilbert, Stone, Dendy Sadler and Tissot are represented, as are also, of course, the Pre-Raphaelite brotherhood.

RAYMOND SMITH,
Director

THE IVEAGH BEQUEST PICTURES
AT KENWOOD

THE pictures at Kenwood House were collected by the late Lord
Iveagh who, on his death in 1927, bequeathed them, together
with the house, to a Trust for the benefit of the public. In 1949,
owing to difficulties in administration, the Trustees handed the
house and the contents over to the London County Council in
accordance with the terms of the Kenwood Act of 1929.

Kenwood House owes its present appearance principally to the
transformation carried out from 1767 onwards by Robert Adam
for the first Earl of Mansfield. Lord Mansfield, or William Murray,
as he was before he received a peerage, was Attorney-General and
Lord Chief Justice and was one of the most celebrated lawyers of
the 18th Century. As a talker he was admired by Pope, as an
opponent he was feared by Chatham; and he suffered for his support of religious toleration by having his house in Bloomsbury
Square burnt by the mob during the Gordon Riots of 1780. Mansfield bought Kenwood House from Lord Bute in 1754, and thirteen
years later called in Robert Adam to improve it. Adam was partly
tied in his designs by the existing building, which he had to incor-
porate in the new house, but his alterations and additions were
made with such skill that there is no clash between his own work
and that of his predecessors. The general effect of the House has,
however, been somewhat impaired by additions made by the second
Lord Mansfield between 1793 and 1797.

The most important additions made by Adam were the great
library, with its anteroom, the portico on the entrance front and
the decoration of the garden front. The library, which is one of
Adam's finest inventions, is a rectangular room with an apse at each
end, cut off by an entablature supported by two fluted Corinthian
columns. The decoration includes stucco work by Joseph Rose,
with painted panels by Antonio Zucchi (1726–95), who later married Angelica Kauffmann.

In 1925 Lord Iveagh bought the house and installed in it the collection of pictures which he had formed mainly in the 80's and 90's of the 19th Century. These consist primarily of important English paintings of the 18th Century, but there are also a few very remarkable specimens of the Dutch, Flemish, French and later Italian Schools.

The two great English portrait painters of the 18th Century are represented by magnificent examples. The Gainsborough of *Lady Howe* reveals in the highest degree his exquisite handling of paint in the tradition of the Venetians and Van Dyck. In the portrait of *Lady Brisco* he appears in more formal vein, but the landscape in the background is a splendid example of his treatment of accessories. The smaller portrait of *Miss Brummel* is a characteristic instance of his treatment of children and provides, therefore, an interesting comparison with Reynolds' treatment of similar subjects. His later landscape style can be seen in *Going to Market*, though this picture has suffered from repainting. Towards the end of his life Gainsborough devoted rather more time to the painting of subject pictures, and the *Two Shepherd Boys with Dogs Fighting* reveals his skill in this vein and at the same time avoids the sentimentality which sometimes obtrudes itself in his paintings of this kind.

Sir Joshua Reynolds, also, appears in many different moods. His early portrait of *Kitty Fisher as 'Cleopatra'* is characteristic of the more staid handling of his early period. It also illustrates another principle enunciated by Reynolds in his *Discourses* and regularly applied in the portraits, for the attitude is borrowed exactly from a painting of Cleopatra by Trevisani in the Spada Gallery, Rome. Another early portrait, representing Lady Mary Leslie as Saint Agnes, reminds us that in the 18th Century one could choose equally to be depicted as a queen of antiquity or a christian saint. Yet another allegorical portrait of a later period, showing *Mrs. Musters as 'Hebe'*, is a fine specimen of the formula which Reynolds invented for giving a dignified representation to even an indifferent model. Another example of this formula, but this time based on a Van Dyck pose rather than an allegorical *alias*, is the portrait of *Lady Louisa Manners*.

It is, however, as a painter of children that Reynolds is seen to the best advantage at Kenwood. The double portrait of *William Brummel and George Bryan Brummel* has the rare advantage of being in excellent condition and not veiled by yellow varnish. It proves to a striking degree that Reynolds was as happy in rendering the naïveté of children as in depicting his more pompous sitters. This quality is even more apparent in the *Master Philip Yorke* (Pl. 27a) where, however, time and the taste of 19th-Century collectors has spread a golden veil over the original colours, which it would, unfortunately, be dangerous to remove.

Reynolds, following the precept of 17th- and 18th-Century doctrine, believed that 'history painting' was a nobler form of art than the portraiture to which the greater part of his life was devoted, and the *Venus chiding Cupid* and the *Gipsy Fortune-Teller* are among the relatively rare examples of his experiments in this idiom.

Reynolds' junior contemporary, George Romney, is represented by a number of works which illustrate well his somewhat facile manner of portrait painting. In the *Mrs. Musters* he tackles the subject directly and successfully, but a different approach is seen in the so-called *Spinstress*, which is a portrait of Lady Hamilton, posed at a spinning-wheel. This portrait, which at one time was one of the most admired pictures in England, illustrates Romney's particular vein of sentiment, which so strongly appealed to his contemporaries.

English landscape painting was evidently of less interest than portraiture to Lord Iveagh, but the landscape by Morland and the admirable early Turner *Fishermen upon a Lee Shore in Squally Weather*, exhibited at the Academy in 1802, show that he did not wholly neglect it. The next generation is represented by several extremely interesting paintings by Sir Edwin Landseer, including a brilliant study of *Hawking*, and a composition of the *Russell Brothers riding Ponies*, in the naturalistic vein which aroused the admiration of Delacroix when he saw Landseer's early work on his visit to England.

Van Dyck, the great predecessor of Reynolds and Gainsborough in portraiture in this country, appears at Kenwood in two examples, *James Stuart, Duke of Richmond*, dating from his English period, and the *Henrietta of Lorraine*, an unusually sumptuous composition, dated 1634.

The number of Dutch paintings at Kenwood is small, but their quality is exceptionally high. The seascapes by Van de Velde the Younger and Van de Capelle, the view of *Dordrecht from the River Maas* by Cuyp, and the early *Portrait of a Man* by Frans Hals would be notable in any collection of Dutch painting, but here they are overshadowed by the Rembrandt *Self-Portrait* and the Vermeer *Guitar-Player* (Pl. 27b). The Rembrandt *Self-Portrait*, probably painted about 1665, is one of the noblest of his later works. Recent cleaning has revealed once more its silvery tone and the expressive freedom of its handling. The Vermeer *Guitar-Player* is remarkable amongst other things for its condition, since it is on its original stretcher and has never been relined. This is a particularly important factor for a painter like Vermeer, who calculated both the geometrical balance of his composition and the exact relations of his colours with unusual care. The design of the Kenwood painting is exceptionally bold, with the placing of the figure in one corner and the balancing of this positive mass by the blank wall in the upper right-hand corner. The paint still has the richness to be seen, for instance, in his *Milkmaid*, but the modelling of the form shows a tendency towards the simplicity of the works associated with his later period.

The catholicity of Lord Iveagh's taste is shown by the inclusion in the collection of a few rococo paintings, which form a striking contrast with the Dutch and English pictures so far considered. The French 18th-Century school is represented by two fine *Fêtes Champêtres* by Pater, and a pair of decorative paintings representing pastoral scenes by Boucher. The Venetian rococo figures in two small but exquisite Guardis of the *Grand Canal*.

Lord Iveagh's principal aim in installing his collection at Kenwood was to re-create the house of an English collector of the later 18th Century, and in this aim he was to a remarkable degree successful. The pictures cover a considerable part of the field admired by English connoisseurs of the same period. In a collection formed at that date there would, no doubt, have been many examples of Roman and Bolognese Schools, but it would have required an almost inconceivable historical objectivity on the part of Lord Iveagh to have collected these in the 1880's, when they stood at the very lowest point of reputation. Otherwise the taste of the 1770's is well represented, contemporary English portraiture dominating the scene, while the more recent fashion of Dutch painting plays its part, and only the liking for French and Venetian rococo can be considered slightly eccentric.

The house is open in summer from 10 a.m. to 6 p.m. on week-days, 2.30 to 6 p.m. on Sundays. In winter it shuts at dusk. Closed on Good Friday and Christmas Day. Admission free except on Wednesdays and Fridays when 1s. is charged.

M. E. TIBBS,
ANTHONY BLUNT

THE ROYAL HOLLOWAY COLLEGE PICTURE GALLERY

THE formation of this collection of pictures was begun by the founder of the College, Thomas Holloway, and completed by his brother-in-law, Sir George Martin-Holloway, who chose and purchased the greater number and presented the collection as a whole to the College. The particular significance of the collection is therefore that it reflects the taste of an average Englishman of the mid-19th Century.

Most of the pictures are by British artists and there is an overwhelming preference for landscape and 'story' pictures. This resulted sometimes in the purchase of 'the picture of the year' at the Royal Academy, e.g. Luke Fildes's *Applicants for Admission to a Casual Ward* and Edwin Long's *Babylonian Marriage Market*, and certain examples of artists who are at present out of fashion, e.g. Landseer's *Man proposes, God disposes* and Briton Rivière's *Sympathy*, familiar in many nurseries. But there are also some real treasures: Constable's *View on the Stour*, Gainsborough's *Going to Market*, *Early Morning*, Turner's *Van Tromp going about to please his Masters*, Morland's *Cottage Door*, *Press Gang* and *Carrier preparing to Set Out*, landscapes by Nasmyth, Old Crome and David Roberts; and such characteristic pictures as Frith's *Railway Station* and Millais's *Princes in the Tower* and *Princess Elizabeth*, as well as an admirable Norwegian landscape by L. Münthe and other smaller works of merit.

Inspection of the pictures can usually be arranged by application to the Principal, and the gallery is open free to the public on Thursday afternoons except in June and August and for a few days in the Christmas and Easter vacations and on other occasions when it is required for College purposes.

EDITH C. BATHO,
Principal

29.a RUBENS Venus, Mars and Cupid

29.b REMBRANDT Girl at a Window

30.a WATTEAU Les Plaisirs du Bal *Dulwich College*

30.b POUSSIN Education of Jupiter *Dulwich College*

31.*a* CANALETTO View in Venice *Sir John Soane's Museum*

31.*b* HOGARTH Canvassing for Votes *Sir John Soane's Museum*

32   LEONARDO DA VINCI

The Virgin and Child with S. Anne

Royal Academy Diploma Gallery

THE ROYAL ACADEMY OF ARTS
DIPLOMA AND GIBSON GALLERIES

THE constitution of the Royal Academy, founded by King George III in 1768, requires that each newly elected Academician shall present to the Academy 'a picture, bas-relief or other specimen of his abilities', before his Diploma can be submitted to the Sovereign for signature and he can be later admitted to full membership by a General Assembly of Academicians. Thus began the permanent collection of the Royal Academy, which also acquired by gift or purchase at various times, among a number of works by foreign as well as native masters, the famous cartoon of the *Virgin and St. Anne and two Children* by Leonardo da Vinci (Pl. 32), the fine copy by Marco d'Oggiono of Leonardo's *The Last Supper*, the great marble relief of the Virgin with the Infant Christ and St. John by Michelangelo, Rosso's drawing after the lost Leda of Michelangelo, and 15 sketches of landscape by J. Constable, R.A.

When the Royal Academy obtained possession of Old Burlington House in 1867, it proceeded to build its main galleries (for temporary exhibitions) on the garden site to the north, and the Diploma Gallery as an additional storey above the house. Part of the cost of this gallery was met by a bequest of money from J. Gibson, R.A.; with it came a number of his sculptures, for which a special gallery was provided. Niches on the façade of these galleries above the old house contain statues of Phidias, Leonardo, Flaxman, Raphael, Michelangelo, Titian, Reynolds and William of Wykeham. After the completion of the main galleries to the north, the three galleries holding the permanent collection were opened to the public in 1878: since then they have been open free every weekday from 11 a.m. to 4 p.m., except during the two great wars of this century. A fourth gallery on the west side was added in 1883.

The Diploma Works, now more than 300 in number, form a collection of great interest to students of the British Schools of painting and sculpture in the past 180 years. Among them may be mentioned works by the following artists: Sir J. Reynolds (portraits), R. Wilson (self-portrait), Sir T. Lawrence (portrait), Sir W. Beechey (portrait), J. Hoppner (self-portrait), J. Flaxman (relief), J. M. W. Turner (landscape), Sir H. Raeburn (*Boy and Rabbit*), J. Constable (landscape), W. Etty (*Nymph and Satyr*), Sir J. E. Millais (portrait), G. F. Watts (*Punishment of Cain*), J. S. Sargent (*Interior in Venice*), Sir F. Brangwyn (*Market Stall*), Sir W. Orpen (*Le Chef*), Sir A. Munnings (*Horse Fair*), A. E. John (portrait), W. R. Sickert (*Sta. Maria della Salute*).

Other important works by Hogarth, Reynolds, Gainsborough, Zoffany and Constable are in the private rooms of the Academy, and are only shown for special reasons submitted to the Secretary.

W. R. M. LAMB,
Secretary

SIR JOHN SOANE'S MUSEUM

THIS Museum comprises the collection of antiquities, paintings, sculpture, drawings, models, MSS. and books formed by Sir John Soane, the architect, between about 1792 and his death in 1837. It is one man's collection. Moreover, it is still arranged in the manner in which Soane arranged it, and still installed in the house (13, Lincoln's Inn Fields) which he designed for the purpose, and for his own occupation, in 1812. There is, perhaps, no museum in Europe which, in contents and arrangement, so jealously preserves the concept of a museum as understood in the 17th and 18th Centuries.

Soane, of course, was one of the latest, and by no means the greatest of the English collectors. He stands right at the end of the long tradition which started with the Earl of Arundel and includes such famous and noble names as Burlington, Leicester, Bessborough and Carlisle or, later in the 18th Century, Yarborough, Cawdor, Towneley, Blundell and Hamilton. Soane was far less wealthy and influential than these, being only a markedly successful professional man. But in his time it had become possible to collect without undue extravagance or the exertion of great influence. England was, by then, full of antiquities, MSS. and paintings, constantly passing through the salerooms; and it was mostly from the salerooms that Soane procured the materials of which his museum is composed. Incidentally, he frequently benefited by the dispersal of older and greater collections, and the museum contains marble urns from the Bessborough, vases from the Englefield and Cawdor collections, and paintings which had belonged to Jonathan Richardson and Lord Bute.

The composite whole which Soane created is, thus, a microcosm of the English collecting world, constructed by an architect with a very understandable bias towards his own art. This architectural bias led Soane to give special emphasis to arrangement and to consider his museum as a 'Union of the Arts', under the aegis of the mistress art of architecture. Within this 'union' painting has its place, and although Soane's collection is neither large nor uniformly important, it is of great interest as a reflection of the taste of his time and contains a certain number of works of the first rank.

Soane does not seem to have acquired any important paintings until about 1801, when he was forty-eight and when his work at the Bank of England had assured him of fame and prosperity. In that year he bought a small Zuccarelli. In 1802, he bought a Fuseli and, in the same year, a set of 8 pictures which, if he had bought nothing else, would have rendered his collection important— Hogarth's *Rake's Progress*. For these he paid £570 at the sale of Alderman Beckford's collection from old Fonthill. In 1803, he bought a Turner water-colour, and three years later, the large Canaletto *Venetian Scene* (Pl. 31a) which is another of the Museum's principal adornments, but little else was added until, in 1820, he bought Reynolds' *Snake in the Grass*, and in 1823 doubled his Hogarth stakes by acquiring, on Mrs. Garrick's death, the four *Election* scenes (Pl. 31b).

By this date, the Museum was so well stocked with marbles, casts and framed architectural drawings that there was little room for further collecting. This obstacle, however, was removed when, in 1824, Soane acquired the adjoining house, No. 14, Lincoln's Inn Fields, rebuilt it and constructed behind it a picture gallery whose walls open out like the pages of an enormous book, so that the visitor, by careful manipulation, may view three times as many pictures as, at first sight, the gallery may be supposed to contain.

From the date of this addition, Soane was able to collect more rapidly and bought at least one picture every year. For the most part, his choice fell upon painters of no great quality who could minister to his pleasure in anecdote and illustration. John Jackson, John Wood, Augustus Callcott, Henry Howard, George Jones and Francis Danby are the kind of artists he favoured, and Howard he commissioned to paint allegorical panels for the dining-room and library ceilings. By far the most important paintings added at this period are Turner's *Van Tromp's Barge* and the portrait of Soane by Sir Thomas Lawrence.

It is evident that Soane never felt himself rich enough (or perhaps was not sufficiently stirred by painting) to reach out for the kind of canvases which would have been most appropriate to the collection. There should, one feels, be at least one Claude, a Poussin and a Salvator. The Bolognese masters should be represented, but they are not and, indeed, the most important Italian painting in the Museum is certainly Giulio Clovio's illumination to Cardinal Grimani's commentary on the Epistle to the Romans, bought by Soane in 1827. A head excised from a Raphael cartoon for tapestry (emanating from Jonathan Richardson's collection) is of slight interest and there is an insignificant 17th-Century painting of an old man, probably Neapolitan. From the 18th Century, however, there are three Canaletto Venetian scenes, two merely school pieces, but the third (from the Calonne and Beckford collections) a large canvas comparable with the best Canalettos in this country.

Among Italian drawings in the Museum the most important are the set of views of the Pæstum Temples by G. B. Piranesi; some are attributed to his son, Francesco. There are two albums of Italian drawings, one associated with Vasari and the other ("Margaret Chinnery's Album") containing miscellaneous drawings, two of which have recently been assigned to Filippino Lippi.

French painting in the Soane collection is represented by one important Watteau—*Les Noces*, a wedding scene in a woodland setting with a hill-town in the background. This painting Soane bought very cheap. It was in bad condition in the early 19th Century and was severely restored, with much over-painting, in the 1860's. It was cleaned in 1949 when much of the original work was reclaimed by the removal of varnish and over-painting.

There is also a sanguine sketch of a dog, certainly by Watteau, though attributed, since Soane's time, to Rubens. Otherwise, the French school is represented only by a large number of architectural compositions by C. L. Clérisseau, an artist who, like Piranesi, was held in high esteem by English architects and was consequently collected and prominently exhibited by Soane.

English paintings are by far the most numerous in the collection and among these the two great Hogarth series—*A Rake's Progress* and *An Election*—stand out as the most important. Hogarth painted the *Rake* shortly before 1735, the date of the engravings. The

Election belongs to about 1754–55 and thus represents his last period. Hanging in the same room these two sets of painting illustrate very strikingly Hogarth's development in the twenty middle years of his career, from a rather diagrammatic type of composition in which a flattened pyramid always prevails, to the vigorous, dynamic organisation represented by the *Election* cycle. The interest of the *Election* paintings is enhanced by the fact that they hang in superb rococo frames which, no doubt, were made to the order of Garrick.

The English 18th Century is also represented by an oil sketch by Thornhill for one of the ceilings at Hampton Court and by Sir Joshua Reynolds' *Snake in the Grass* (or *Love and Beauty*) for which Kitty Fisher was the model and of which there are or were replicas in the National Gallery and the Hermitage. The painting is in an irretrievably bad condition, having suffered, like so many of Reynolds' canvases, from the painter's unfortunate selection of materials. Reynolds is also represented by a drawing and two sketch-books dating from his Italian visit, documents of considerable importance which still await publication.

Two drawings by James Barry, several by J. H. Mortimer (including a self-portrait), water-colours by Francis Wheatley and William Hamilton and temperas (Indian scenes) by William Hodges illustrate the later years of the century, while at the end of it we come to J. M. W. Turner who is well represented by an early water-colour of *Kirkstall Abbey* (1798), another of *The Valley of Aosta* (1803) and the fine 'second period' oil-painting, *Van Tromp's Barge Entering the Texel*, purchased by Soane from the painter in 1831.

With the 19th Century we find Soane buying, without too much discrimination, from his painter friends and Academy colleagues, such men as Sir Francis Bourgeois, Henry Fuseli (a typically melodramatic piece), Sir William Beechey, Edward Bird (anecdotal, in the manner of Wilkie), William Hilton, Sir Augustus Callcott (including a huge imaginary Italian landscape which Soane commissioned) and George Jones (the large Turneresque *Opening of New London Bridge*, commissioned by Soane and introducing his portrait). A favourite painter in Soane's latest years was Henry Howard to whom we owe the painted ceiling panels in the dining-room and library as well as several sentimental Shakespearian compositions.

The Soane family portraits form an interesting series in themselves. The earliest portrait of Soane is a pencil drawing by Nathaniel Dance, showing him at twenty-one. At twenty-six, in Rome, he was admirably painted by C. W. Hunneman and at forty-two was drawn by his old master George Dance. At fifty he had both himself and his sons painted by William Owen, and at seventy-five John Jackson painted him and (posthumously) Mrs. Soane. Finally there is the well-known Lawrence portrait (one of the painter's last) showing Soane at seventy-six. Besides these, there are two excellent Downman drawings of Soane's mother and his younger son, as well as a group of Mrs. Soane and the boys by Van Assen, who also painted Fanny, the family pet, whose remains are deposited in the Monk's Tomb. Fanny is also the subject of a small oil painting by James Ward.

A number of minor paintings and drawings remain unmentioned in this brief account which must, in any case, conclude with a reminder that Soane was primarily an architect and interested in architectural things, and that the collection of some 20,000 drawings of strictly architectural character gives the Museum an importance which (the Hogarths apart) one would hardly claim for it on the strength of its paintings, sculpture and objects of art alone. These, nevertheless, have a special (perhaps unique) interest among English collections in that they represent the collecting career of one man, his whole and entire collection from which, since his death in 1837, nothing has been removed and to which nothing has been or will be added.

Sir John Soane's Museum is open free from Tuesday to Saturday inclusive 10 a.m. to 5 p.m. throughout the year except for the month of August. It is closed on Sundays, Mondays and Bank Holidays.

JOHN SUMMERSON,
Curator

3.*a* BLAKE The Whirlwind of Lovers *Birmingham, City Art Gallery*

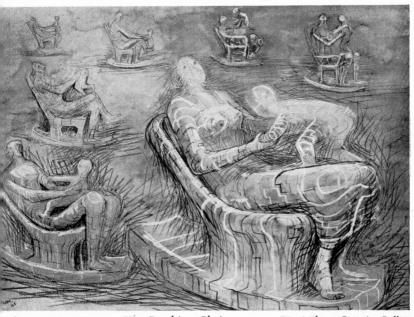

3.*b* HENRY MOORE The Rocking Chair *Birmingham, City Art Gallery*

34.a   VAN GOYEN   View of an Estuary   *Birmingham, City Art Gallery*

34.b   HOLMAN HUNT   Two Gentlemen of Verona   *Birmingham, City Art Gallery*

III

The Provinces

THE BOWES MUSEUM

THE Bowes Museum, in the small country town of Barnard Castle, Co. Durham, is less known outside the north of England than its importance deserves. Its remoteness from the main traffic routes is a partial explanation but does not account for the ignorance of its existence so frequently expressed.

The building is on a grand scale befitting the importance of its collections. Its situation amid the beautiful scenery of Upper Teesdale, and surrounded by its own park with flower beds, lawns and majestic trees, gives it a special charm.

There are about 1,000 paintings, and, like the many other objects of art the Museum contains, they embrace most of the European Schools. The pictures are not all of first-rate quality, but the surprise is that there are so many of exciting interest.

The collection was acquired by John Bowes and his French wife. John Bowes began collecting in 1830. From then onward, and particularly after his marriage in 1854 when his wife entered with even greater enthusiasm, the acquisitions developed into a vast collection. This led to a desire by his wife to found a Museum and endow it. The result was the Bowes Museum, one of the finest gifts of its kind ever made in this country. Neither Mrs. Bowes nor her husband lived to see the completion of the Museum, but in 1885 John Bowes bequeathed a handsome endowment which has enabled it to be maintained without help from other sources.

It is only possible to draw attention to a few of the pictures of special interest. Among those of the Italian Schools chief attention might be drawn to the small panel by Sassetta (1392–1450), *The Miracle of the Holy Sacrament*, from the predella to a polyptych painted for the chapel of the Arte della Lana at Siena between 1423 and 1426. A portrait of Lelio Torelli, by Domenico Caprioli, dated 1528, is an important example of portraiture of that period. *The Harnessing of the Horses of the Sun*, by Giovanni Battista Tiepolo, is a fine example of decorative painting.

Among the other Italian pictures may be mentioned a *Circumcision* by Girolamo da Santa Croce, painted about 1530; a *Holy Family* by Lorenzo Sabbatini (1530–77); *The Rape of the Sabine Women* by Giuseppe Porta or Salviati (late 16th Century); *The Infant Saviour and St. John* by Pietro Liberi (1605–87); *The Beheading of John the Baptist* by Mattia Preti (1613–99); and a portrait of Cardinal Ottobuoni (Pope Alexander VIII, d. 1691) by F. C. Trevisani (1656–1746).

The Spanish paintings are a fascinating collection. The most important were purchased from the collection of the Conde de Quinto by John Bowes in 1862. They include a number of exceptionally fine paintings and many by lesser artists whose works are rarely to be seen in this country. Outstanding is the superb *St. Peter* by El Greco (Pl. 37*b*), which must have been painted in the early 1590's. *The Prison Scene* by Goya (Pl. 37*a*), painted shortly after 1810, is remarkable for the way a group of prisoners have been placed under a deep archway with silvery light beyond contrasting with the deep shadow of the interior; it is poignant yet beautiful. Also by Goya is the portrait of the poet Melendez Valdes, painted in 1797, which shows the artist at his best in that aspect and period of his art; it is intimate and serene. The authorship of a third painting, *The Portrait of Goya's Brother*, has been questioned.

Among other Spanish pictures are a version dated 1602 of the portrait of José de Siguenza in the Escorial Library attributed to Pantoja de la Cruz, and two paintings by Pereda. Of the two pictures by José Antolinez one, the *Christ on the Mount of Olives* (1655) is the earliest dated example of his work. The large (Black) *Madonna of Monserrat with a Donor* is by Fray Juan Rizi (1595–1675), *Belshazzar's Feast* by Juan Carreno (1614–85) is an impressive work; and Juan de Valdes Leal (1622–90) is represented by a fragment of an altarpiece, other parts of which are scattered in the Prado and the Museums of Seville, Grenoble and Dresden. There are also signed works by F. Camilo, Antonio de Puga and Pedro Muñoz (the two last being the only signed examples by these artists).

There are several important pictures of the early Netherlandish and German Schools, including a triptych, *The Crucifixion*, by the Master of the Virgo inter Virgines, *c.* 1470–80, and a panel of the same subject by Jacob Cornelisz van Oostsannen (c. 1470–1533). A small triptych of *The Entombment* might be ascribed to Adriaen Ysenbrandt, c. 1550, and a delightfully homely *Holy Family* bears the monogram of Willem Key (c. 1550).

Four wings of a large carved altar-piece painted with scenes of the Passion, appear to belong to the Westphalian School, though it is also strongly influenced by Dirk Bouts.

Another German panel is by the Master of St. Severin and is painted on both sides : one with *The Adoration of the Magi* and the other *The Raising of Lazarus*. Among other paintings of these Schools may be mentioned a Martin Heemskeerk (1498–1574), *Christ at the Sea of Tiberias*, a small portrait by Katharina van Hemessen (16th Century), *The Death of St. Paul the Hermit* by Martin de Vos (1532–1613), *A Flemish Lady* by Simon de Vos (1603–76), *Ulysses and Nausicaa* by Lucas van Uden, dated 1635, and a large *Family Group* by Van Hulle (1594–1665).

The French School includes a portrait of Elizabeth de Valois ascribed to F. Clouet (c. 1510–72), a landscape by Jean Dughet (1615–75), another by F. Boucher, dated 1743, and a small *Avenue with Figures* by J. H. Fragonard (1732–1806). A monumental portrait of the Bishop of Mechlin, by P. de Champaigne, is dated 1642, and there are several portraits of Louis XIV and members of the court, including Madame de Maintenon by J. Jouvenet (1664–1717). There is also a series representing Napoleon and his associates, one of which is a large painting of *Napoleon taking the Oath of Fidelity to the Constitution* by J. L. David, and there is a small pencil self-portrait of the artist.

Baron F. P. S. Gerard was the painter of *Charles X in Coronation Robes* and Baron A. J. Gros the painter of *The Duchesse d'Angoulême*. There is a fine *View from Ornans* by Gustave Courbet (1819–77); two oils and two pastels are by E. L. Boudin (1825–1908), and a *Fruit and Flowers* is by Fantin-Latour, and dated 1866.

The English School is not happily represented. Among the most interesting are portraits of Bishop Butler by Thomas Hudson (1701–79), Mrs. Thrale by Sir Joshua Reynolds, *A Female Portrait* by Hogarth, and a portrait of Catherine Stephens, the singer, painted about 1820, by Sir Thomas Lawrence. The *View of Elmsett Church*, by Thomas Gainsborough, has been presented by Mr. F. J. Nettlefold and the water-colours, *Windsor Castle* by Paul Sandby, G. F. Robson's *Durham* and others are from the same donor. Helped by the National Art Collections Fund, the Museum has acquired a *View of Barnard Castle* by Thomas Girtin, *c.* 1800.

A few English School pictures have been acquired on long loan. These include pastel portraits of Peg Woffington, Mrs. Stillingfleet, and John Vanderbank by Hoare of Bath (*c.* 1740), and some later 18th-Century examples by Ozias Humphreys. An illustration of *Edwin and Emma* by John Downman, dated 1788, is not only a good example of that feature of Downman's work but has a local setting.

The pictures mentioned will give an idea of the wide range of the Bowes Museum collections. Many typical examples by well-known artists have not been included.

Open 10 a.m. to 4 p.m. during winter, 10 a.m. to 6 p.m. during summer.

THOMAS WAKE,
Curator and Secretary

BATH

THE HOLBURNE OF MENSTRIE MUSEUM owes its origin to a bequest made in 1882 of the collection belonging to Sir Thomas William Holburne. It is housed in the Pavilion built in 1796 in Sydney Gardens 'Vauxhall'. Among the pictures is an interesting group of 18th-Century portraits, including works by Gainsborough and Hoppner. Thomas Barker of Bath is well represented in all his manners by portraits, landscapes and genre pictures. The earlier schools are less richly displayed, but there is an interesting German 16th-Century *Judgment of Paris* in the manner of Lucas Cranach, a *Kermesse* after Pieter Bruegel the Elder, small *Tavern Scenes* by Adrian van Ostade and others, and portraits by Cornelius Johnson. From the 17th-Century Italian and French Schools there are several small sketches of religious paintings and a large canvas of *Rinaldo leaving Armida*, probably by the rare French artist François Perrier. In addition to oil paintings there is an extensive collection of miniatures, porcelain and other objects of art.

Open 11 to 1 and 2 to 4 on Mondays, Tuesdays, Thursdays, Fridays and Saturdays.

THE VICTORIA ART GALLERY in the Municipal Library contains a large collection of English water-colours, principally of subjects connected with Bath. Its small collection of oil paintings includes an important Flemish Primitive, which is probably an early copy after Hugo van der Goes.

Open 10 to 5 on Tuesdays, Thursdays and Saturdays.

BIRMINGHAM CITY ART GALLERY

THE Birmingham Art Gallery was first opened to the public in August 1867, when it was housed in a room in the Free Library. In 1877 the collection had considerably increased and was shown temporarily at Aston Hall, the fine 17th-Century house, which has now been arranged as a private house museum with appropriate pictures and furnishings. When the extensions were made to the Council House towards the end of the century, a space was allocated for the Art Gallery and the new rooms were formally opened in 1885. In 1905 John Feeney bequeathed a large sum for the erection of further galleries, which were opened in 1912, and in 1919 six more rooms were added, but unfortunately in 1940 seven galleries were destroyed by a 1,000-pound bomb. These are now in process of rebuilding, and experiments are now being made with a view to the installation of the best methods of lighting and display.

Although the Gallery was maintained and administered by the Corporation, no money was voted from public funds for the purchase of works of art. In the great age of *laissez faire* everything was left to private enterprise. Birmingham has good reason to be proud of the public spirit of her citizens who have not only presented works of art from their own collections, but have supported generously the Public Picture Gallery Fund and the Feeney Charitable Bequest to which the Gallery is indebted for some of its most important acquisitions. In 1933 the Association of the Friends of the Art Gallery was inaugurated which enables those with more modest means to contribute to the collection. In 1946 it was, however, decided that the Art Gallery Committee should no longer have to rely entirely on private generosity for the acquisition of works of art and a sum of £1,000 was voted from the rates to be spent on pictures and other museum objects; in 1947 the grant was raised to £5,000. It is difficult to formulate a precise policy in buying, but broadly speaking the Committee has aimed at strengthening the collection of English pictures, at acquiring more contemporary work and also at buying examples of the work of the European painters at present so poorly represented.

The permanent collection is chiefly known for the paintings of the Pre-Raphaelites and those of Burne Jones, the oils and water-colours of David Cox, and English water-colours of the 18th and 19th Centuries.

Birmingham patrons supported the Pre-Raphaelite painters in the early days before they became popular and in 1853 Holman Hunt was awarded the Birmingham Society of Artists prize for his picture *Strayed Sheep*, now in the Tate Gallery. There are well-known pictures by the three original members of the Brotherhood, Holman Hunt, Millais and Rossetti. *Two Gentlemen of Verona* (Pl. 34b) and the *Finding of Christ in the Temple*, both by Holman Hunt, were painted in the early years of Pre-Raphaelitism when the fervour of the movement was still at its height. Millais' *Blind Girl*, of 1856, is perhaps the most distinguished picture of the School in the Gallery. Rossetti is represented by two large pictures, *Our Lady of Pity* and *Beata Beatrix*, both of which are late works and not truly Pre-Raphaelite in character. Unfortunately there is only one of his remarkable early water-colours, *Sir Galahad*, but the collection of his drawings is of exceptional quality.

A feature of the Gallery is the representative collection of the works by painters associated with the Brotherhood. *The Last of England* by Ford Madox Brown inspired by the emigration of the sculptor, Woolner, to Australia, in 1852, is almost universally known, whilst *The Long Engagement* by Arthur Hughes always excites admiration for its technique, although it is derided for its sentimentality. Amongst the works of lesser-known artists are *The Stonebreaker* by Henry Wallis, with its curious unearthly colour, *The Woman of Samaria* by William Dyce, and pictures by James Smetham, Walter Deverell, John Brett, Frederick Sandys and R. B. Martineau.

The Pre-Raphaelite drawings, which number several hundreds, were many of them acquired from Fairfax Murray. It is appropriate that the collection should also include a number of water-colours and drawings by John Ruskin, the great champion of the Pre-Raphaelites.

The Gallery is very rich in the works of Burne-Jones, who was a native of Birmingham. Some of the best known are the series of panels designed as a frieze for No. 1, Palace Green, the house built for the Hon. George Howard by Philip Webb; and the large water-colour *The Star of Bethlehem* commissioned by the City in 1887, later to be reproduced in tapestry for Exeter College, Oxford. Others which deserve special mention are *Phyllis and Damon*, the *Pygmalion series* and the *Holy Grail*, the last recently presented by Mrs. Burney, a daughter of Sir George Lewis. An interesting possession is the sensitive portrait of Burne-Jones by G. F. Watts.

It seems apposite in this connection to mention the series of pictures by J. F. Lewis, whose work is so closely allied to the Pre-Raphaelites in technique. They include the well-known *Lilium Auratum* and the recently acquired water-colour of the *Artist's House in Cairo*.

English painting of the 17th, 18th and early 19th Centuries is not so well represented. Portraits by Lely and Kneller are hanging at Aston Hall in an appropriate 17th-Century setting. One of the more interesting recent acquisitions is *Susannah and the Elders* by Lely from the collection of the Duke of Grafton, of which there are various other versions which show the strong influence of Rubens and of the Bolognese School in the early painting of Lely. There are por-traits by Reynolds, Gainsborough and Romney, including the charming small picture of *Mrs. Luther* by Reynolds. But the most interesting of the 18th-Century pictures are two by Zoffany depict-ing scenes from Garrick's play, *Lethe*, in one of which the actor himself is represented; they came from the collection of Sir George Beaumont. Another small picture of some historical interest is a copy by Gainsborough from a picture by Salvator Rosa which was once in the collection at Houghton.

Of the landscape paintings, the most distinguished are *The View of Okehampton* by Richard Wilson, the *Pass of St. Gothard*, by Turner, painted about 1811, and a *Cloud Study* by Constable. The *Pigs* by George Morland is a particularly good example of that artist's work, while the large collection of oil paintings by David Cox includes such well-known pictures as the *Welsh Funeral*, *Rhyl Sands* and *The Skylark*.

The fine collection of English water-colours contains good examples of the work of all periods. One of the earliest is the *View of Mæcenas Villa at Tivoli* by James Skelton. Other distinguished drawings by the early topographers are the *View of Rome* by William Pars, dated 1766, a lovely little *View of Stirling* by Thomas Hearne and *St. Albans* by Paul Sandby. A group of drawings by Francis Towne includes both English and Italian subjects of high quality. The more classical tradition is seen in a composition by Alexander Cozens on a larger scale than is usual with that artist. Amongst the drawings by J. R. Cozens is the *Valley of Sion*, signed and dated 1780. A recent acquisition of special interest is the *View on the Dee* by Wilson composed on classical lines, which is a study for the oil painting belonging to Lord Tollemache. Turner is unfortunately not well represented, but the *View of Salisbury* is an excellent example of his early topographical work commissioned by Sir Richard Colt Hoare in 1789, whilst *Cochem on the Moselle* is a brilliant impressionistic study probably painted in the 1830's. The *View of Hawes* by Girtin, for which there is a small pencil sketch in the collection, is identical with one in the Hickman Bacon collection, and is remarkable for its subtle tones. The Gallery owns two other water-colours by this distinguished artist. John Sell Cotman is not well shown, but there is a charming early study of the interior of *Walsoken Church* and a good pencil sketch. De Wint, on the other hand, is represented by a fine series of water-colours of various dates.

The fashion for continental views in the early 19th Century is reflected in the collection by good examples of the work of Samuel Prout, James Holland and Shotter Boys, whose view of Dresden is a memorial to that great city, now almost destroyed. Other items of interest are the 6 water-colours by William Blake, including the well-known *Whirlwind of Lovers* (Pl. 33a), the two *Views of Ancient and Modern Rome*, painted in 1836 by Samuel Palmer, the friend and admirer of Blake; and the original drawings by Caldicott for John Gilpin. There is also a good selection of drawings by Charles Keene and some interesting work by Le Gros.

Water-colours of more recent date, but based on the old earlier English tradition, include some good examples of the work of Wilson Steer and some fine early Sargent figure drawings. There are also water-colours by a number of contemporary artists, including John Nash, Paul Nash, Gilbert Spencer, Eric Ravilious, John Piper and Henry Moore (Pl. 33*b*).

Pictures by members of the New English Art Club are prominent and include six paintings by Wilson Steer showing the various aspects of his work, impressionistic sketches, a girl's head and a large landscape with figures. Walter Sickert's early work is seen at its best in the *View of Dieppe*, painted in 1901, whilst *The Miner* represents his later work when he was making use of photographs.

The Crystal Gazers by Henry Tonks, shows the influence of the Pre-Raphaelites in the choice of subject, tempered by his interest in impressionistic effects of light and texture. An early Ethel Walker, *Bronze and Silver*, *The Nurse* by Harold Gilman, and a *Still Life* by William Nicholson, should also be noted together with the portraits by Augustus John, including that of *King Feisal*, and a highly decorative landscape by J. D. Innes.

A number of good drawings have been acquired in the last two or three years, including three by Augustus John, of which the *Head of Delius* is of special interest. A portrait drawing of *Steer* by Tonks, a nude study by Ethel Walker, two excellent drawings by Sickert and a group of drawings and pastels by Sir George Clausen, illustrate the exacting standards of draughtsmanship of the New English Art Club.

Of the work of the more advanced guard there is a *Still Life* and a lovely small *Landscape at Aix* by Matthew Smith, landscapes by Stanley Spencer and paintings by Ivon Hitchens, James Tunnard, John Piper, Graham Sutherland, Barbara Hepworth and William Scott.

Although the strength of the collection is in English painting, efforts are being made to increase the representation of works of the European Schools. One of the most important possessions is the altar-piece by A. Isenbrandt, a triptych representing *The Nativity, the Adoration and the Presentation in the Temple*, with small grisaille figures on the backs of the wings. Another important early picture is the *Dead Christ* by Cima. More recent acquisitions include a large landscape by Jan van Goyen (Pl. 34*a*) of unusually good quality signed and dated 1642, an interesting picture by Orazio Gentileschi of *The Rest on the Flight into Egypt*, of which a smaller version is now in the Louvre. Another picture which hung for some time in the Louvre is attributed to a Neapolitan painter, Bartolomoneo Passante, a pupil of Ribera. It was once in the collection of King Louis Philippe, and was for many years on loan at the Louvre, where it was labelled Velasquez. It depicts the *Angels appearing to the Shepherds*. A charming small Venetian picture by Luca Carlevaris also deserves special mention. Of more recent date there are two outstanding pictures, *Venus* by Courbet and the *Church at St. Moret*, a late work by Alfred Sisley, the only French Impressionist picture in the collection. Every effort is being made to extend the scope of the collection, not only by purchase which is inevitably a slow process, but by means of loan exhibitions and loans from private individuals. At the present time the bulk of the Lockinge Collection is hanging at Birmingham, notably the Pesellino Cassone panels, the triptychs by Gerard David and *The Enchanted Castle* by Claude Lorrain. Amongst other loans are an early Rembrandt *Portrait of His Father* and a fine Ruisdael landscape, whilst English portraits lent by Lord Rothschild include *The Morning Walk* by Gainsborough, *Mrs. Lloyd* and *Garrick between Tragedy and Comedy* by Reynolds. Such pictures set a very high standard for those who are commissioned to buy for the City.

MARY WOODALL,
Keeper of Department of Paintings

THE BARBER INSTITUTE OF FINE
ARTS OF THE UNIVERSITY OF
BIRMINGHAM

THE Barber Institute of Fine Arts contains what is perhaps the most recently acquired art collection of first importance in England. When it was opened by Her Majesty Queen Mary in 1939 there were only 13 paintings and 20 drawings, with a few pieces of sculpture, objects of art, articles of furniture and textiles. Since then many additions have been made and the collection is now many times greater. But it is still small and practically everything is comfortably displayed in four large galleries and two rooms of drawings. All is of high quality; indeed, the Institute must be unique among museums in having no storerooms filled with doubtful and second-rate works.

Though facilities have been made for the public to visit the Institute, it is not a public gallery. It belongs to the University of Birmingham and its first purpose is to serve the members of the University. That was the intention of its founder and the principle which has guided the Trustees in the control of its affairs. It owes its existence to the judgment and generosity of Dame Martha Constance Hattie Barber. Her husband, Sir Henry Barber, Bart., had during his lifetime been actively concerned with academic affairs in Birmingham and became a Life Governor of the University. A solicitor himself, his particular interest was the Faculty of Law, which was then coming into being, and he provided the endowment for the Professorial Chair of Law in the Department of Legal Studies which preceded the establishment of the Faculty. Lady Barber, who shared to the full her husband's interests, thus came into personal touch with the University and its future.

When Sir Henry Barber died, Lady Barber was left with considerable wealth and sought some imaginative way in which to use it. She had always been interested in the fine arts and was herself a skilled needlewoman with an expert knowledge of lace. At her house, Culham Court, she and her husband had made a collection of fine examples of textiles and furniture. This interest, combined with her close contact with the University of Birmingham, shaped the decisions which brought the Barber Institute into being. The modern university in Birmingham was already a flourishing institution. But, like others whose foundation date from the late 19th Century, its development had laid greater emphasis on the scientific and technical than on the liberal and humanistic arts. Lady Barber felt that her purpose might well be to do something to redress the balance. In order to effect this, she decided to concentrate rather than disperse her resources. Instead of giving a little here and a little there —all of which would no doubt have done some good—she chose to devote the main part of her wealth towards some single purpose, and the idea of establishing an Institute of Fine Arts where some place would be found for the performance of music, seemed the best way of expressing her wishes. To this end she established the Barber Trust, with its original Trustees nominated by herself.

Lady Barber had hoped to take an active personal part in the working out of the Trust, but, after a severe illness, she died in 1932, before much of a practical nature had been done. Her will, however, made her wishes clear, and two of the Trustees she had appointed, Mr. C. D. Medley, the first chairman, and the late Sir Charles Grant Robertson, then Vice-Chancellor of the University, were personal friends who had full knowledge of her intentions. The will empowered the Trustees to establish the Institute: to erect and equip, on land provided for that purpose by the University, a building which should serve both as a Museum and a Music Room which should 'belong to and be used by the University for the study and encouragement of art and music'. At the same time a Professor of Fine Arts who should also be Director of the Institute was to be appointed. As Professor he would be head of the Department of Fine Arts and responsible to the Senate of the University; as Director he would control the Institute, and the Museum contained therein, though in this capacity his responsibility would be to the Trustees.

The double nature of the Institute was thus formed at the start. The teaching would be that of an orthodox University department,

but its scope and its influence were to be extended by the art collections, available to all members of the University whether concerned with the department or not. The presence of a Music Room,
in which Lady Barber's Trust provided the necessary funds for
occasional recitals of chamber music by artists of the first class, further
widened the circle of interest. But the whole was to be an integral
part of the University, and the galleries and their contents not a
public or semi-public museum but the University's private collection.

In the Trust Deed Lady Barber laid great stress on the quality of
the collections—the phrase she used was 'works of art of exceptional
and outstanding merit'. In making their acquisitions the Trustees
were to be guided solely by this principle of high quality, and in
general, no restrictions were made as to the nature of the works of
art or their country and period of origin. Indeed, the character of
the Deed suggested that the scope of the collections should be the
widest possible, and in addition to paintings and drawings, which
would automatically be included, Lady Barber specifically mentioned 'furniture, tapestries, needlework, lace, medieval manuscripts, finely printed books and other works of art'. Only in three
respects were there prohibitions. The Trustees may not purchase
'pottery or china'; works which date from later than the end of the
19th Century are excluded; and gifts, other than those from Lady
Barber herself, may not be accepted.

In 1935 the first Director-Professor, Dr. Thomas Bodkin, was
appointed, and he has ever since been the adviser of the Trustees
in building up the collections. Lady Barber's standard of outstanding and exceptional merit has been remembered. The aim has
been not merely to represent artists and schools by work which can
be proved to be authentic, but to represent them with the best
examples obtainable. The collections as they stand at the moment
are little more than a nucleus and reflect in some measure the state
of the art market over the past fifteen years or so. But already there
is enough to give the Institute its own individuality. As the Trust
provides a regular annual income subsequent purchases will help to
make this quality even more apparent.

The most important of the acquisitions have been the paintings,
and already all the main European Schools are represented. In

35.a CIMA DA CONEGLIANO Crucifixion   Birmingham, Barber Institute

35.b RUBENS Landscape near Malines   Birmingham, Barber Institute

Birmingham, Barber Institute

26 *a* GIOVANNI BELLINI Portrait of a Boy

Birmingham, Barber Institute

26 *b* REMBRANDT An Old Warrior

relation to its importance the Italian still perhaps falls behind the others in quantity. But there is enough to show that a good start has been made. The earliest picture is a 13th-Century *Crucifixion*, exhibited at Burlington House in 1930, and attributed with the reservations common to pictures of this period to Giunta Pisano. It is followed by two Sienese trecento panels, a *St. Francis* from a dismembered polyptych by Ugolino da Siena and a moving head of *St. John the Evangelist* by Simone Martini. This small group of Sienese pictures is rounded off by a *Madonna with SS. John the Baptist and Michael* by Matteo di Giovanni.

There are only three Florentine pictures in the collection, a Botticelli, a Signorelli and an Andrea del Sarto. The most important of these is the Botticelli *Madonna and Child with the Infant St. John*, a late work which is most probably the original version of the studio picture in the Pitti which repeats its composition in reverse.

Venice is much more fully represented. Two paintings by Giovanni Bellini, both included in the 1949 Bellini Exhibition at Venice, the charming early *St. Jerome in the Wilderness* and the little *Portrait of a Boy* (Pl. 36a) from the Holford Collection make an excellent start. This is splendidly maintained by the magnificent *Crucifixion* by Cima da Conegliano (Pl. 35a) described by Raimond van Marle as 'one of the finest and most inspired pictures I know from the hand of the master'. These earlier works are followed by an impressive Tintoretto *Portrait of a Young Man* and, still more distantly, by a *Regatta on the Grand Canal* which shows all the liveliness and bustle of Guardi's later work.

There are a few early Netherlandish pictures including Mabuse's *Hercules and Deianira*, dated 1517, and a portrait of an ecclesiastic by Quentin Massys. Bruegel's *Two Peasants Binding Faggots*, from the collection of Prince Paul of Yugoslavia, is a little-known but unquestionably authentic work by the master. But as the collection stands at the moment, the most thoroughly represented period is the 17th Century. Of the Flemish pictures the finest and most impressive is the late Rubens *Landscape near Malines* (Pl. 35b) which had disappeared during the 19th Century and re-appeared only a few years ago. The Dutch paintings include several portraits. There is the early Hals, *A Man Holding a Skull*, and Rembrandt's *Old*

N

Warrior (Pl. 36*b*) signed and dated 1651, and, by slightly lesser artists, Flinck's little *Boy* in a delightful landscape and Nicolas Maes's elegant *Portrait of a Lady*. Nearly all the other facets of Dutch art during the century are triumphantly exemplified: landscape by Ruisdael and van de Cappelle, still-life by Jan Davidz de Heem, genre by Cornelis Dusart and full-dress subject painting by Jan Steen with his remarkable *Wrath of Ahasuerus*.

Though the representation of the Spanish School is small, only 2 paintings, the large Murillo *The Marriage Feast at Cana*, is undoubtedly one of the artist's most important works outside Spain. The other picture, a portrait by Goya of his mother, is a very early work. There is much more from France. The most important of the 17th-Century pictures is Poussin's *Tancred and Erminia*, a work only recently re-discovered, but apart from characteristic paintings by Mathieu Le Nain and Lancret, all the other French paintings date from the 19th Century. There are fine and typical landscapes by Corot and Courbet and the large *Portrait of Carolus-Duran* by Manet. Later still there are Monet's *L'Eglise de Varangeville* and two landscapes, of Brittany and Tahiti, by Gauguin. Toulouse-Lautrec's *La Songeuse* belongs to the last years of the century and comes very near to Lady Barber's stipulated time limit.

In making the collections the Trustees have shown no special favouritism towards English painters, but it is perhaps natural that the national school should receive special attention. A miniature of *Henry, Prince of Wales* by Isaac Oliver belongs to the early 17th Century, but all the other works are later. Reynolds's *Portrait of Dr. Richard Robinson* is one of the artist's outstanding works; indeed, it was described by Horace Walpole in 1775 as 'the best portrait he ever painted'. Gainsborough is even more splendidly shown. *The Harvest Wagon* is considered by many to be his finest landscape, a view which Gainsborough himself would have understood for in a letter to his friend Walter Wiltshire, to whom he gave the picture, he wrote, 'I think this is one of my best compositions.' Gainsborough's portrait art is also well exemplified by *The Hon. Harriet Marsham* and *G. F. Tenducci*, both late works. A group of four landscapes by Wilson, Crome, Turner and Constable make a good complement to the portraits; and two aspects of later 19th-Century painting are shown in Whistler's *Symphony in White No. III* and Orchardson's portrait of his wife.

These are not all the paintings, but enough have been mentioned to give some idea of the catholicity of selection. They are well supplemented by a small but well-chosen collection of drawings of which the outstanding feature is a group of four by Rembrandt. Among the other artists included are Fra Bartolommeo, Tintoretto, Veronese, Tiepolo, Guardi, Longhi, Rubens, Van Dyck, Van Goyen, Potter, Claude, Ingres, Degas, Gainsborough, Rowlandson, Turner and a number of later 19th-Century English draughtsmen such as Charles Keene, John Leech and Phil May.

The scope is still further widened by the sculpture and objects of art, which include works from many different civilisations and periods.

These collections, with a few tapestries and pieces of French and English furniture, are contained in a well-proportioned and dignified building, designed by Mr. Robert Atkinson, F.R.I.B.A., which is adjacent to the main part of the University at Edgbaston. The galleries are open during term to all members of the University. In 1947 the Trustees decided to make the collections more generally available, and since then there has been a public day on the first Saturday of each month, when the Institute is open from 10 a.m. to 4 p.m. A short handbook has been published which includes a summary list of all acquisitions and there is also a full and detailed catalogue of the paintings and drawings.

The Institute can look forward to a great future. Only the income from Lady Barber's Trust has been used in making the many acquisitions of its early years. If the wise guidance it has had in the past should continue to be maintained—and there is no indication of any reason to the contrary—it may well become a force and an example among British institutions.

A. McLAREN YOUNG,
Assistant Curator

BRIGHTON ART GALLERY

THE Gallery was opened in 1873, in buildings that are part of the Royal Pavilion Estate. The Central Gallery was originally the tennis court, the other rooms part of the royal stables and coach-houses. Sickert wrote in a letter—

> the gallery which is still *the* example of proper picture hanging. Pictures considered as permanent factors in the architecture of a room, and not as items in a lending library. The life sized or larger than life portraits or drama—pictures, hang on the frieze above the picture-rail. Below are perhaps a couple of lines of cabinet pictures. . . . This, the traditional grand style of hanging that nothing can ever replace. . . .

The nucleus of the collections is the bequest of Henry Willett, a familiar name to students of Friedländer and the early editions of Berenson. From him came most of the large collection of early paintings, chiefly of the Netherlands. There are an important *Virgin and Child with Angels*, by Albert Cornelis of Bruges (*c.* 1532) (Pl. 40a) one of the only two works of this master, a moving *Raising of Lazarus*, by Jan Lievens, which hung in Rembrandt's house, and works by Henri de Bles, Bernard van Orlay, Joachim de Patinier, Jan Mostaert, Aert de Gelder, Jan Weenix, Peter Pourbus, Van Balen, Van Bassen, E. van de Velde, Van der Aelst, Gerard Dou, Van Goyen, Wybrand Hendriks, Abraham Storck, Van der Borcht, Nikolas Maes, Van der Neer, Louise Moillon, Michael Wohlgemuth, Martin Schongauer, and portraits of the Electors Frederick and John of Saxony by Lucas Cranach. Of the Italian School there are a *Tobias and the Angel* by Jacopo de Sellaio, a *Virgin and Child* by Bartolommeo Vivarini, a *Hercules and Omphale* by Luca Giordano and landscapes by Zuccarelli. Of English artists there are a small but excellent Richard Wilson landscape, portraits by Zoffany (Pl. 40b), Angelica Kauffman, George Dance, Hoppner, Raeburn, John Russell, and important portraits of George IV by Lawrence. There is a group of Early English water-colours, a larger collection of modern British water-colours, including works by John and Paul

Nash, Bawden, Henry Moore, Gross, Hennell, Michael Rothen-
stein, Ardizzone, Ravilious, Hodgkins, Methuen, Muirhead Bone,
Pitchforth, Steer, Ricketts, Short, Hilder, Suddaby, Brabazon, Du
Plessis, Duncan Grant, Claude Flight, and Minton, 18th-century
engravings, modern British drawings and prints, Japanese prints,
and the original drawings and water-colour sketches by Augustus
Pugin, made between 1818 and 1822 for John Nash's *Views of the
Royal Pavilion*, 1826. A number of 19th-Century painters, including
John Phillip, John Linnell, Muller, Holland and Herring, have
been grouped together under the heading 'Victorian Painting'.
The modern paintings include works by Brangwyn, Gertler, Whit-
ing, Munnings, Meninsky, Wadsworth, Connard, Tryon, Grant,
Blanche, Clausen, Lucien Pissarro, G. W. Lambert, Richard Wynd-
ham, Algernon Newton, Ethel Walker, Laura Knight, Robert
Bevan, Le Bas, Lawrence Gowing, Ivon Hitchens and Frances
Hodgkins.

A mural painting by Rex Whistler, removed from the walls of a
house in Brighton where it was painted shortly before 'D-Day',
his last important work, represents *H.R.H. the Prince Regent awakening the spirit of Brighton*.

The Willett collection of pottery has some important groups of
various English wares, and there is also a group of modern pottery
designed or decorated by Eric Ravilious and Graham Sutherland,
which shows the continuance of the English tradition in our own
day.

There are examples of English and foreign glass, Japanese pottery
and Georgian wax portraits and an important collection of Primitive
Art, chiefly of the Western Pacific and Africa.

About ten special exhibitions are held every year.

The Gallery is open on weekdays from 10 a.m. to 7 p.m. ; on
Sundays from 2.30 p.m. to 5 p.m.

CLIFFORD MUSGRAVE,
Director

CITY ART GALLERY, BRISTOL

THE buildings of the City Art Gallery, now completely surrounded by those of the University of Bristol, were given by two members of the Wills family; the first part opened in 1904 by Sir George Wills, afterwards Lord Winterstoke, and the extension, opened in 1930 by his brother H. H. Wills. Combined originally with a much older institution, Bristol Museum, founded in 1821, the Art Gallery was separated in 1945.

The collections include examples of pictorial and industrial arts, and attention may be called to the following outstanding examples.

There is a very large collection of works by local artists, chief of whom is W. J. Muller (1812–45) (Pl. 38b). He was the son of the first Curator of Bristol Museum and started his artistic career by drawing objects in his father's collections. His principal work, *Eel Bucks at Goring*, shows strong influence by Constable.

A number of important works were purchased in 1932 from the Royal West of England Academy, a sister institution founded in 1844, which included a large panel *The Nativity* by Jacob Jordaens, originally in the Harford collection, a signed portrait of Queen Henrietta Maria by Van Dyck and an interesting series of portraits in pastel, including those of several early Presidents of United States, by James Sharples (1750–1811) and members of his family. His widow, Ellen Sharples, was founder of the Royal West of England Academy.

A triptych altar-piece by Antonio da Solario (signed and dated Venice, 1514) (Pl. 38a) has been reassembled with the co-operation of the National Gallery. The centre panel containing the portrait of the donor—Paul Withypool, a Bristol cloth merchant, was purchased and the wings have been lent by the National Gallery.

The munificent bequest of F. P. M. Schiller, K.C., Recorder of Bristol, 1935–46, included beside the well-known collection of some 400 pieces of Chinese porcelain of superb quality, a number of small Old Master paintings including works by Ambrogio da

Predis, Corneille de Lyon, Bernard van Orley and others, and a very interesting conversation piece by Sir Joshua Reynolds.

Recent purchases include a *Tavern Scene* by Adrian Brouwer, which was once in Rubens' collection, a small work by John Constable and choice drawings by Gainsborough, Cotman and William Blake.

A start has been made in building up a representative group of work by contemporary painters, in which valued help has been given by the National Art-Collections Fund, the Contemporary Art Society and the recently formed Association of Friends of Bristol Art Gallery. Amongst artists included may be mentioned W. R. Sickert, Lord Methuen, Harold Gilman, Henry Moore, Graham Sutherland, William Roberts, Ivon Hitchens, Barbara Hepworth, Frances Hodgkin, John Piper, Augustus John and Gwen John.

In the Industrial Arts, the Gallery is particularly strong in ceramics and glass, noteworthy Bristol products of the 18th Century; there is also a good collection of textiles and some fine furniture. Some of these are exhibited in the Georgian House, built in 1789-91 by John Pinney, a West Indian merchant, which was given to the city by the late Canon R. T. Cole, F.S.A., and is furnished as a Bristol merchant's house of the late 18th Century.

Another fine Elizabethan house—the Red Lodge—which was given to the city some years ago, is also under the Gallery's care. It is at present (1949) undergoing extensive repair, but will be reopened shortly.

The Gallery is open free 10 a.m. to 6 p.m. weekdays; 2.30 p.m. to 5 p.m. Sundays.

H. W. MAXWELL,
Director

THE FITZWILLIAM MUSEUM,
CAMBRIDGE

THE Fitzwilliam Museum was founded in 1816 by Richard, 7th Viscount Fitzwilliam of Merrion, who bequeathed to the University of Cambridge his collections of works of art, with £100,000 to provide a building to house them. It thus takes its place among the earliest public museums to be founded in England.

The collections thus bequeathed were varied and extensive. Pictures to the number of 144 included a Titian, a Paul Veronese, a Palma Vecchio and a Rembrandt, besides other Italian paintings, family portraits, and works of the Dutch and Flemish Schools largely inherited from the Founder's maternal grandfather, Sir Matthew Decker. A vast assembly of prints by the most celebrated engravers of all countries included a series of Rembrandt's etchings unsurpassed in England at the time. The splendid library contained many fine 18th-Century books, 130 medieval manuscripts, and an outstanding collection of autograph music by Purcell, Handel and other famous composers.

The original museum building, opened in 1848, was designed by George Basevi, after whose untimely death in 1845 the work of continuation was entrusted to C. R. Cockerell, though the present form of the entrance hall, finished later, is due to E. M. Barry. Three extensions, necessitated by great increases in the collections, were opened between 1924 and 1936, designed by the London firm of Smith & Brewer.

The chief collections now comprise Egyptian, Greek and Roman Antiquities, Coins and Medals, Paintings, Prints, Drawings, Ancient and Modern Manuscripts, Ceramics, Textiles, Medieval and Renaissance Objects of Art, Music, both manuscript and printed, and a Library. Several of these are of outstanding importance. The Coin Collection, amounting to nearly 70,000 coins, medals and seals, is second in England only to that in the British Museum, as is the Collection of Prints, especially rich in portraits; the Department of

37.*a* GOYA Prison Scene   *Barnard Castle*

37.*b* EL GRECO St. Peter   *Barnard Castle*

38.*a* SOLARIO   Virgin and Child with Donors   *Bristol*

38.*b* MULLER   River Avon and Bristol Cathedral   *Bristol*

39.*a*   IVON HITCHENS   Landscape   *Cardiff*

39.*b*   RICHARD WILSON   Caernarvon Castle   *Cardiff*

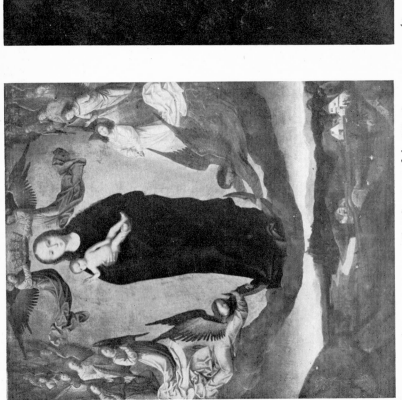

40.a ALBERT CORNELIS Glorification of the Virgin
Brighton

40.b ZOFFANY Woman and Child
Brighton

Ceramics is surpassed in England only by the British Museum and the Victoria and Albert Museum and is especially strong in English pottery; while the Music Collection contains the best series of auto-graph compositions in England after the British Museum and the Royal Library at Windsor.

The Fitzwilliam Museum, like many similar institutions in England, is entirely the creation of private generosity, both as regards buildings and collections, continued without a break from the time of the Founder to the present day. The formation of the picture collection took place mostly during the 19th Century, and in its interest and balance is thus principally representative of the taste of 18th- and 19th-Century collectors. It numbers close on 1,000 paint-ings, of which nearly 200 are Italian, about 150 Flemish, 220 Dutch, almost 300 English, about 80 French and the remaining 50 Spanish, German, etc. Owing to restrictions of space, a selection only of this number is exhibited, occupying 11 galleries on the upper floor of the Museum.

The collection is strengthened by the addition of a few choice loans. Among pictures lent by the Trustees of the Cook Collection are a Rembrandt, a Van Dyck and an early Velasquez, while a number of paintings by the French Impressionists have been lent by Captain S. W. Sykes. Reference is not made to these loans in the ac-count which follows, which is confined to the permanent collection.

ITALIAN SCHOOLS.

The collection is mainly representative of the Sienese, Florentine and Venetian Schools. With the pictures are shown Italian medieval and Renaissance illuminated manuscripts, drawings, maiolica and bronzes.

The dissemination of Byzantine culture in Italy is illustrated by a 13th-Century *Crucifixion* of the Sienese School, and another of Sienese origin of the School of Pietro Lorenzetti (active 1305–48). Truer to the characteristic spirit of medieval Siena are the three splendid panels from an altar-piece, *St. Ambrose, St. Michael and St. Augustine*, with angels above (about 1320) (Pl. 42*a*). The figures of the three saints are by Simone Martini (1283–85 (?) –1344), the foremost

Sienese painter of the 14th Century, whose influence was felt far afield throughout Europe; the figures of the angels are regarded as the work of his studio. This is among the principal Italian medieval paintings in England. A small painting under glass (*verre églomisé*), *The Virgin and Child with Saints*, is closely related to the work of Simone Martini. Among other 14th-Century Sienese painters represented are Luca di Tommè (fl. 1355–99) and Andrea Vanni (about 1332–1414). Of the 15th Century is Giovanni di Paolo (1403(?)–82).

The authoritative artistic spirit of Florence is first seen in a small panel of the *Virgin and Child enthroned* by Lorenzo Monaco (about 1370(?)–1425). Though still medieval in character, the weighty forms in their architectural setting, with their air of individual vitality, bespeak the tradition which was to lead to the greatest art of the Renaissance.

The best Florentine pictures in the collection are two small panels of the Early Renaissance by Domenico Veneziano (about 1410–60), *The Annunciation* (Pl. 42*b*) and the *Miracle of St. Zenobius* (St. Zenobius, Bishop of Florence—among other miracles he restored to life a little child run over and trampled by an ox-cart in the streets of the city). These come from the predella of the large altar-piece of the *Virgin and Child enthroned with Saints* in the Uffizi Gallery in Florence.

The essential nature of Florentine painting as a figure art is illustrated by the imposing, if somewhat grim, *Virgin and Child enthroned with Saints* by Cosimo Rosselli (1439–1507), showing the plasticity of form and the organic sense of movement sought by the Renaissance painters of the second generation. Greater ease and success mark the almost life-size nude of *St. Sebastian*, of the School of Lorenzo di Credi (1459–1537), of a generation and more later.

Among the remaining Florentine paintings the *Virgin and Child* by the Master of the Castello Nativity (active later 15th Century) may be singled out for its beauty of colour and fine landscape background; the *Virgin and Child enthroned with Saints* by Bartolommeo di Giovanni (active at the end of the 15th Century) for its quality as an example of tempera painting; and the group of 'cassone' panels for their variety and vivacity. A frequent convention in pictures of this narrative type is the depiction of a sequence of scenes from a story as though taking place simultaneously. A 'cassone', or chest, one of the principal forms of Renaissance furniture, stands in the Gallery.

A few fine drawings by Botticelli, Michelangelo and others supplement the representation of the Florentine School provided by the paintings.

The district of Umbria, south of Florence, was another active centre of painting in Renaissance Italy, the home of Raphael and of his master, Perugino. A red chalk drawing of the *Holy Family* by Raphael (1483–1520) is a reminder of his inimitable perfection; while a small *Virgin and Child* by an unknown follower of Perugino (1446–1542) gives a general idea of the character of that master's works. Another Umbrian painting is the *Virgin and Child with St. John Baptist* by Pinturicchio (1454–1513).

The sensuous and romantic painting of North Italy had its principal centres at Padua and, later, Venice. A painter who studied at Padua and founded an influential school at his native town of Ferrara, is Cosimo Tura (about 1430–95); his *Crucifixion with the Virgin Mary and St. John*, though much damaged, remains a moving treatment of the subject.

The Venetian School had become an independent centre by the end of the 15th Century under the leadership of Giovanni Bellini. The lyrical character of its painting at this time is illustrated by the large *St. Lanfranc of Pavia enthroned with Saints*, by Cima (about 1495–1517/18), and the *Virgin and Child with Saints and Donor* by Basaiti (active 1500–21). The landscape in the Basaiti, now part of the picture instead of a mere background to the figures, is evidence of a new feeling for nature.

Venetian paintings of the earlier part of the 16th Century, with the new visual world they explore and their new oil technique, are splendidly exemplified in two pictures by Titian (1480(?)–1576), *Tarquin and Lucretia* (Pl. 41b) and *Venus and Cupid with a Lute Player*. Almost contemporary with this great master is Palma Vecchio (1480–1528), whose imposing *Venus and Cupid* is transitional between the earlier type of Venetian painting and that of Titian, as is the Giorgionesque *Adoration of the Shepherds* by Sebastiano del Piombo (1485–1547).

The magnificent character of mature Venetian painting is also seen in a work of another of the great masters of the school, Paolo Veronese (1528–88), *Hermes, Herse and Aglauros* (Hermes, the lover of Herse, transforms her jealous sister, Aglauros into a block of stone with a touch of his caduceus). The third of the trio in whom Venetian painting culminates, Tintoretto (1518–95), whose work leads on to the Baroque of the 17th Century, is seen in a large *Adoration of the Shepherds* and a *Portrait of a Young Man*, the best Italian portrait in the collection. Drawings by Titian and Tintoretto are shown in the display case.

The painting of the late 16th Century is represented by two works of the Bolognese School, the academic *St. Roch and the Angel*, by Annibale Carracci (1560(?)–1609), and the *Ecce Homo* by Guido Reni (1575–1642), a remarkable piece of virtuosity. Three pictures illustrate the development of painting to full maturity in the 17th Century, *The Betrayal* by Guercino (1591–1666), a *Holy Family* by Sassoferrato (1605–85), and a landscape by Domenichino (1581–1641).

Two small views by Canaletto (1697–1768), *The Court of the Doge's Palace* and *St. Mark's*, and two little sketches by Francesco Guardi (1712–93), may serve as an introduction to Venetian 18th-Century topographical painting, which is also exemplified by views of Venice and Florence by Canaletto's nephew and imitator, Bellotto (1720–80).

FLEMISH AND DUTCH SCHOOLS.

These are represented from the early 15th Century to the end of the 17th. With the pictures are shown medieval illuminated manuscripts, and drawings.

As rare as it is exquisite is the drawing of *St. Veronica* by Robert Campin (1375–1444), of the School of Tournai (known also as the 'Maître de Flémalle'), after the Van Eycks the most important figure of early Flemish painting. The character of Flemish painting about the turn of the 15th Century is illustrated by the *Transfiguration* by Aelbert Bouts (1458–1548) and by the triptych by an unknown painter (centre, *Descent from the Cross*, left wing, *Presenta-*

tion of the Virgin, right wing, *Marriage of the Virgin*). Of fine quality is the *Virgin and Child* by Joos van Cleve (about 1485–1540, also known as the 'Master of the Death of Mary'), imitating North Italian models, which derives from the important 16th-Century centre of Antwerp.

The fertile 17th-Century painting of Flanders and Holland is well represented. The incomparable vitality of Rubens (1577–1640) is to be seen in 8 small oil sketches and several drawings; some fine drawings also illustrate the mastery of his pupil Van Dyck (1599–1641). A large *Self-Portrait* (Pl. 41a) dated 1650, and a few splendid drawings, display the unique powers of Rembrandt (1606–69).

Most of the many aspects of Dutch 17th-Century painting are to be seen in this collection. Its great school of landscape is represented by the work of two of its leading masters, Jacob Ruisdael (1628/9–1682) and Meindert Hobbema (1638–1709), besides that of other painters. Among the best of numerous examples of genre painting, are works by Jan Steen (1626–79), Gerard Dou (1613–75), Frans van Mieris the Elder (1635–81), and Adrien van der Werff (1659–1722). Portraiture includes, besides the Rembrandt, a *Portrait of a Man* by Frans Hals (1580/1–1666), another lively male portrait by Van der Helst (1613–70), and other works. Among the architectural subjects are two by G. A. Berckheyde (1639–98), and there are numerous examples of the flower-painting which reached such high perfection.

SPANISH SCHOOL.

The representation of this school is very limited, and consists of paintings of the 15th and 17th Centuries. The strong influence of Flemish painting in Spain in the 15th Century is evident from several pictures, but most strikingly in the *Road to Calvary* by Antonio and Diego Sanchez (active late 15th Century). The *Adoration of the Shepherds* by Luis Tristan (1585–1640), a pupil of El Greco, echoes the work of this solitary genius of 16th-Century Spanish painting. The greatest master of the 17th Century after Velasquez, Esteban Murillo (1618–82), is represented by his earliest known work, *The Vision of Fra Lauterio*, and a large painting of *St. John the Baptist with the Scribes and Pharisees*.

FRENCH SCHOOL.

French painting is sparsely represented before the 19th Century. With the paintings are shown medieval illuminated manuscripts and drawings.

The classicising tendencies of the 17th Century are indicated by two landscapes by Gaspard Poussin (1613–75), and a *Holy Family* by Charles le Brun (1619–90), together with drawings by Nicholas Poussin (1594–1665) and Claude le Lorrain (1600–82). Some small figure paintings by Lancret (1690–1743), Greuze (1725–1805), etc., together with a group of the exquisite drawings of Antoine Watteau (1684–1743), provide a sample of 18th-Century painting, which is further illustrated by the Beauvais tapestry of *Apollo and Clytie*, one of a set woven (1756–61) after the designs of Boucher (1703–70.)

The revived classicism of French art after the Revolution is reflected in the brilliant drawing by Ingres (1780–1867) of *Mr. and Mrs. Joseph Woodhead and the Rev. Henry Comber as a Youth*, 1816. The landscapes of a near contemporary, Corot (1796–1867), display more of the romantic elements of this period, with a freshness and intimacy reminiscent of Constable. Corot's works, with the massive realism of the pictures of Courbet (1819–77) lead on to Impressionism.

The Impressionist version of the perpetual theme of landscape, light and atmosphere, is very well typified in the *Garden at Pontoise* (1882) by Camille Pissarro (1830–1903), with its pervading shimmer of sunshine. Similar possibilities of colour are exploited to obtain the brilliance and heat of the small *Rue St. Vincent* by Seurat (1859–91). Of a different type is the exhilarating *Landscape* (Pl. 43a) by Renoir (1841–1919), who is seen in another phase in the *Portrait of a Girl*. A rather slight example of Cézanne (1839–1906), with his research after solid form, is the landscape *La Forêt*. The masterly Degas (1834–1917) is represented by an unfinished painting, *Au Café*. Among other Impressionist paintings are two by Vuillard (1868–1940), and two by Bonnard (1867–1947).

ENGLISH SCHOOL.

The representation of the English School is continuous, though not complete, from the first half of the 16th Century to the present day. With the paintings are shown medieval illuminated manuscripts, drawings, portrait miniatures and modern bronzes.

The beginnings of the modern tradition of painting are represented by the portrait of *William Fitzwilliam, Earl of Southampton*, by an unknown follower of Holbein (1497–1543), who first came to England in 1526. This may stand as representative of the three special peculiarities of English painting—the lateness of its start, the long dominance of foreign masters, and the predominating importance of portraiture, which lasted until the end of the 18th Century.

The degeneration of the average portrait into a mere costume piece by the end of the 16th Century is illustrated by two anonymous portraits of Elizabethan ladies, though evidence of the existence of better work is seen in the *Portrait of a Man*. By contrast, the fine quality of the portraiture produced by the contemporary miniaturists can be appreciated from a number of examples of the work of Nicholas Hilliard (1547–1619) and Isaac Oliver (1557/67–1617), exhibited in the display case.

The improvement which took place in the 17th Century under the Stuarts is exemplified in the portrait of *Archbishop Laud*, from the studio of Van Dyck (1599–1641), who settled in England in 1632. His style is also reflected in the *Portrait of a Cavalier*, attributed to Henry Stone (d. 1653).

The Van Dyck tradition was transmitted to later generations, to the permanent enrichment of English portrait painting, by another foreigner, Peter Lely (1618–80), who came to England in 1641. The sound painting of this prolific artist is well demonstrated by the *Portrait of a Lady*. The English portrait painters of the 18th Century owed much to the technical traditions established by his example, exemplified here in the *Portrait of an Unknown Man* (1693) by Charles Beale (b. 1660) and in the *Self-portrait* by Jonathan Richardson (1665–1746).

The work of the last foreigner to dominate painting in England, Godfrey Kneller (1646–1723), is not represented in the collection. Like Lely, his technical training was valuable to the native English

School which succeeded him, in which the leading figure was William Hogarth (1697–1764). The new warmth of human interest and the vigorous freshness of method which he introduced are seen in the portraits of *George Arnold*, his daughter *Frances Arnold* and the *Unknown Man*. The conversation-pieces for which he was celebrated are exemplified in the *Musical Party* and the small portrait of *Benjamin Hoadly*.

The lesser painters of Hogarth's generation are represented by Joseph Highmore (1692–1780), George Knapton (1698–1778) and W. Hoare (1706–92), the latter with portraits of the mother and father of the Founder of the Museum. The Founder is seen in a lively portrait by Joseph Wright of Derby (1734–97), a provincial painter of a later generation who remains characteristic of the earlier 18th Century; Lord Fitzwilliam is portrayed in 1764, at the age of nineteen, in the rich gown worn by nobleman undergraduates on special occasions.

The new spirit in English portrait painting of about the middle of the 18th Century, in which the somewhat frigid earlier portraits awaken to a mobility of attitude and expression which seems to bring their sitters into our own world, is due to two of the outstanding masters of the English School, Reynolds and Gainsborough, the dominating figures of 18th-Century painting.

Sir Joshua Reynolds (1723–92), first President of the Royal Academy, is seen in two early portraits, *Mrs. Angelo* (1759/60) and *Henry Vansittart* (about 1767), and a third, unfinished, of *Edmund Burke and the Marquess of Rockingham*. As original as the freedom of conception of these paintings is the new visual beauty of their treatment.

Thomas Gainsborough (1727–88), of East Anglian origin, is represented by several works of his early years, when he was established in Ipswich, and one of his maturity. Of the former, the *Heneage Lloyd and his Sister*, has a double interest from the large part which landscape plays in it. The *Hon. W. Fitzwilliam* (1775), an uncle of the Founder, finely executed though faded, indicates the excellence of Gainsborough's mature powers of characterisation.

Though George Romney (1734–1802) challenged the preeminence of Reynolds and Gainsborough in 18th-Century London,

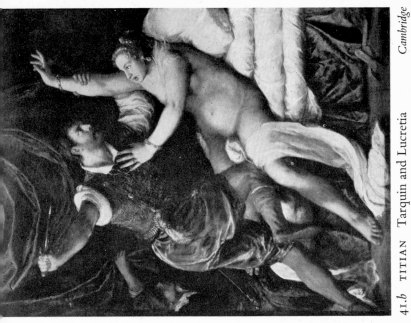

41.a REMBRANDT Self-portrait   Cambridge

41.b TITIAN Tarquin and Lucretia   Cambridge

42.a SIMONE MARTINI SS. Augustine, Michael and Ambrose   *Cambridg*

42.b DOMENICO VENEZIANO Annunciation   *Cambridg*

his best work only will stand comparison with them. The *Portrait of a Young Man* gives some idea of the telling simplicity of his method.

The painting of Thomas Lawrence (1769–1830) carried the traditions of 18th-Century portraiture over into the 19th Century. After the gravity of his predecessors he sought rather brilliance and animation in his portraits, of which a graceful example may be seen in the *Samuel Woodburn*, a celebrated picture dealer through whom the Founder of the Museum acquired some part of his collection.

Lawrence's distinguished Scottish contemporary, Henry Raeburn (1756–1823), is represented by the exceptionally happy portrait of *W. Glendouwyn*. His celebrated fellow-countryman, David Wilkie (1785–1841), better known for subject pictures, is seen in the portrait of *John Cowper*, an Edinburgh beggar. (Drawings by Wilkie are shown in the water-colour gallery.)

The age of Reynolds and Gainsborough also saw the rise of the English School of landscape painting, which at length broke the monotonous dominance of portraiture. Unrivalled anywhere in Europe for a hundred years, this school preserved a fine tradition of painting in England long after its decline in portraiture. The formation of the school follows on from the achievements of Richard Wilson (1714–82), a master of atmospheric luminosity, whose landscapes combine picturesqueness of motive with strict design. Two paintings illustrate his qualities, the *Italian Landscape with River and Temple*, and the *Bridge of Augustus at Rimini*.

The landscapes of Gainsborough have also contributed to the formation of the English School. A fine example of his early style is seen in the landscape background to the *Heneage Lloyd and his Sister* already referred to. Two drawings in black and white chalk on blue paper (water-colour gallery) show his mature style. While Wilson embodies Italian principles, Gainsborough carries on the landscape traditions of Flanders and Holland.

The principal successors of Wilson—Crome, Turner and Constable—are all represented in the collection.

John Crome (1768–1821), the founder and head of the Norwich School, is the final and most finished sample of 18th-Century landscape painting. The *Welsh Landscape* shows the large simplicity, atmospheric quality and fine colour of his mature style.

J. M. W. Turner (1775–1851), whose genius is one of the most remarkable in the whole history of painting, outclasses all his predecessors in the depth and strength of his conceptions, and in his later years arrived at a painting of pure light almost freed from the trammels of form. His characteristics are best displayed in the collection of water-colours (water-colour gallery, and Room I); but one oil, *The Trossachs* (1810) shows him closely imitating Wilson, though in its poetical feeling it is pure Turner.

John Constable (1776–1837), one of the great originators in the history of painting, introduced a masterly naturalism which makes earlier landscape appear almost conventional by comparison. His methods, which effected a real revolution in the outlook of painters, in France perhaps even more than here, are exemplified in three pictures, *Hampstead Heath* (Pl. 43b), the small *Parham's Mill*, *Gillingham* (1824) and *Salisbury*. Water-colours and drawings are shown in the water-colour gallery.

The English water-colour school (examples in the water-colour gallery) is closely connected with landscape painting. It originated in the latter part of the 18th Century mainly with topographical work done for engraving. The best of this early work is represented by the drawings of Paul Sandby (1725–1809), M. A. Rooker (1743–1801), Thomas Malton (1726–1801) and Edward Dayes (1763–1804). Almost contemporary with it are the noble landscapes of J. R. Cozens (1752–87), one of the greatest of English painters to use water-colours.

But it was Thomas Girtin (1775–1802) in whose hands water-colour became a medium rivalling oils both in range and in strength, and possessing a particular beauty of its own. His lead was followed by Turner, who used water-colours throughout his life with brilliant skill. Their principal successors in the flourishing school they founded are John Sell Cotman (1782–1843), who almost rivals them, P. de Wint (1784–1849), and David Cox (1783–1859). Among modern painters, the most distinguished work in this medium has been done by P. Wilson Steer (1860–1942).

An art of figure painting also developed in England towards the end of the 18th Century. The outstanding personality in this, William Blake (1757–1827), was a man of powerful visionary imagination, which he realised pictorially through an exceptional gift of creative design. He is well represented by numerous water-colours and engravings, besides volumes of his own writings de-signed, etched and printed by himself.

The productive art of the 19th-Century painters, though varied and accomplished, remained at a low level artistically and imagin-atively. It embraces, however, a remarkable phenomenon in the talent of Alfred Stevens (1817–75), draughtsman, painter and sculptor, endowed with a brilliant sense of style and great facility of invention. His powers are seen in the portrait of *Leonard Coll-mann*, and in drawings shown in the water-colour gallery. The average level is also somewhat relieved by the deeper and truer feeling of the Pre-Raphaelites and their followers. This movement, founded in 1848 by J. E. Millais (1829–96), W. Holman Hunt (1827–1910) and D. G. Rossetti (1828–82), is represented by draw-ings by all three of these artists in the water-colour gallery, and by paintings by Rossetti, Ford Madox Brown (1821–93), an inde-pendent but associated painter, and Arthur Hughes (1832–1915), one of the followers.

French influence, especially the *plein-air* vision of the Impres-sionists, revitalised English painting towards the end of the century. From this fertile development came P. Wilson Steer (1860–1942), the greatest English landscape painter since Turner and Constable. W. R. Sickert (1860–1942) was educated in the same school, from which J. S. Sargent (1858–1925) also drew inspiration. Both oil paintings and drawings by these artists are on exhibition.

The foremost English painter of the present day, Augustus John (b. 1879), remarkable both as draughtsman and painter, is repre-sented by 6 oil paintings and numerous drawings. Another painter of distinction of this generation whose work is well represented is William Nicholson (1872–1949), and among those of a younger gen-eration are Harold Gilman, Charles Ginner, Duncan Grant, Henry Lamb, Stanley Spencer, Ethel Walker and Christopher Wood.

Open 10 a.m. to 4 p.m. weekdays, 2 p.m. to 4 p.m. Sundays, September to April; 10 a.m. to 5 p.m. weekdays, 2 p.m. to 5 p.m. Sundays, May to August.

J. W. GOODISON,
Assistant Director

THE NATIONAL MUSEUM OF WALES, CARDIFF

DEPARTMENT OF ART

THE Department of Art has developed with, and as an integral part of, the National Museum since its foundation in 1912. Structurally, the Museum has grown slowly and is not yet quite completed; this has resulted in the Department of Art, amongst others, being handicapped by lack of adequate exhibition-space. Acquisitions, nevertheless, are constantly being made, in the several aspects of Fine and Applied Art with which the Department is concerned. Here, however, we must concern ourselves only with paintings.

The principal strength of the paintings in this collection is in the British Schools of the 18th and 20th Centuries. There are, however, a few 17th-Century portraits, including one of a lady signed by the very rare painter Gilbert Jackson, a good signed Cornelius Johnson of Sir Thomas Hanmer and a Closterman of one of the Aubreys of Llantrithyd.

The 18th-Century pictures are about evenly divided between portraiture and landscape of the British School, with an emphasis on Wales either through artist or subject-matter. There are only two important foreign paintings, but their importance is considerable; one is the celebrated *Portrait of Richard Wilson, R.A.*, by Anton Raphael Mengs; the other is a very splendid *Group of Sir Watkin Williams-Wynn and Others*, by Pompeo Batoni. The British portraits include three by Richard Wilson, of which one is signed; a signed Nathaniel Hone; a very grand full-length by Romney of Viscountess Bulkeley; and an unusual life-size group by Zoffany, for which the artist's receipt, dated 1770, exists. These last two are deposited on long loan by the respective descendants of the sitters.

Richard Wilson himself, as might be expected, is nobly represented. He was a native of Wales, which he constantly revisited

188

throughout his later life and where he died. In addition to the three portraits already mentioned, there are a dozen landscapes painted in Italy and at home. The most distinguished of these are: the early *View of Dover*, 1745; the signed *View at Tivoli*, the *Villa Madama* and the *White Monk* of his Italian years; the *Pembroke Castle*, the *Caernarvon Castle* (Pl. 39b), the *Dolbadarn Castle* and the *View of Cader Idris* painted during (or as a result of) his Welsh travels.

Another Welsh landscape painter, of the generation after Wilson, is John Inigo Richards, R.A., represented here by his highly picturesque *Chepstow Castle* and his more matter-of-fact *Halswell House*. The early years of the 19th Century produce an interesting group of small landscapes by Ibbetson, Thomas and Benjamin Barker, and Loutherbourg, a beautiful little Constable *Cornfield*, a vast Copley Fielding *Caernarvon Castle*, of 1819, already showing the influence of Turner; and a deeply moving group, *The Sisters*, of about 1805, which may be attributed with some confidence to Opie.

On the whole, the middle and later 19th Century is not represented very fully and the paintings of that period are not at present on exhibition; limitations of space make it necessary to exclude these from the galleries and to place the best of them on loan in other Institutions.

The painting of the present century, on the other hand, is represented in considerable variety. There is, for instance, a good Wilson Steer, *The Schoolgirl*. Augustus John, O.M., R.A., the most eminent living Welsh painter and the outstanding figure in the older generation of British art, is shown by several paintings: his portraits of himself, *Dorelia*, W. H. Davies and the young poet Dylan Thomas, and his still-life *Cinerarias*, are all outstanding. Another celebrated Welsh veteran, Sir Frank Brangwyn, is represented by two very large decorative panels and by two delicate little early seascapes. Of the Welsh moderns, there are very interesting works by Ceri Richards, Sir Cedric Morris, Kyffin Williams, Evan Walters and Alfred Janes; an exquisite Gwen John; and two by J. D. Innes, who had a strong influence on Augustus John nearly forty years ago. Other moderns who are represented in the permanent collection are Stanley Spencer, R. V. Pitchforth, Henry Lamb and Ivon Hitchens—the last by one of his best abstract landscapes (Pl. 39a).

In the same gallery as these modern paintings, but separated from them, hangs a large and very splendid pastel by Degas, *Le Tub*, at present deposited on loan.

The water-colours on exhibition have been selected to show the development of the British School in that medium continuously from the end of the 17th Century down to the exponents of the contemporary idiom.

Open weekdays 10 a.m. to 5 p.m.; Thursdays (April to October) 10 a.m. to 8 p.m.; Sundays 2.30 p.m. to 5 p.m.

JOHN STEEGMAN,
Keeper, Department of Art,
National Museum of Wales

CHELTENHAM ART GALLERY AND MUSEUM

THE Cheltenham Art Gallery and Museum owes its inception to a gentleman of Dutch extraction named the Baron de Ferrieres, who gave to the town in 1898 a collection of 43 paintings, some of the Dutch School, including Gabriel Metsu's *A Man and a Woman at Wine*; Jan Steen's *The Lean Kitchen* and *The Fat Kitchen*; Gerard Dou's *Portrait of Himself*; all of which are of such a high standard as to have taken their place in the great display of Dutch art at the Royal Academy in 1929. These are Little Masters of first-rate importance. There are other Dutch examples of this period, some of which have a greater popular appeal—Rachel Ruysch (1664–1750), *Flower Piece*; Godfried Schalcken (1643–1706), *Portrait of Rachel Ruysch;* Hendrick Martensz Sorgh (1611–70), *Christ with Martha and Mary*; Philips Wouverman (1619–68), *Dutch Horse Fair*; Melchior de'Hondecôeter (1636–95), *Poultry.*

In this collection there is also a Danish example by Heinrich Hansen (1821–90), *Knight's Hall, Palace of Fredericksborg, near Copenhagen.* The French School is represented by Vernet's *Landscape with Cascade and Bridge* and the Belgian by Baron Leys' *Interior of Tavern, with Blind Fiddler.*

Hung with the pictures given by the Baron de Ferrieres is a Dutch example formerly attributed to Willem van de Velde the Younger, the attribution of which has been recently changed to Cornelis Verbeeck. It is a view of a Dutch Fleet; the date, 1623, and the remains of the artist's signature were recently discovered on the painting, which has been restored and reframed.

Opening out of the Dutch room is a larger gallery which is used for hanging eight or nine temporary exhibitions throughout the year. Occasionally it is possible to make a display from the Gallery's permanent collection of British paintings and water-colours.

D. W. HERDMAN,
Curator

DERBY ART GALLERY

THE most notable feature of the Derby Art Gallery is its collection of paintings by Joseph Wright, A.R.A. (1734–97), commonly known as 'Wright of Derby'. This painter of portraits, conversation pieces, genre works as well as landscapes has not in the past received adequate notice from critics and students and in the national collections he is represented hardly at all. (The exception is the very fine *Experiment with an Air Pump* in the Tate.)

Derby Art Gallery possesses more than 30 oil paintings and the most important of them are permanently on view. Mention might be made of *The Orrery*, a good example of his genre work, and also *The Wood Children*, a fine example of an 18th-Century conversation piece. Among the portraits is an attractive work *Mrs. Sarah Carver and her daughter Sarah*. Although not primarily a landscape painter, he was much interested in landscapes by moonlight and the Gallery possesses a number of striking works on this subject. An extremely fine painting in similar vein is *The Rainbow* and this would assuredly compare favourably with Gainsborough or Constable.

The Derby Art Gallery also contains a unique collection of 'Old Derby Pictures', although in this collection topographical interest has been considered before artistic merit.

The Gallery is open daily 10 a.m. to 6 p.m. and on Sundays 2.30 p.m. to 4.30 p.m.

A. L. THORPE,
Curator

LEEDS CITY ART GALLERY AND
TEMPLE NEWSAM HOUSE

THE city of Leeds is well provided for in the field of the fine arts with its two art museums. The great Tudor-Jacobean mansion of Temple Newsam, bought from Lord Halifax by the Corporation in 1922, and during the last ten years remodelled as a museum of decorative arts, is situated 5 miles from the centre of the city. It is perhaps the ideal compromise between the museum and the country house. The City Art Gallery, founded in 1888, is centrally situated and contains the major portion of the collection of pictures. The collections are divided between the two institutions, but generally speaking, Temple Newsam contains the 17th- and 18th-Century British paintings, set against the background of fine Jacobean and Georgian rooms, furniture and decorative arts, and the Art Gallery contains the remainder of the pictures, drawings and prints.

The collections are mainly British, but there are a number of fine works by other European artists. At Temple Newsam among the 17th-Century paintings are: a portrait of *Elizabeth Daughter of James I* by Van Somer; the dated portrait of *Oliver Cromwell* (1649) by Robert Walker, and a portrait of *Thomas Howard, Earl of Arundel* by Daniel Mytens. The two last named come from Naworth Castle. William Dobson is represented by one of his rare female portraits *Mrs. Charles Scarbrough of Windsor*. Lely and Kneller are also represented, the former by a masterly portrait *Young Man with Red Hair* which came from Holkham Hall, and the latter by a pair of full-length portraits of *William* and *Mary* which belonged to Temple Newsam. Perhaps the most important picture from the original Temple Newsam collection is the huge sporting picture of *The 3rd Viscount Irwin* by Francis Barlow (1626–1702), the father of English sporting painters.

There are a number of 18th-Century portraits, perhaps most notable being the group of Ingram family portraits by the German artist Philippe Mercier (1689–1762), who lived at York for a few years about 1740 and executed a number of commissions for the then owner of Temple Newsam. This is one of the most important groups of paintings by this artist. In addition, there is another very lovely canvas by him of *The Daughters of Lord Fauconberg* on long-term loan from Newburgh Priory. A very fine portrait by Romney of *Lady Anne Wombwell* comes from the same source.

Among the earlier 18th-Century portraits is a large and imposing canvas by the Swedish-born Michael Dahl (1656–1743) of *The 5th Viscount Irwin and his Wife*, and a portrait of *Mrs. Elizabeth Ingram* by Bartholomew Dandridge (1691–1754). Thomas Gainsborough, Sir Joshua Reynolds, Francis Cotes and Allan Ramsay are also represented in portraiture, together with the native-born Benjamin Wilson, by whom there is a charming *Conversation Piece* and a portrait of *The 4th Earl of Chesterfield*.

Landscape and decorative painters of the 18th Century are well represented but perhaps a little overweighted on the side of the latter. A group of twenty canvases of battle scenes and romantic landscapes, which formed part of the Temple Newsam collection, are believed to be by the Venetian, Marco Ricci (b. 1680). If this attribution is correct, some of the larger paintings must be among his finest productions. Two decorative panels set in the chimney-pieces in the Long Gallery are by another Italian decorative painter Ioli. Richard Wilson is represented by a version of his *Boys Bathing* and a smaller painting. The Norwich School is admirably, if not extensively, represented in paintings by John Sell Cotman's *On the Banks of the Yare* (Pl. 45a); John Crome's *Wherries on the Yare*, and *Mousehold Heath*; and a *Landscape* by James Stark. A lively sketch by John Constable, *Vale of Dedham*, is dated Sept. 5th, 1814. A recently acquired painting by Henry Robert Morland (*c.* 1730–97), *The Fair Nun Unmasked; A Tigress* by George Stubbs; Francis Wheatley's *Return from Market*; an early Gainsborough landscape; and paintings by Thomas Barker and George Morland should also be noted. A large painting of *The Pantheon*, of which only the portico now remains in Oxford Street, is by Thomas Patch.

Some 19th-Century paintings, a few 'moderns' and some English water-colours are usually shown at Temple Newsam, but for the sake of convenience in this article they will be considered as part of the City Art Gallery collection.

The Leeds Gallery is particularly notable for its very comprehensive collection of English water-colours beginning with Alexander Cozens. A number of famous local collectors like Sir Michael Sadler, Mr. Sydney Kitson and a monetary benefactor, Mr. Alfred Bilbrough, have helped to build up this collection which includes many superb examples of masters of English water-colour. It is doubtful whether there are much better examples of the work of J. R. Cozens, John Varley, Peter de Wint, Thomas Girtin, Thomas Hearne and Thomas Rowlandson than can be found here. But outstanding in this section is the large collection of water-colours and drawings by John Sell Cotman. There are no less than 22 finished water-colours, including famous examples like *A Ploughed Field*, *Bedgellert Bridge*, *The Harvest Field*, *Walsingham Priory* and *The Brick Kilns*. In addition are some 750 sketches and drawings by him which formed the Kitson collection recently given to the city. This gift also included 17 water-colours by William Turner of Oxford, as well as many etchings by Cotman and his associates. A large group of drawings by Phil May, the native cartoonist, is another noteworthy part of this fine collection of 18th-, 19th- and 20th-Century English drawings.

The Charles Roberts collection, given in 1937, consists of a number of paintings by French artists chiefly connected with the Barbizon School. Corot, Diaz, Mesdag, Cazin, Leon Richet, Courbet and Fantin Latour are outstanding.

French painting is perhaps inadequately shown here to give anything like a comprehensive picture of the developments of the last 100 years, but in addition to the Roberts collection are good examples of Auguste Renoir *Après le Bain*; André Derain *Barges on the Thames*; Pierre Bonnard *Mother and Child*; Alfred Sisley *River Scene*; Edouard Vuillard *Mlle Nathanson in the Artist's Studio;* Othon Friesz *Honfleur* and Fantin Latour *La Causerie*.

In common with most regional galleries founded during the last quarter of the last century, the one at Leeds has its fair share of 'Academy' pieces of the times. Among these are *The Return of Persephone* by Frederick, Lord Leighton; *Scotland for Ever* by Lady

Butler; *The Bridesmaid* by J. J. Tissot; and a small version of *The Shadow of the Cross* by Holman Hunt.

In 1925 an extension to the Gallery, built by Mr. Sam Wilson, was opened to accommodate the collection of this local gentleman. The pictures consist of a number of canvases by Frank Brangwyn, including a set of large decorative panels painted for the British section of the International Exhibition in Venice in 1903. Sir William Orpen, Professor Georg Sauter, Mark Fisher, Buxton Knight, A. J. Heymanns and H. le Sidaner, appear to have been favourites of this local collector. One outstanding picture in this pleasantly designed extension is a large *Romantic Landscape* by James Pryde.

As would be expected, there are a number of local artists represented in the Leeds Gallery. Some of them, though little known elsewhere, are not without merit. Julius Cæsar Ibbetson (1759–1817) is, of course, quite widely known and well represented here. Charles Henry Schwanfelder (1773–1837), who was one time animal painter to George III; Joseph Rhodes (1782–1859), a landscape and genre painter; John N. Rhodes (1809–42), a topographer; John William Inchbold (1830–88), and Atkinson Grimshaw (1836–1893), both of whom came under the spell of the Pre-Raphaelites; and William Robinson (1799–1839) and William Frederick, the portrait painters, can all be studied at Leeds.

But the last two decades have witnessed a concentration on contemporary British painting with the result that most of the outstanding and progressive painters are well represented. In some instances, a small collection of an artist's work has been brought together to represent his development. Thirteen paintings, as well as a number of drawings, by W. R. Sickert, illustrate the whole period of his life from the large *St. Mark's* of about 1882, *The Blackbird of Paradise*, and *The New Bedford* of the '90's, *St. Jacques, Dieppe* and *The Little Trianon* to the later works like *Juliet and the Nurse*, and *The Venture* of the *English Echoes* series.

Matthew Smith and Stanley Spencer are each represented by 6 paintings of different periods. Notable among these groups are Smith's *The Little Seamstress, Lilies, Model Waking* and Spencer's *Separating Fighting Swans* (Pl. 45b); *Shepherds Amazed* and *The*

Family. Edward Wadsworth, who like Smith was a native of Yorkshire, has 7 paintings in the collection, Graham Sutherland 9 and Christopher Wood 5. Practically all the great names which have been in the van of 20th-Century British paintings are to be found here.

For the time being, while the Dulwich Gallery is being rebuilt, the Leeds Art Gallery is the temporary home of the most important paintings from the Dulwich collection. Sixty-seven paintings, most of which have been cleaned, are already on exhibition, others will be added from time to time. How long they are likely to remain, cannot at present be anticipated. It may still be some years, but in the meantime they are exhibited at Leeds.

Other collections do not come within the scope of this article but reference should be made to the fine groups of English pottery, with an extensive collection of Leeds ware, and the Chinese ceramics covering the whole period from the Chou dynasty to Chien Lung.

City Art Gallery. Open weekdays 10.30 a.m. to 6.30 p.m.; Sundays 2.30 p.m. to 5 p.m.

Temple Newsam House. Open 11.30 a.m. to 6.15 p.m. in summer; 11.30 a.m. till dusk in winter.

ERNEST MUSGRAVE,
Director

LEICESTER ART GALLERY

T HE Leicester Art Gallery was first opened to the public in the museum buildings in 1885. The nucleus of a collection had been created four years before this and had subsisted on private subscription. From 1885 the Gallery received a regular financial support from the Corporation, which was augmented by bequests of money and pictures. In 1934 the creation of a permanent Department of Art in the Museum ensured a greater uniformity of policy and, although there are many deficiencies, the collection today is fairly well representative of the main trends in English painting during the last four centuries. The oil paintings may be said to fall roughly into three main groups; portraiture from the 17th Century to the present day—19th-Century landscape, narrative and allegorical paintings, and finally, works by artists of the modern Schools ranging from Whistler to Matthew Smith.

Although its quality varies considerably, the collection of portraits is interesting. In accordance with an accepted policy of purchasing works of art which have a local interest, the Museum and Art Gallery Committee has bought several good portraits of local families. Most of the best Elizabethan and early 17th-Century portraits are of the Leicestershire nobility and city officials; they include portraits of the Heyrick family ranging from the 17th Century to the early 19th Century, of the 4th Earl of Huntingdon and a full-length portrait of George Villiers, the 1st Duke of Buckingham, by Cornelius Johnson. From the late 17th Century there is a notable portrait by Sir Peter Lely of Sir Thomas Lee, Bart., M.P., (1635–91) (Pl. 44a). In addition to several unattributed early 18th-Century works there is a portrait of James Wigley of Scraptoft by Joseph Highmore dated 1741. Reynolds is represented by two portraits, the first of unproved authenticity of an unknown man, formerly called Wilson Gale Braddyll, the second of a Leicestershire character Charles Boothby Skrymshire, 'Prince Boothby'. Other good late 18th-Century portraits are by Wright of Derby,

John Jackson, Sir William Beechey, George Morland and Francis
Cotes. A fine early 19th-Century sketch portrait may be ascribed
with a fair degree of certainty to John Constable. Finally, this group
is brought up to date by a vigorous portrait of Admiral Fisher by
Augustus John and another of Viscount Allenby by Sargent.

The most noteworthy example of late 18th-Century landscape
painting may be found in a romantic *High Tor, Matlock* by Joseph
Wright of Derby, and an attractive work entitled *Landscape with
Bathers* by Richard Wilson, which appears to be a later version of
the National Gallery picture of the same name. In 1948 the Gallery
bought a small sketch *Noon West End Fields, Hampstead*, by John
Constable; the finished work is in the National Gallery of Victoria,
Melbourne. Amongst these greater names the quiet brooding landscapes of Sir George Beaumont (1753–1827) of Coleorton Hall in
Leicestershire hold their own and indeed are perhaps more noteworthy than a necessarily limited representation of paintings by
artists of renown who may be seen at their best in London and elsewhere. The scope of his work ranges from the intensely dramatic
Peel Castle in a Storm to peaceful Midland landscapes. It is in the
same light that we should view hunting scenes by the Leicestershire
artist John Ferneley (1781–1860).

Amongst the many 19th-Century narrative and allegorical paintings we should mention William Etty's *Sabrina and her Nymphs*, a
work well illustrative of his skill in depicting the nude and G. F.
Watts' *Fata Morgana*, which the artist presented to the Gallery in
1889. Other aspects of Victorian art find expression in Lord
Leighton's *Perseus on Pegasus hastening to the Rescue of Andromeda*
and another version of W. P. Frith's lively and popular *Railway
Station*.

The Leicester collection covers a wide range of English artistic
achievement since the beginning of the present century. From
Whistler's *Thames, Nocturne in Blue and Gold*, we may pass to a river
scene by Walter Greaves and two sketches by W. R. Sickert, the
first a humorous conversation piece *The Bart and the Bums*, the
second a landscape of Dover. Both Duncan Grant and Vanessa Bell
are well represented, the former by a Lewes landscape, and the latter
by a portrait *Spanish Lady*. The Gallery has landscapes by Adrian

Daintrey and John Nash, and in 1947 it acquired the metaphysical *Nostalgic Landscape* painted by Paul Nash between the years 1923 and 1938. Other modern works of interest are by Vlaminck, Mark Gertler, John Tunnard, John Piper, Geoffrey Tibble, Graham Sutherland, Ivon Hitchens and Matthew Smith.

Open 10 a.m. to 5 p.m. during winter; 10 a.m. to 7 p.m. during summer.

B. M. WALKER,
Keeper of Art

43.*a* RENOIR Le Coup de Vent   *Cambridge*

43.*b* CONSTABLE Hampstead Heath   *Cambridge*

44.a LELY Sir Thomas Lee   *Leicester*

44.b CHARDIN La Récureuse   *Glasgow, Hunterian Museum*

LINCOLN: USHER ART GALLERY

THE Usher Art Gallery was founded on a bequest left to the city by the late James Ward Usher, a jeweller of Lincoln. It was opened in 1927 by the then Prince of Wales. It is a fine palladian-style building designed by Sir Reginald Blomfield, most beautifully situated with lawns sloping upward to the Cathedral which towers above it. A portion of the old ditch which once surrounded Roman Lincoln still remains in the grounds within 20 feet of the eastern wall of the Gallery and adds the interest of ancient history to the charm of the setting. Usher was a discriminating collector special-ising in miniature portraits, European and Chinese porcelain and fine antique watches. The whole of these collections were be-queathed to the city, and the Usher Art Gallery was conceived primarily as a means of permanently exhibiting them.

The financial bequest to the city, however, made it possible to provide a building which is much more than a storehouse for the Usher collection. The Gallery is not large—the total area of its eight rooms is 8,000 square feet—but this collection occupies only one room and space remains for the general collection of pictures and *objets d'art* which is being built up by the City Corporation.

There is no considerable endowment for making purchases but careful regard for a particular policy and the allocation of reason-able funds from rates have resulted in the building up of a collection of which the city is proud—particularly in view of the short time during which the Gallery has been in existence. There have been valuable donations.

Among its pictures is a collection of works by Peter de Wint. This has been built up during the last dozen years and has already gained recognition as the most important collection of works by this artist. De Wint was not born in Lincoln but he had intimate ties with the city. He visited the Lincoln home of William Hilton, R.A., his fellow-apprentice in the London studio of the engraver John Raphel Smith. He married Hilton's sister and bought property in

Lincoln in which the Hilton family, and he while resident in Lincoln, lived for many years. The house still stands and is marked by a tablet placed upon it to commemorate the centenary of De Wint's death (he died June 30th, 1849).

De Wint's important place in the ranks of the English water-colourists is marked by a predominance of water-colours in this special collection. There are upwards of 60 of them, half of this number being important larger works including such well-known pictures as *Lincoln Cathedral*; *River Scene with Elms*; *Cottage at Aldbury*; *Gloucester* 1860 *and Lowther* 1839. The remainder are studies representing many styles and periods of the artist's work. It may surprise many people to discover that the 'pure' De Wint in fact had such varied manners (Pl. 46*a*).

The large representation of De Wint's work in oils will particularly delight the art historian for it is not easy elsewhere to study him in this medium. It is interesting to see him in the toils of a Romantic impulse, so foreign to his real nature, in the large *Mountainous Scenery with Rainbow* and then to see him in oils working with freedom and vivacity which his well-known water-colours have made so familiar.

William Hilton also is well represented in the Gallery, especially by his portraiture which is not generally so well known as his historic painting. Hilton and De Wint, the men whose lives had so much in common but whose work was so different, can be well studied and compared at Lincoln.

These are the most important pictures in the Usher Art Gallery; another considerable collection by James Bourne (1773–1854) and a few oil paintings by Charles Shannon (1863–1937) represent the work of two other Lincolnshire artists. Among other paintings of local interest is a view of the Newport Arch, Lincoln, signed N. D., and attributed to Sir Nathaniel Dance (Pl. 46*b*).

Among the general collection, modern painting is not yet largely represented but in acquiring works regard is being paid to the need for a wide purview.

Open free on weekdays 10 a.m. to 5 p.m. ; 2.30 p.m. to 5 p.m. Sundays.

F. J. COOPER, Director

THE WALKER ART GALLERY,
LIVERPOOL

THE Walker Art Gallery was opened to the public in 1877, but the impulse which led ultimately to its erection had its origin many years earlier. In addition to the decorators and other craftsmen employed by the flourishing local potteries, a small but active artistic community had existed in Liverpool right through the 18th Century. Towards the end of the century, notably in 1769 (inspired apparently by the foundation of the Royal Academy in the previous year), several attempts were made to co-ordinate their activities, to bring their work to the notice of the public and to encourage the arts generally by the formation of an Art Society. They all proved ephemeral until the foundation in 1810 of the Liverpool Academy of Arts, which not only established an art school but held an annual exhibition, not restricted to local work but open, like the Royal Academy, to artists in every part of the country. The exhibition took place from year to year in various more or less suitable quarters, and from 1830 the Corporation officially recognised its importance by making an annual grant of £200. It continued till 1867, when internal differences among the local artists brought it to an end, and the Liverpool Academy became, as it still remains, a closed society, limited, except for a few honorary members, strictly to Merseyside painters and their work.

The exhibition had, however, become by this time a popular feature of the city's life, and the public missed the water when the well ran dry. Accordingly the Corporation, reflecting the electors' interest, took up the responsibility which the Academy had dropped, and in 1871 they opened in the Public Museum, which had been built in 1860, the first 'Liverpool Autumn Exhibition'. With municipal prestige and publicity behind it, the show became so popular that the question arose of the provision of a more appropriate building. In 1873 Alderman Andrew Barclay Walker, whose beer is still brewed at Warrington, became Mayor of Liverpool and signalised his mayoralty by offering to supply the necessary building at his own expense; and on September 6th, 1877, its doors were cere-monially opened to the public. In due course the donor received the honour of knighthood, and his statue in white marble by John Warrington Wood, the sculptor of the effigies of Raphael and Michelangelo which flanked the entrance of the new Gallery, was placed conspicuously at the head of its principal staircase.

It is clear, then, that the primary purpose of the Gallery at its inception was not so much to house a permanent collection as to provide accommodation for the great annual show, which came to be familiarly known as the 'Academy of the North', and that Walker's generosity was inspired rather by the example of Burling-ton House than by that of the National or any provincial Gallery. The exhibition usually lasted from September to December, and allowing for its collection, hanging and dispersal occupied the time of the staff and the walls of the Gallery for some six months of the year. How then was the staff to be engaged and the vacant walls filled during the remaining half-year? The problem had not been entirely overlooked, for when the Earl of Derby had unlocked the front door on the opening day, he proceeded at once to unveil the first picture of a permanent collection. The City had already acquired a few paintings by gift; most of these were gathered in the Gallery and they attracted further gifts. The annual exhibition itself, however, provided the real solution of the problem, for it became immensely popular and, in the days when the richer ship-owners, cottonbrokers and merchants still lived within easy reach of the centre of the city, was an important social function in the life of Liverpool. The charge for admission and for catalogues, as well as the commission on the considerable sales, resulted in a hand-some profit, and this profit, in order to encourage artists to submit their work, was spent year by year in the purchase of pictures from the exhibition, which were added to the ever-growing permanent collection.

This, together with occasional donations and bequests, was the principal means of acquisition for the first half-century of the Gallery's history. In the absence of any other source of revenue this procedure was perhaps inevitable, but it was certainly unfortunate for the organising committee, under the honest but misguided belief that it was getting the best work available, based the exhibition on the current shows in Burlington House and limited the exhibits to academic and conventional work. The movement which brought new life and brilliance into French art in the '70's and inspired the New English Art Club in the '80's was ignored, and the later reaction against Impressionism which inspired the Camden Town Group and the London Group was rejected with horror. Admission was refused (and their work therefore not purchased) even to local artists who showed unconventional tendencies: to Wilson Steer, for instance, who was born just across the Mersey in Birkenhead, and to Augustus John, who did some of the finest work of his early manhood while an art-master in Liverpool. Consequently after fifty years of accumulation the public collection consisted almost wholly of anecdotal and photographic paintings of the late 19th Century, of which the ever-popular '*And when did you last see your father?*' is the best-known example. It lacked almost entirely any representation either of the British masters of the 18th Century or of progressive contemporary painting.

There were a few exceptions. First, William Roscoe, an enlightened citizen of Liverpool at the beginning of the 19th Century, a man of great ability and wide interests, anticipated even the Prince Consort in his appreciation of Italian and Flemish painting of the 14th, 15th and 16th Centuries and collected the so-called 'primitives'. After his death in 1821 his pictures were purchased for the Liverpool Royal Institution, a home of learning which Roscoe had helped to found in 1817, and of which he was the first President. In 1892 the Institution lent these pictures to the Walker Art Gallery, and in 1914 the loan was confirmed by a legal agreement expiring in 1948. The following year the Institution was disbanded, and its last remaining proprietors presented the pictures to the Corporation. This collection, which included priceless examples of the work of Simone Martini (Pl. 48*b*), Vincenzo Catena, the Master of the Virgo inter Virgines, Jan Mostaert, Ercole de' Roberti, Luca Signorelli, Lorenzo Vecchietta and others, forms now a most important part of the permanent collection of the Gallery.

Secondly, thanks to the energetic advocacy of Philip Henry Rathbone, three important Pre-Raphaelite paintings were purchased, chiefly by subscription, between 1881 and 1891: Millais' *Lorenzo and Isabella* (Pl. 47*b*), Rossetti's *Dante's Dream* and Holman Hunt's *Triumph of the Innocents*. The two last are not typically Pre-Raphaelite, for they are late works, painted after the movement had lost its original impetus, and are notable rather for their acreage than their æsthetic quality, but Millais' youthful *tour-de-force* is a landmark in the history of the Brotherhood. Paintings by Burne-Jones, Ford Madox Brown and John Brett were afterwards added.

Thirdly, the acquisition was encouraged by gift, bequest and even occasional purchase of the work of earlier Liverpool artists. George Stubbs is the outstanding name among Liverpool-born painters, but he left the city at an early age, and William Daniels, William Huggins, Alexander Mosses, Robert Salomon, Charles Towne, Samuel Walters, W. L. Windus and others represent the flourishing school which worked on Merseyside during the first half of the 19th Century.

Finally, the range of the collection was widened in 1923 by the bequest of the collection made by Mr. James Smith of Blundell-sands, near Liverpool, which included 30 paintings by George Frederick Watts, 6 pieces of sculpture by Auguste Rodin and many etchings by Palmer, Whistler and Seymour Haden.

In 1929 the City Council for the first time made an annual grant from the rates for the purchase of works of art. This grant has since been maintained without a break (though naturally it was reduced during the war) and has made it much easier to acquire contemporary work from other sources than directly from the artists in the autumn exhibition. Then in 1932 Lord Wavertree bequeathed a large sum to the Gallery which his father had built, and the use of both capital and interest has made possible the purchase of works by the older and more expensive masters. With these funds at their disposal the Committee set out to fill as best they could the historical gaps at each end of the collection. The funds would not permit the acquisition of costly works of the continental schools, but during the past twenty years, as the result of careful purchase aided by single gifts and two recent bequests of local collections, the city's collection has come to include at least the adequate representation of nearly every phase of British art and of nearly every important British painter from Tudor times to the present day.

As the collection grew, the Autumn Exhibition became an increasing embarrassment, for it involved removing annually the greater part of the permanent exhibits from the walls of the Gallery and storing them for about four months of each year in the cellars. Obviously the Gallery was not large enough to perform its dual function effectively. During the first quarter of the century two gifts and two bequests of money had been received, amounting in all to £31,000. With these funds, supplemented by the accumulated interest and part of the Wavertree bequest mentioned above, an extension comprising five large rooms and one smaller was built at the rear of the original structure, connected with it by two enclosed bridges over a lane which bounded it. This addition was opened by H.R.H. Prince George (afterwards Duke of Kent) on October 3rd, 1933.

Immediately on the outbreak of war in 1939 the Corporation handed over the whole Gallery to the Ministry of Food, and it served as local headquarters for the control of food and fuel till July 1949. At the moment of writing preparations are being made for its complete redecoration and some reconstruction, but its reopening can hardly be expected before the spring of 1951.

The sixty-fifth Autumn Exhibition, which was nearly ready for opening in September 1939, had of course to be abandoned, but the authorities kept the flag flying by renting a hall in Bluecoat Chambers, an early 18th-Century building in the heart of the city, and a continuous series of smaller exhibitions began there in November, selected from the permanent collection, gathered from local sources or borrowed from such bodies as C.E.M.A. (now the Arts Council), the British Council, the Ministry of Information and the Art Exhibitions Bureau. The hall was destroyed by bombing in May 1941 (miraculously during the brief weekend interval between the dispersal of one exhibition and the hanging of the next), but later a smaller repaired room was taken in the same building and the exhibitions resumed, defying Hitler among the ruins. The present (June, 1950) is the 136th of this wartime and post-war series.

Exhibitions, however, vital though their function is to the service offered by any art gallery, especially in familiarising the public with every phase of contemporary painting, are passing things. More important is the fact that the additions to the permanent collection of the Gallery exceed in quantity and excel in quality those acquired during any similar period since its opening.

Among these acquisitions the collection bequeathed in 1945 by Miss Emma Holt is of outstanding importance—it will suffice to mention the names of Gainsborough, Reynolds, Turner, Raeburn and Romney, all of whom were either unrepresented or inadequately represented before. The collection was formed by her father, George Holt, the well-known shipowner, and was bequeathed not to the Gallery but to the city, together with Miss Holt's residence, where under the terms of the will it is intended that it shall as far as possible be shown. It will, however, come under the care of the Committee which controls the Gallery, and is therefore mentioned in this survey.

Next in importance comes the Walter Stone collection of sporting pictures, bequeathed by Miss Mary Stone, sister of the collector, in 1944, and containing typical hunting, racing and shooting subjects by Henry and Samuel Alken, H. B. Chalon, John Dalby, J. F. Herring, J. N. Sartorius, Dean Wolstenholme and others. This collection would enhance the interest of any Gallery of British art, and it provides the nucleus for a more complete representation of its subject-matter. Under the conditions of the will it must be kept in a separate room, but there is no reason why pictures of the same genre, with the addition of such typically British sports as fishing, boxing and cricket, should not be shown in adjoining rooms, so as to make ultimately a comprehensive gallery, within the Liverpool permanent collection, of British sporting art.

Another specialised group, developed during the war, deserves mention. In 1940 Captain Fenwick-Owen lent to the Gallery three early paintings by Alfred Stevens after Raphael and his collection of drawings by the same artist, which included five studies for the decoration of Deysbrook House, on the outskirts of Liverpool, which the artist carried out in 1847. Two years later this collection was purchased, and because of Stevens' association with Deysbrook

45.a JOHN SELL COTMAN   On the Banks of the Yare

45.b STANLEY SPENCER   Separating fighting Swans

46.*a*   PETER DE WINT   Cornfields   *Lincoln*

46.*b*   Attrib. to SIR NATHANIEL DANCE   Newport Arch, Lincoln   *Lincoln*

47.*a* RICHARD WILSON Snowdon   *Liverpool*

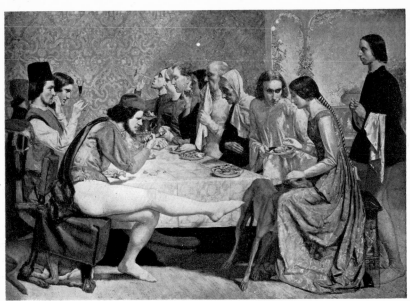

47.*b* MILLAIS Lorenzo and Isabella   *Liverpool*

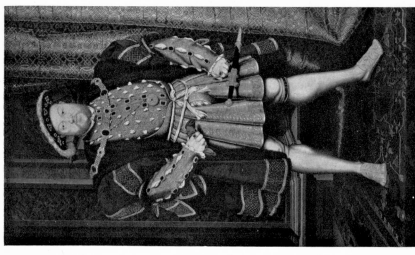

and his work with Cockerell at St. George's Hall (not forgetting his skill as draughtsman and craftsman), the opportunity has since been taken to acquire other examples of his work both in painting and the crafts. The group now includes 3 portraits and about 100 drawings, casts from and models for sculpture, the studio table which he designed for his own use and which later belonged to Sargent, and doors, mirrors, a buffet and a mantelpiece from Dorchester House.

It remains to summarise the main features of the permanent collection, including single donations and purchases as well as the groups already described. The importance of the Roscoe collection has been mentioned, but the bulk of the exhibits illustrate the development of British painting from its beginnings. This is no place for a catalogue, and it will be enough to say that the 16th Century is represented by contemporary portraits of Henry VIII (Pl. 48a) and Elizabeth; the 17th by Highmore and Lely and Dutch portraits of English subjects; the 18th and 19th by Wilson (Pl. 47a), Reynolds, Stubbs, Gainsborough, Zoffany, Romney, Raeburn, Turner, Constable, Lawrence, Cox, Stevens, Watts and the Pre-Raphaelites; the last generation by Steer, Sickert, Gilman, Gore, Bevan, Conder and others. This takes no account of the Liverpool school or of water-colours, prints and sculpture, and it is perhaps invidious to mention living artists, except to state that their work is headed by the distinguished name of Augustus John.

There are obvious gaps among these artists in every period, but it is confidently hoped that before long they will be filled.

FRANK LAMBERT,
Director

THE MANCHESTER CITY ART GALLERIES

THE GALLERIES

THE Corporation of Manchester maintains seven Art Galleries and Art Museums in different parts of the city. Brief notes on these and their contents are given as an introduction to a general account of the city's collection of pictures.

THE CITY ART GALLERY, MOSLEY STREET, MANCHESTER, 2

The building was designed in the Greek revival style by Sir Charles Barry, later the architect of the Houses of Parliament, as the headquarters of *The Royal Manchester Institution for the Promotion of Literature, Science and the Arts*. It was opened in 1829. The Institution soon began to concentrate almost exclusively on the Arts, and not only arranged exhibitions and lectures, but also built up its own collection of paintings. In 1882 the Governors of the Institution presented the Gallery and the whole of its art collections to the city, on condition that for the following twenty years £2,000 a year should be provided from the rates for the purchase of works of art.

The building has long ceased to be large enough for present needs, and in 1938 the city acquired the block of property behind the Gallery with a view to building an extension which would more than double the Gallery's present size. The war followed and the extension is yet to be built.

The City Art Gallery houses the best of the city's collection of paintings and sculpture. The Greg collection of English earthenware is also shown here.

THE GALLERY OF ENGLISH COSTUME, PLATT HALL, RUSHOLME, MANCHESTER, 14

Platt Hall, a red brick Georgian house finished in 1764, was in use before the war as a Branch Art Gallery. In 1947 it was re-opened as a Gallery of English Costume, consequent upon the city's acquisition of the vast collection of Englishwomen's costume formed by Dr. C. Willett Cunnington.

THE FLETCHER MOSS BRANCH ART GALLERY, EAST DIDSBURY, MANCHESTER, 20

This house, formerly a parsonage, was built about 1800. Its windows show the Gothic taste kept within discreet limits. The grounds form a small but charming public garden. This gallery is now used to show the best of the city's collection of water-colours.

WYTHENSHAWE HALL, WYTHENSHAWE PARK, MANCHESTER

The earliest part of the hall (which was presented, with its large park, to the city in 1926 by the present Lord and Lady Simon of Wythenshawe) dates from the 16th Century, and there are a number of later additions.

It is now used for the display of 16th- and 17th-Century furniture together with a number of paintings of the same period. The 19th-Century library is used to show Chinese porcelain, and a gallery on the first floor contains the Greg collection of early dolls and dolls' houses.

HEATON HALL, HEATON PARK, MANCHESTER

This elegantly decorated hall is the work of James Wyatt, begun about 1772 when he had just begun to rival Robert Adam in the latter's own style of classical design. The most elaborate painted decoration is found in a cupola room on the first floor which was decorated in the Etruscan gusto by Biagio Rebecca.

The portion of the hall now used as a Branch Art Gallery contains English paintings, water-colours, and furniture of the Georgian period. A selection of English silver from the Elizabethan period onwards, including some rare and important pieces from the Lloyd Roberts Bequest, is shown here, as well as English glass, porcelain and Wedgwood ware.

QUEEN'S PARK BRANCH GALLERY, HARPURHEY,
    MANCHESTER, 9

Although this building was opened in 1884 as a Natural History Museum, it has been in use as a Branch Art Gallery since 1906. Paintings and water-colours, chiefly 19th and 20th Century, are shown, and here also is the Old Manchester collection of pictures, maps, models and other objects illustrating the past history of the city.

This Gallery is also the home of the Rutherston Loan Scheme, described below.

THE HORSFALL MUSEUM OF ART, EVERY STREET,
    MANCHESTER, 4

Ancoats Hall, now the Horsfall Museum of Art, was built about 1820 on the site of the Elizabethan home of the Mosleys. It was the centre of an educational movement begun about 1876 by T. C. Horsfall under the influence of Ruskin's teaching. He maintained a private museum in this building until 1918, when he transferred the collections and the lease of the house to the city.

Since that time the work of this museum has been largely concerned with children.

THE COLLECTION OF PAINTINGS

The main part of the collection is concentrated at the City Art Gallery in Mosley Street; unless another locality is named, every painting mentioned in the following description will usually be found there. The greater part of the collection consists of English paintings from the 17th Century to the present day. There is a small group of 15th- to 17th-Century European paintings and another of 19th- and 20th-Century French paintings.

EUROPEAN PAINTINGS, 15TH TO 17TH CENTURIES

Although this part of the collection is little more than an introduction to the more complete representation of English painting that follows, a few of the pictures it includes are not without interest. Florentine painting at the end of the 15th Century is represented by the large circular *Adoration* which was attributed to Piero di Cosimo by Dr. W. Bode in his catalogue of Sir Otto Beit's collection, to which the painting formerly belonged. Domenico Feti's effective portrait of the actor *Giovanni Gabriele* is a smaller version of the portrait which was once in the Hermitage collection.

The 17th-Century paintings from the Netherlands include a Van Dyck *Holy Family*, an excellent portrait of an old woman by M. J. van Mierevelt, dated 1636, a pleasant *Merry Company* by Ochtervelt, and typical landscapes by Jan Wynants and Isack van Ostade.

ENGLISH PAINTING, 17TH TO 19TH CENTURIES

The most impressive of the 17th-Century paintings is probably the large canvas depicting *Sir Thomas Aston at the Deathbed of his Wife*, painted in 1635 by John Souch of Chester, an artist of whom less is known than the very real gifts shown in this somewhat macabre painting would seem to merit. A fine example of later 17th-Century portraiture is Joseph Michael Wright's *First Earl of Inchiquin*, a painting curiously reminiscent of Largillière in its handling.

The 18th-Century portraits include examples by Hogarth, Hudson, Reynolds, Dance, Devis, Hone and Northcote—the *Portrait of a Moor* by the last named being an unusually sensitively painted example of this artist's work.

The beginning of English landscape painting is shown in a group of 4 paintings by Richard Wilson. Of these, *Cicero's Villa* (Pl. 50a) is a splendid example of the classical type of composition which Wilson learnt in Italy but to which he added his own delight in the mellow glow of afternoon sunshine. *On the Strada Nomentana* is a version of the Villa Adriana theme of which Wilson painted so many variations, while the *Landscape with Ruins* is a large decorative canvas with an English subject. The more personal and romantic approach to landscape of Wilson's last period is well shown by *A Welsh Valley*—a distant view of Cader Idris from the valley of the Mawddach, of which another version is in the Walker Art Gallery, Liverpool.

The progress of landscape painting can be followed through paintings by William Marlow (whose *Italian Town* is a specially good example), Gainsborough, Ibbetson, Morland and others, to the innovations of Turner and Constable. Turner is represented here by one very large painting (the seascape called *Now for the Painter* when shown at the Royal Academy in 1827) and Constable by some small oil sketches among which is a jewel-like *Hampstead*. Two quiet and poetic small landscapes by De Wint continue the story. Outstanding among a group of landscapes by David Cox is the brilliant and original *Rhyl Sands*, which more closely resembles French painting of a generation yet to come than any other work of Cox's contemporaries.

An unusual aspect of the isolated genius of William Blake is seen in the series of 18 portraits of poets and authors, painted in a mixed medium which Blake called tempera, for the library of his friend and patron Hayley at Felpham. Each head occupies the centre of a long canvas; on either side of the head are designs of figures or emblems connected with the subject's works—Shakespeare's head, for example, being framed between scenes from *Hamlet* and *Macbeth*.

Another isolated figure, that of William Etty, is represented by 15 paintings, including one of his most satisfactory subject pictures, *The Storm*, as well as a sensitively modelled self-portrait, the vigorously handled *Study of a Peacock*, and a number of typical nude studies. At the Queen's Park Branch Gallery is the gigantic *Ulysses and the Sirens*, one of Etty's largest compositions.

The Pre-Raphaelites and their associates are strongly represented, each of the principal figures by several works. Outstanding among these are Holman Hunt's *The Hireling Shepherd* (Pl. 50b), Ford Madox Brown's *Work* and Millais' *Autumn Leaves*. The official academic art of Victorian England is represented by such works as Frith's *Derby Day* (the Gallery possesses Frith's autograph letter explaining why this version is superior to the version now in the National Gallery), and Leighton's *Captive Andromache*, with which Walter Greaves' *Chelsea Regatta* makes a refreshing contrast.

FRENCH 19TH-AND 20TH-CENTURY PAINTINGS

This small group includes typical paintings by Corot, Boudin, Sisley and Pissarro; a brilliant study of dancers by Forain; an interesting early harbour scene in the impressionist manner by Gauguin; a rich and vigorous landscape painted by Vlaminck in 1908, full of the first enthusiasm of the *fauves*; a Derain portrait, and an abstract composition by Léger. Somewhat apart from the main trend is *The Concert*, painted in London by Tissot.

ENGLISH PAINTING, 20TH CENTURY

This is well represented in the collection. The first wave of reaction against Victorian academic art is shown by numerous examples of the work of Sickert (Pl. 49*a*), Steer, Augustus John, Innes and others. Work by Gilman, Gore and Bevan follows, and nearly every name of importance in English painting as it follows the route from Camden Town to Euston Road is to be found here. Particular attention might be drawn to the works by Wadsworth, Hillier, Matthew Smith, Piper and Pasmore, while both Paul Nash's *Nocturnal Landscape* and Ben Nicholson's *Au Chat Botté* (Pl. 49*b*) are key works in their respective painters' careers.

ENGLISH WATER-COLOURS

The City Art Galleries have not set out to collect English watercolours, since Manchester is fortunate in the presence of the extremely large and rich collection contained in the independently governed Whitworth Art Gallery. Gifts and bequests made to the City Art Galleries in the past have, however, built up a series of water-colours which, though small compared with that at the Whitworth Gallery, is sufficient to represent the main trend of English water-colour from Sandby to the present day.

Outstanding in this series is a group of more than twenty Turners, most of which are of extremely high quality. These range from the crisp clarity of the early *River in Spate* and *View of Exeter* to the luminous haze of the *Heidelberg Sunset* and other golden visions of Turner's later years.

All the best of the city's water-colours, including the Turners,

are shown at the Fletcher Moss Branch Gallery at East Didsbury.
The small rooms of this early 19th-Century parsonage make so
pleasantly intimate a setting for the enjoyment of water-colours
that the whole of the available space is now normally devoted to
their display.

THE RUTHERSTON LOAN COLLECTION

In 1925 the late Charles L. Rutherston, of Bradford, presented
the city with his collection of some 800 20th-Century works of art
in order that it should be used as a lending 'library' for schools, art
schools and universities in the north of England. The collection has
since doubled in size, and each school term over 1,400 works of art
are now sent on loan to over 100 educational institutions.

The original gift included important paintings by Steer, Sickert,
Augustus and Gwen John, Wyndham Lewis, John and Paul Nash
and many other English painters. The many water-colours and
drawings include large series by John, Wyndham Lewis and Paul
Nash. Subsequent additions have tended to keep abreast of more
recent developments in English painting, and to add original
etchings, aquatints and lithographs by such continental painters as
Picasso, Matisse, Derain, and Rouault.

The Loan Scheme is administered from the Queen's Park Branch
Gallery and during the school holidays works from the Rutherston
collection are exhibited there.

The city also owns a fine collection of mezzotint portraits and
early English colour engravings, and some notable sculpture,
mainly by contemporary artists.

The City Art Gallery, the Gallery of English Costume, Platt
Hall and the Horsfall Museum of Art are open on weekdays from
10 a.m. to 6 p.m. and on Sundays from 2.30 p.m. to 5 p.m. The
Queen's Park Gallery is open on weekdays from 10 a.m. to 6 p.m.
in summer; from 10 a.m. to dusk in winter and on Sundays from
2.30 p.m. to 5 p.m. Heaton Hall, the Fletcher Moss Museum and
Wythenshawe Hall close at 8 p.m. in summer and at dusk in
winter.

DAVID BAXANDALL,
Director, Manchester City Art Galleries

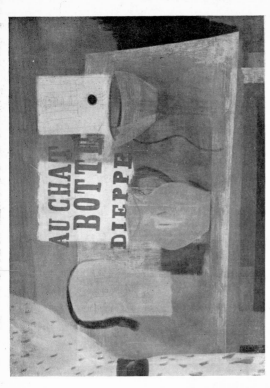

49.b BEN NICHOLSON Au Chat Botté
Manchester

49.a SICKERT Victor Lecour
Manchester

50.a RICHARD WILSON Cicero's Villa   *Manchester*

50.b HOLMAN HUNT The Hireling Shepherd   *Manchester*

THE ART COLLECTIONS AT THE
NORWICH CASTLE MUSEUM

THE Norwich Art Galleries are part of the Norwich Castle Museum which was opened to the public in 1894. Although Norwich had possessed a Museum since 1825 and, in the course of years had become the owner of a few pictures, it was not until 1894, when the collections were transferred to the commodious premises attached to the Norman Castle, that a gallery was devoted entirely to the display of pictures. As was usual at that time, a number of portraits of local celebrities figured largely in the collection, of which the backbone consisted of the work of artists of the Norwich School purchased and presented by the East Anglian Art Society, a policy encouraged by the then Curator of the Museum, James Reeve, who was one of the first to realise the importance of the work of the Norwich School in the development of landscape painting. In 1898, Jeremiah James Colman, who had also collected Norwich School pictures, on the advice of James Reeve, bequeathed a number of paintings to the gallery, and they remain some of its most prized possessions today. By 1904, three additional rooms had been added for the display of water-colours. Subsequently Sir Henry Holmes, another city magnate, bequeathed a selection of his Norwich School pictures, and in 1946 Russell J. Colman, son of Jeremiah, bequeathed the whole of his large collection which consisted of pictures collected by his father with the addition of a large series of oils and water-colours by John Sell Cotman. He also gave to the city a sum of money for the erection of galleries to contain the collection, but the building has necessarily been delayed owing to economic conditions. At the time of writing, owing to lack of accommodation, the Trustees of the Colman Bequest have only been able to hand over to the Corporation the finest of the Cotman water-colours, to which reference is made later in this article.

The city of Norwich produced in the early 19th Century the only School of Painting, properly speaking, ever to flourish in Great

Britain, and it is therefore fitting that the collections in its public Art Gallery should consist mainly of the work of the men forming the Norwich School of Painting. The School was founded by John Crome in 1803, and although some of the members of the School called themselves portrait painters, their surviving work is largely landscape, views of the quiet Norfolk countryside painted in a naturalistic manner showing little or no trace of the classical tradition of landscape painting.

The fact that these men worked together, learning from one another, sometimes painting the same scene, leads to a certain similarity in their pictures, particularly in the case of the minor men, so that sometimes a painting may be definitely attributed to the Norwich School, although not to any particular artist.

John Crome, the greatest in achievement of all the Norwich men, owed much to the great 17th-Century Dutch landscape painters, the two Ruisdaels, Hobbema, Cuyp and Van de Velde. But his first inspiration came from Richard Wilson, as is evidenced in his early work of which the little oil painting called *Morning—Castle in Ruins* is a typical example. Dutch influence is strongly seen in his *Back of the New Mills* (Pl. 51*b*) and *On the Wensum*, both Norwich scenes, where reflections play a large part in the build-up of the pictures. Crome's lovely luminous skies are the main features of two very different pictures, *Yarmouth Jetty* (Pl. 51*a*), a beach scene, and *Moonlight on the River at Bruges—Ostend in Distance*, one of the few pictures which remind us of Crome's one trip abroad.

The Gallery is fortunate in having the loan of two other paintings inspired by his visit to Paris in 1814; *The Boulevard des Italiens* and *The Fishmarket at Boulogne*, both well-known pictures which have remained in the Gurney family since they were purchased by Mr. Gurney, of Keswick, near Norwich, soon after they were painted.

Marlingford Grove, 'the green Crome', is a wonderful painting of trees, profoundly moving and beautiful, yet simple and unpretentious in subject. For brilliance of colour few pictures in the Gallery can equal *The Burdock*, a still-life of slender flowers, etc., posed against the majestic curves of the burdock's luxuriant green leaves; the subject was undoubtedly inspired by the Dutch flower pieces, but is much broader in treatment.

John Crome was among the first English artists to practise etching extensively, and a complete set of his etchings with almost every state of each plate is in the possession of the Gallery, which also contains a number of his water-colours, monochromes and pencil drawings.

Through the generosity of Jeremiah James Colman and Russell J. Colman, the work of John Sell Cotman (1782–1842), the second great head of the Norwich School, is extraordinarily well represented; indeed, without seeing these pictures, it is impossible to judge Cotman's work or form any estimate of his contribution to art. Cotman was undoubtedly the most temperamental of all the Norwich men, and the most brilliant colorist; his technique was so modern that his pictures could be shown in exhibitions today and would not be remarked except for their brilliance and competence. Just as Crome's trees are felt to have roots, so Cotman's buildings seem to stand on solid foundations, for he was a fine draughtsman, having served a weary apprenticeship in the drawing of hundreds of castles, churches, etc., commissioned by Dawson Turner of Great Yarmouth on his three tours in Normandy.

The two best-known oil paintings by Cotman are the classical pair known as *The Baggage Wagon* and *The Mishap*, both painted during his most inspired period, 1827–29. They are so utterly different in conception, colour and technique from any other Norwich School paintings that it is difficult to account for them. It is evident that Cotman owed much to Rubens and probably also to Gainsborough, but he is so very individualistic in his methods that he cannot be fitted in to the general pattern of the Norwich School at all. Another gem of this same period is *Cader Idris*, a little poem in paint of sunshine and atmosphere. Dramatic cloud effects are seen in *Boats off Yarmouth* and *Scene in Normandy*, in contrast to the quiet architectural study of *Old Houses at Gorleston* (Pl. 52b).

But Cotman was primarily a painter in water-colour, and the water-colours in the recent Colman Bequest are an incomparable collection. Starting with the quietly patterned yet forceful early works, such as *Durham* and *Trentham Church*, we come to the glories of his Yorkshire period such as *Devil's Elbow, Rokeby Park* (Pl. 52a). Never was so much conveyed to the eye with a minimum of colour and a minimum of brush work. It and the monochrome *Storm at Sea*, also in the Gallery, were chosen by the late Laurence Binyon for the exhibition of British Art shown in Tokio, 1932. Cotman used his water-colours almost in the oil manner, a fact particularly noticeable in such strong pictures as *Storm on Yarmouth Beach*, where the great, heavy blue cloud seems ready to burst at any moment, and *St. Benet's Abbey* with its hot yellows and browns. *Greta Bridge*, a very lovely drawing, quiet and still, is a larger version of the same subject in the British Museum. From the architectural point of view, *The Gateway of the Abbey Aumale*, *The Statue of Charles I* and the *Abbatial House* are the most satisfying, but every one of the 37 water-colours already received from the Colman collection is a gem.

Of the work of Cotman's two sons there are good examples in the Gallery. Miles Edmund (1810–58), the elder son, has a most satisfying oil painting in rich warm tones called *Boats on the Medway*, and in at least one of his water-colours, *Hayboat on the Thames*, he almost equals the excellence of his father in this medium. Both father and son were drawing masters at King's College, London. The younger son, Joseph John (1814–78), had a prolific output, largely topographical in interest, and towards the latter part of his life luxuriated in a riot of colour—purple, blue and hot orange, with flaming yellow predominating. To this period may be assigned several of the water-colours on exhibition, while the charming study of the Norfolk country scene entitled *Strumpshaw* shows him at his best.

Another artist of the School who owed much to John Sell Cotman was John Thirtle (1777–1839), who painted entirely in water-colour. He frequently introduced the rainbow into his pictures, of which *King Street, Norwich*, with the river in the foreground, is a good example. Many of his water-colours are almost monochromes in reddish-brown, but whether this effect was intentional or due to the passage of time has led to much discussion. Also by this painter are two studies in natural colour of *St. Benet's Abbey* on the Bure, always a favourite subject with artists of all ages.

The Gallery contains three outstanding works by Joseph Stannard

(1797–1830) who, with his brother Alfred, was very much influenced by Cotman. The largest canvas depicts *Thorpe Water
Frolic*, a very large regatta held on the river just outside Norwich
in the early years of the 19th Century. It is full of incident and in
great contrast to his serene painting of *Yarmouth Sands*, where a
beautiful group of three figures is posed against a deserted beach
and a wide expanse of blue sky. The other picture by this artist,
whose output was very limited owing to his early decease, is called
A Stiff Breeze and shows boats heeling over in a choppy sea.

It is John Crome, however, whose domination can be seen in
the work of the greater part of the Norwich School men. His son,
John Berney Crome (1794–1842), who painted many moonlight
scenes of no great merit, could on occasion almost equal his father
in broadness of design and excellence of execution, and his large
canvas *Scene near Bury St. Edmunds* is of this calibre. A simple
subject, treated in a straightforward manner is *Burgh Castle, near
Yarmouth*. Two other pupils of Crome, whose work is well known
outside Norwich, are James Stark (1794–1859) and George Vincent
(1796–1831). Both subsequently moved to London, and although
Stark's pictures in his Windsor period seem to have been painted
more easily, they lose something of the depth and dignity of such
pictures as *Intwood*, of which there are two versions in the collection.
The Forest Oak is a magnificent study of trees, but probably *The
Forest Gate* shows Stark at his best, with a clear golden light illumin-
ating a very satisfying landscape composition. George Vincent was
an unequal painter, but his work at its best is very good indeed.
The Valley of the Yare and *Fish Auction, Yarmouth Beach* are very
different subjects, both competently painted, but the picture with
the greatest appeal is called *Trowse Meadows*, for which a preliminary sketch in oils is also in the Gallery. It is a joyous sunlit scene
painted in all the fresh colours of a June day. *Beachy Head with
Pevensey Bay in the distance* is another large canvas from his
brush.

It is impossible in a short article to mention the other members
of the Norwich School, but the work of Henry Bright (1810–73)
and John Middleton (1827–56) will be specially noticed for its broad
and modern treatment. Middleton painted almost entirely in water-

colour, but there are several large oils by Bright, including *Upper Sheringham* and *St. Benet's Abbey*. There are also good examples of the two topographical artists, David Hodgson (1798–1864) and Henry Ninham (1793–1874), whose paintings of old Norwich are valuable records.

The Gallery contains the beautiful *Glebe Farm* by John Constable (1776–1837), another version of the National Gallery picture, and several smaller Constable pictures in oils and water-colour. It is hoped at some future time that it will be possible to show the work of Gainsborough in landscape, so that the collection will be representative of the art of East Anglia and not only of Norfolk.

Modern local artists whose pictures are on exhibition include Sir Alfred Munnings, P.P.R.A., Sir Arnesby Brown, R.A., Geoffrey Birkbeck, Edward Seago and Walter Dexter, R.B.A.

Open on weekdays 10 a.m. to 5 p.m., October to May; 10 a.m. to 6 p.m., June to September. Sundays 2.30 to 5 p.m. Free except on Tuesdays and Fridays when a charge of 3*d.* is made.

G. V. BARNARD,
Curator

NOTTINGHAM MUSEUM AND ART GALLERY

THE Castle Museum and Art Gallery, Nottingham (opened in 1878), displays as well as pictures, ceramics, wood and metal work, lace and textiles and Nottingham medieval alabasters.

Its paintings are chiefly English and Dutch. The Nottingham-born artists, Thomas and Paul Sandby and R. P. Bonington are well represented: the Sandbys by a large collection of gouaches and water-colours and Bonington by oil paintings (including his *Abbey of St. Bertin, St. Omer* and *Fisherfolk on the Coast of Normandy*), water-colours and numerous pencil drawings.

Oil paintings of special interest are Charles le Brun's *Hercules and Diomedes* (originally commissioned by Cardinal Richelieu), Richard Wilson's *Mount Snowdon*, Kneller's so-called *Dr. Thoroton, The Haywain* by Wheatley, and James Ward's *Bull, Cow and Calf.*

Other oil paintings are mainly of the Netherlands and English Schools. Among the former may be mentioned works attributed to Bloemaert, Jan Both, 'Velvet' Breughel, Hondecoeter, J. Lingelbach, Molenaer, Neeffs, Niemann, Ouwater, Pynacker, Steenwijck, B. van de Neer, W. van der Velde, P. van der Werff, Verboeckhoven, Wijnants, Teniers, Wouvermann. English artists represented include George Chambers, W. Dyce, Etty, Herring, J. C. Ibbetson, Loutherbourg, Morland, Orchardson, J. Phillip, G. F. Watts and, among more recent painters, Sir Arnesby Brown, Charles Cundall, R. O. Dunlop, Mark Gertler, Dame Laura Knight, Harold Knight, Neville Lewis, Bernard Meninsky, Nevinson, Ben Nicholson, Sir William Nicholson, Winifred Nicholson and Stanley Spencer.

Open 10 a.m. to dusk in winter, 9 p.m. in summer (6 p.m. Fridays), Sundays 2 to 5 p.m.

C. F. PITMAN,
Curator

THE ASHMOLEAN MUSEUM,
OXFORD

Even the casual visitor to a museum or gallery, after completing a general survey of its contents, can hardly fail to evince some curiosity as to its history, development, and benefactors—in a word, the circumstances and personalities responsible for its formation and growth. If that is true of almost any notable collection, no matter how recent its beginnings, it is doubly true, for instance, of the Florence or Vienna Museums whose origins date back far into the past, and the full history of which might easily fill a volume. Among the public museums of this country the Ashmolean is generally recognised as the oldest, and though it is only right to emphasise that the Ashmolean of today bears its ancient name rather by collateral than by direct descent, an historical approach seems clearly indicated even for this brief account of its picture galleries only, the most recent offshoot of Elias Ashmole's original foundation of 1683.

Of Ashmole, the son of a Lichfield saddler, born in 1617, the reader should at least be told that, as an ardent supporter of the Royalist cause, he rose to lucrative appointments after the Restoration, and that, both as an antiquarian and in his capacity as Windsor Herald, he made substantial contributions to historical scholarship. With these interests, however, he contrived to combine a passion for alchemy, astrology and Hermetic philosophy, and it was these pseudo-scientific proclivities in a man of strange opposites that were mainly characteristic of the collections in his possession. When in 1683, James, Duke of York, afterwards King James II, performed the opening ceremony of the old Ashmolean Museum on Broad Street, the collections which it contained, Ashmole's gift to the University of Oxford, were chiefly in the nature of a cabinet of rarities illustrating the natural sciences as they were then understood. Certain paintings, it is true, were also included in it—not, however, for painting's sake, but purely as memorial portraits. In a place of honour, of course, hung Ashmole himself—a fine, ceremonial three-quarter length by John Riley, sumptuously framed with carving by Grinling Gibbons; and beside him were certain of his friends and associates, but more especially members of the family of John Tradescant, traveller, and collector of curios, whose accumulated treasures later descended to Ashmole, and constituted the bulk of his donation to the University. The quality of these portraits is very uneven, but among them are a number that have been associated with the name of Emanuel De Critz, an artist of Flemish extraction, whose work, though by no means of the highest order, has yet come to be recognised as having a peculiar beauty of its own, much period flavour, and a charming sense of domestic intimacy. Thus, the pictures in question have justly claimed their place within the Gallery, and hold it today by no means only on the strength of their interest of association.

To the mainly scientific, or pseudo-scientific, character of the Ashmolean in its initial stages archæological interests were to some extent added during the 18th Century. But as long as the Museum remained in the Broad Street building the Tradescant *Wunderkammer* underwent little change; it never assumed anything of the character of a *Kunstkammer*, by then a recognised type of museum on the Continent. The arts remained alien to it from start to finish, and what little collecting of pictures as there was in Oxford, centred, apart from the Colleges, in the Bodleian Library.

On reaching the second quarter of the 19th Century we must shift our attention to where, on a different site and along different lines, important new developments were gradually materialising. The legacies of Sir Robert Taylor, Dr. Francis Randolph and Sir Robert Newdigate, benefactions destined on the one hand for the foundation of an Institute of Modern Languages, and on the other for the accommodation of the Arundel-Pomfret collection of statuary, resulted between 1839 and 1845 in the erection of the fine neo-classical building at the juncture of Beaumont Street and St. Giles, in the western portion of which (originally known as the University Galleries) the present-day Ashmolean Museum is housed. So far as the Fine Art collections are concerned, however, the latter name was not adopted until very much later, not indeed until 1908 when the University's archæological department, into which the Tradescantian rarities other than zoological had been absorbed, and the independently constituted University Galleries were amalgamated under a single administration.

From the way in which they have here been accorded pride of place, the Tradescant and Ashmole portraits might perhaps be mistaken for the nucleus around which the later collection of pictures grew up; but actually such was not the case. This distinction belongs to a very miscellaneous contingent of some 60 items, transferred to the new building from the Bodleian Library. Less than 10 of them have stood the test of time as exhibits worthy of permanent display, and even of these only one has just claim to be anything of a masterpiece. A work of undoubted eminence, however, is Sir Joshua Reynolds' portrait group of the architect, James Paine, and his son, a picture of dignified design and sensitive characterisation, dating from the painter's early maturity. Unfortunately, when this canvas was presented to the University in 1834, it was separated from its counterpart in which the architect's wife and daughter are represented, the two compositions being skilfully balanced to their mutual advantage. The latter picture, however, has also found its way into a public collection, and is now preserved in the Lady Lever Art Gallery at Port Sunlight.

It must not be implied that the Bodleian pictures consisted preponderantly of portraits, but there are in fact three further such among its items of more enduring importance. Brief mention should at least be made of a second, but much larger, Reynolds, representing the 2nd Duke of Grafton; and of an interesting self-portrait of the Commonwealth painter, Robert Walker. But of more general appeal is the *David Garrick* of Pompeo Batoni, which shows the great actor as a man in middle age, of witty and distinguished countenance, and with an open book beside him which has been recognised as a contemporary edition of Terence's *Andria*. The picture was painted in Rome in 1764 during Garrick's temporary withdrawal from the strain of the stage and the cares of management. Of the remaining Bodleian pictures the two most worthy of attention are the charming *Shorescape* of Adam Willaerts, and Pieter Codde's *Young Cavalier*. Willaerts, though a Fleming by birth, worked principally at Utrecht, mingling Dutch and Flemish elements of style, and making a speciality of fish-market scenes, of which the present example shows the additional features of sea and shipping. The Pieter Codde, signed and dated 1625, is unlikely in spite of its small size to escape the visitor's eye, or to fail to delight it with its perfection of finish and almost enamel-like surface. A pupil of Hals, Codde is more generally known for his larger-sized pictures of *genre*, and the Ashmolean example, therefore, is something of a rarity.

If, when all is said, the beginnings of the collection were comparatively humble, the importance of the Bodleian contingent as a nucleus around which more and better things could gather was to prove itself as early as in 1850. Some twenty years earlier, when the Hon. William Fox-Strangways, afterwards 4th Earl of Ilchester, gave away the first portion of a collection of pictures which he had formed in Italy while in the Diplomatic Service, Oxford had benefited, it is true, by his act of munificence, but the gift had then passed into the comparative seclusion of Christ Church Library. It is perhaps idle to speculate whether this would have happened had then the University Galleries already been in existence. Be that as it may, in 1850, within only five years of its foundation, the new Museum became possessed of the some 40 Italian pictures which constituted the second Fox-Strangways benefaction, and many of which still rank among the proudest treasures of the Ashmolean.

This is clearly not the place for detailed lists or descriptions. What will be more appropriate is to say a few words on the collector's taste, to remark on its very personal direction, and to point out how far it was in advance of its time. In contrast to prevailing fashions, Fox-Strangways showed comparatively little interest in the High Renaissance masters, while those of the 15th Century and the Trecentisti were particularly dear to him. So marked is this preference, when one surveys his donation as a whole, that it comes almost as a surprise to find among them Bronzino's *Portrait of Don Garzia de' Medici*, a masterly work, worthy of any collection, but somewhat out of tune with most of its companions. In his appreciation of the Primitives, Fox-Strangways' discernment must have been largely intuitive, for it far outstripped the scholarship at his disposal. It needed for him an independent judgment to perceive the stern beauty of Barna's *Crucifixion*, the monumental quality of Orcagna's *Birth of the Virgin*, the exquisite tenderness of the *Visitation* attributed to Fra Filippo, or the wonderful gift of poetic narrative revealed in Bicci di Lorenzo's *St. Nicholas assuaging the Storm*, a derivative though it is of the more famous predella of Gentile da Fabriano in the Vatican Gallery. It has remained for quite recent criticism to recognise in a pair of female saints, now given to Francesco dei Franceschi, one of the best examples in the country of the Venetian Gothic. Like a number of further pictures from the Fox-Strangways collection, these had at some time suffered extensive repainting, and it is only since a recent cleaning that their true quality has become visible. The same is true, though to a lesser degree, of Marco Zoppo's *St. Paul*, a companion to the panel in the National Gallery, and a very beautiful *Portrait of a Youth* (Pl. 54a), which is more probably by Mainardi than by Pinturicchio as stated on the label, and may be considered as perhaps the finest example of its type.

But the undoubted climax of the collection has still to be mentioned. Paolo Uccello's well-known panel representing a *Hunt in a Forest* has not only proved its fascination for every student of the Renaissance, but also its universally popular appeal. The veracity of its figures, the brilliant delineation of animal life, above all perhaps its exuberant spirit of youthful adventure, have made it without doubt the most widely known and generally admired work in the Gallery. One of the pioneers of the Florentine School, Uccello is credited with the epoch-making discovery of linear perspective. With this, however, the picture shows little direct concern. Even the use of bold foreshortenings to emphasise the effect of space is less in evidence than in the National Gallery *Rout of San Romano*, and elsewhere. But there is a consummate mastery in its converging design, leading the eye to a remote distance in the forest's depth, which proclaims clearly enough the artist's preoccupation with a new pictorial theory. As a pendant to this wonderful picture, which marks, as it were the very birth of the Renaissance, hangs Piero di Cosimo's *Forest Fire*, a gift of the National Art-Collections Fund in 1933. This is far more than an ideal match in shape and size and general distinction for the first. They are essentially in harmony as being the work of painters discovering new aspects of nature; both are instinct with the spirit of Humanism, and both have something of the very essence of the Florentine genius. Even a strain of belated Gothicism is common to both, a feature not unnatural in the *Hunt*, where new and old are still freely mingled, but more of an eccentricity in the considerably later work of Piero.

Even now, after many subsequent developments, the earlier Italian painters in the Ashmolean definitely outweigh the later, notwithstanding the counterpoise of a number of very remarkable 16th-Century pictures, among which are such a masterpiece as Tintoretto's *Resurrection*, and such an extraordinary rarity as Michelangelo's unfinished *grisaille* of the *Return of the Holy Family from Egypt*.[1] To a great extent, of course, this is still due to Fox-Strangways' precocious understanding of the Primitives, but substantial contributions in the same direction were made by later benefactors as well. Interrupting for a moment our chronological survey, let us anticipate at this point the Fortnum Bequest of 1899, and the two assignments, of 1913 and 1947 respectively, from the collection of James Reddie Anderson, the friend and lakeland neighbour of Ruskin. By comparison with the size and importance of his collections of majolica and bronzes, Fortnum's pictures were not very numerous, but, in addition to a beautiful *Virgin and Child* by Pinturicchio, they included also the exquisite little panel of *St. Jerome in the Wilderness* (Pl. 54b), which is certainly one of the high-lights of the Gallery. Whether it is in fact by Giovanni Bellini himself, or as some critics, not altogether convincingly, maintain, the work of his studio, so much is certain, that there are few things in the Gallery that will provide a memory so lasting and vivid as this ascetic figure of the old hermit, and the peaceful sunlit landscape spread out behind his cave. Outstanding among the Reddie Anderson pictures is a small, but strikingly noble *Virgin and Child* in a style

[1] The former came with the Farrer Bequest of 1946, to which also the Koninck landscape, mentioned below on p. 231, belongs. The latter formed part of the Lawrence collection of drawings by Michelangelo and Raphael, by the acquisition of which in 1846 the University Galleries became famous overnight.

closely approximating to that of Giotto and evidently by a painter of his immediate circle; but another very remarkable piece is a *Baptism of Christ* by the rare Sienese master, Giovanni di Paolo.

In 1855, only five years later than the Fox-Strangways Gift, came that of Chambers Hall, a benefaction which, alike for its size, its Catholicity and its impeccable quality, is individually perhaps the most notable ever received by the Ashmolean. One of the leading amateurs of his day, Chambers Hall spread his interests with equal enthusiasm over the fields of painting, drawing, engraving and sculpture, and to do anything like justice to the importance of his collection as a whole one would need to dwell in turn on each of these branches. As a collector of pictures his preference lay principally with the Flemish School of the 17th Century, the great Venetian view-painters of the *Settecento*, and such English masters of the same period as Hogarth, Reynolds and Richard Wilson. Within each of these sections it is easy to perceive that a type of picture having a special appeal to Chambers Hall was the oil sketch of small dimensions, with breadth of handling and bold brushwork. His Hogarth of the *Death of the Countess*, for instance, shows a brilliance of artistic shorthand which calls to mind the name of Fragonard. Of the greatest interest, too, is a series of compositional and portrait sketches by Rubens and Van Dyck, the former including designs connected with the ceiling of the Jesuit Church at Antwerp, the latter with heads in the group of magistrates in the Town Hall of Brussels. Even more admirable are Rubens' two studies of sunset and moonlight, in which the painter's mastery of colour and extraordinary intensity in the experience of nature are shown to the full. Quite apart from Hall's fondness of the oil sketch in general, the inclusion of these two examples in his collection had surely a very particular significance. Himself a landscape artist of considerable skill, he was never more felicitous in his choice, never more discerning in his judgment than in this particular field. Among his drawings, the series by Claude, one of the choicest that there is, would be evidence enough, to say nothing of his much admired water-colour by Dürer, painted on his journey to Venice in 1494. But other acknowledged masterpieces of landscape are among the more finished oils included in his benefaction: Richard

Wilson's small, but exceptionally sensitive *Lago d'Agnano*, and Constable's *River Valley in the Downs*. Forgetting neither the classic serenity of the Colonna-Northbrook Claude (surely one of the finest examples of the master in England), nor the epic grandeur of Philips de Koninck's *View over Flat Country*, another canvas of impressive size,[1] it would be no exaggeration to say that of the art of landscape the Ashmolean has nothing of greater merit than these small pictures from Hall's possession.

Before leaving Rubens to pass on to one or two other treasures from his collection, it is worth saying a word on the *Apotheosis of James I*, which the donor believed to be a sketch for the famous Whitehall ceiling. If, on this occasion, Chambers Hall's connoisseurship was definitely in error, his sense of quality has yet been fully vindicated. It is now fairly agreed that this is a copy made by no less an artist than Antoine Watteau from a sketch by Rubens which in the 18th Century belonged to Pierre Crozat, and is now preserved in the Hermitage at Leningrad.

As in this chapter the subject of Reynolds has already repeatedly been touched upon, the charming and ever-popular portrait of *Mrs. Meyrick* (Pl. 55a) must be passed over at this point with a haste that it ill deserves. But we have certainly to pause over Guardi's *Campo di S. Zanipolo* (Pl. 53a), undoubtedly one of the finest individual achievements of the painter, and one of the great treasures of the Gallery. It dates from 1782, and was painted as one of a set of four pictures commissioned, presumably on behalf of the Senate, by Pietro Edward, the English-born Inspector-General of Monuments to the Serene Republic, to commemorate a state visit of Pope Pius VI to the Doge. All but the first of this set can still be traced, and of the three others not only the original versions, but also replicas are known. Of the Ashmolean composition, which shows the Papal Blessing in front of the Scuola di S. Marco, a but little inferior version, doubtless also the work of Guardi's own hand, formed part of the late Lord Bearsted's bequest to the National Trust, and may be seen at Upton Park, near Banbury. Versions at Dresden and Stuttgart, on the other hand, serve rather to emphasise

---

[1] See respectively p. 235, below, and p. 229, above.

by contrast, the sparkling brilliance of Guardi's original brushwork, ever at its best when rendering the incomparable pageantry of 18th-Century Venice.

Contemporary art made its first appearance in the Gallery with the Combe Bequest of 1894. Dr. Thomas Combe, Printer to the University, who formed the collection bequeathed by his widow, was a prominent Oxford figure about the time of the Tractarian Movement, and he proved his worth and independence of spirit not merely by supporting this great revival of religious thought, but also by the loyal friendship which he extended to the young Pre-Raphaelites in the storm and stress of their early notoriety. His collection, composed almost entirely of works of this group, covered both the period of the short-lived Brotherhood itself and that of its subsequent developments. It is thus linked by manifold associations with the city in which it was formed and afterwards found its permanent resting place. Perhaps the most notable of his acquisitions, Millais' *Return of the Dove*, painted in 1851, is a case in point. It was this picture, completely typical of the Pre-Raphaelite aims, which was seen in the window of a print shop in High Street by two young undergraduates from Exeter, William Morris and Edward Burne-Jones, and so fired their enthusiasm that (it is said) they resolved then and there to dedicate themselves to art. Again, it was Combe's *Dante painting an Angel* which first opened Ruskin's eyes to the genius of Gabriel Rossetti. This highly finished water-colour is another work in the early and best Pre-Raphaelite style, but it dates from 1853, the year subsequent to the actual severance of the Brotherhood. Earlier than either of the above is Holman Hunt's *British Converts sheltering a Missionary*, which bears the hallmark of its date in the features of Elizabeth Siddal (readily recognisable in one of its figures), though it lacks the secret PRB device in conjunction with the signature. It is regrettable, perhaps, that it was Holman Hunt to whom Combe was most particularly partial; it is certainly regrettable that his *Light of the World* was alienated from the rest of the collection to pass into the semi-darkness of Keble College Chapel. But, even among the half-dozen later and emotionally less-sustained examples of Hunt's work in the bequest, the well-known *Festival of St. Swithun* deserves the popularity it enjoys,

51.*a*   CROME   Yarmouth Jetty   *Norwich*

51.*b*   CROME   Back of the New Mills   *Norwich*

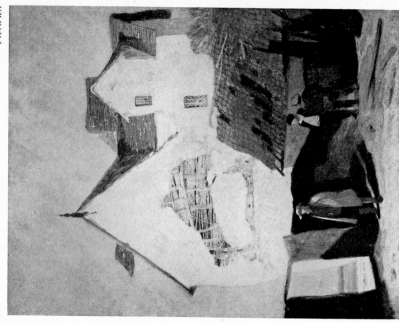

52.*a* JOHN SELL COTMAN Devil's Elbow, Rokeby Park

52.*b* JOHN SELL COTMAN Old Houses at Gorleston

while *Afterglow in Egypt* and *The Plains of Esdraelon* are at least representative of their time, and typical of the decline.

The second phase of Pre-Raphaelitism could be studied in a number of later accessions, notably in what were for many years the loans of Miss May Morris, but became the property of the University after her death in 1939. It is more essential, however, to devote a few lines to the Hindley Smith Bequest of 1940, since to it the largest individual contribution of French painting of the 19th Century is due. In the direction of the Moderns this benefaction extends as far as Matisse, Segonzac, Utrillo, Picasso and even Braque; but its principal accent rests on the Impressionists, while of Corot there are not only typical landscape subjects, but also, what is far more uncommon, a pair of portraits dating from the early '50's. The gem of the collection is easy to determine. Even if in general the work of Toulouse-Lautrec appeals somewhat exclusively to the initiated, *La Toilette* from the Hindley Smith collection, the back view of a woman fastening her hair before a mirror, combines the painter's full power for expressive design and subtlety of colour with a subject free of the slightest taint. Among the first half-dozen masterpieces of the Gallery this picture's place might not be secure; among the first ten its inclusion could hardly be contested.

Of the same year, 1940, as the Hindley Smith Bequest is another important but very different benefaction: the gift of Mr. Theodore Ward made in memory of his wife. This takes us back again to the Netherlands School of the 17th Century which, despite contributions not yet mentioned from the Penrose and T. Humphrey Ward Bequests of 1851 and 1897 respectively, had remained rather sparsely represented, and is still in a sense a somewhat unsatisfactory section of the collection. But as the result of the gift of 1940, a specialised one consisting entirely of still-life pictures, at least one branch of painting in the Low Countries during the century of their great national revival can be studied in the Ashmolean in a series of remarkable quality and abundance. Still-life pictures have in recent years enjoyed a particular vogue, as is plainly shown by the number of specialist exhibitions both in this country and abroad, and by the fast-growing literature on the subject. So comprehensive a collection, however, can seldom have been brought together, and certainly no other has passed intact into a public museum. In such numbers, of course, any theme of comparatively restricted range must necessarily skirt the danger of monotony, however choice each individual piece. In point of fact, no opportunity was lost by the collector of including every variety of still-life available, and to contrast the more elaborate and dynamic style of the Flemings with the more restrained and intimate of the Dutch. Little need here be said of the commoner types, the skilfully varied arrangements of fruit and flowers, or the familiar 'breakfast pieces' and kitchen in-teriors. But a word on the so-called 'Vanitas' may not be out of place, the much rarer type of symbolical still-life which produced certain works of particular beauty. It has aptly been said that its moralising tendency fulfilled within the artistic convention of pro-testant Holland a function not dissimilar to that of religious painting in the South. That it flourished more especially at Leyden, the seat of a great theological University, may therefore well be more than a mere coincidence. What makes the collection as a whole of particular importance to the student is the number of signed and dated exam-ples it contains, and the fact that besides the most distinguished names, such as Willem Kalf, Van Beyeren or Abraham Mignon, one meets also with many now virtually forgotten—painters almost indistinguishable to the layman from their more celebrated con-temporaries, but each with some degree of individuality on closer scrutiny.

It is not proposed to touch here at all on the Gallery's accessions by purchase, numerous though they have been and determined by policy. But even in the briefest account of the growth and develop-ment of the collection of pictures in the Ashmolean, something by way of tribute must be said to the contributions of the late Mrs. W. F. R. Weldon, whose position among its benefactors is a very special one. It is significant that her bequest of 1937, though it included a number of good examples of artists such as Boudin, Fantin-Latour and Jongkind, and a Courbet of exceptional beauty, could hardly be rated as an accession of major importance. The true measure both of her discernment as an amateur and of her liberality as a benefactress emerges from a long series of single gifts, begin-ning as early as in 1915, when her collection was still in active formation, and when, giving her best as was her invariable practice, each successive item transferred to the Museum deprived her own walls of what they could least well dispense with. No less remarkable than her self-denial was the catholicity of her tastes. During the twenty years or thereabouts of her connection with the Gallery, Mrs. Weldon contributed substantially to all the principal schools of painting except the German, which, incidentally, but for a remarkable series of prints and drawings, would still constitute a serious deficiency in the collection. Mention has already been made of the Colonna-Northbrook Claude (Pl. 53b) as one of the finest examples of landscape in the collection, and this was by no means her only important work of French origin. A still-life of kitchen utensils by Chardin has its acknowledged place in critical literature, and it is only by one of the strangest of oversights that the same is not true also of Watteau's exquisite little panel of *Le Repos Gracieux* (Pl. 55b). Hitherto unpublished, its genuineness nevertheless is beyond doubt, and its state of preservation, moreover, particularly good. Next to the French School the Dutch, perhaps, benefited most by Mrs. Weldon's donations, for both the *Ruth and Naomi* of Barent Fabritius and Nicolas Maes' *Sense of Smell* stand out as works of notable interest. To go into further such particulars for the Italian, Spanish and British Schools would only be to labour a point already abundantly clear. In its choiceness the Weldon contribution conforms with the best traditions of the Gallery; in its diversity it is something of an epitome of the collection as a whole.

The Museum is open throughout the year on weekdays from 10 a.m. to 4 p.m., and on Sundays from 2 p.m. to 4 p.m. It is closed from Good Friday to Easter Sunday; for the two days of the St. Giles' Fair (Monday and Tuesday after the first Sunday in September); and for three or four days at Christmas.

K. T. PARKER,
Keeper

PLYMOUTH MUSEUM AND ART GALLERY

THE Permanent collection contains representative works by West Country artists. There is a collection of portraits of famous personalities associated with the Elizabethan period and a very fine group of paintings in the De Pass collection.

The Cottonian collection is housed in this building. The collection contains a number of interesting Reynolds family portraits by Sir Joshua. In addition, there is a large number of drawings by Dutch and Italian masters and an important collection of early illuminated books, missals and manuscripts.

The Water-colour collection is arranged to give emphasis to prominent West Country artists, including Samuel Prout and Francis Towne to name but two. In recent years a collection of contemporary paintings and water-colours has been acquired.

The City Art Gallery is open to the public from 10 a.m. to 6 p.m. daily and from 3 p.m. to 5 p.m. on Sundays.

A. A. CUMMING,
Curator

THE LADY LEVER ART GALLERY,
PORT SUNLIGHT

ART collections made by a single individual have a character, a sense both of uniqueness and of unity, which other collections, made on more orthodox lines by public officials, very rarely achieve. It is this quality which makes a visit to the Lady Lever Art Gallery not only an agreeable but also a stimulating and even a provocative experience. The Gallery and the collection it contains, which are available to the public had their origins in the collections made by William Hesketh, 1st Viscount Leverhulme, for his own delight and satisfaction. Lord Leverhulme was no æsthete, no leisured amateur of the arts. On the contrary, he was an extremely shrewd and vigorous industrialist: one who turned to art not because it offered an amiable occupation for otherwise empty hours, but more urgently because it offered a very real recreation after the cares and obsessions of an active business life.

The 1st Lord Leverhulme was the apotheosis of that much maligned creature, the man who 'knows what he likes'. Certainly he knew what he liked and, being a man of great determination, he was often able to get it. The extraordinary thing is not that his judgment should have faltered, as, judging by contemporary critical standards, it occasionally did, but that it should have been so often and so profoundly right. He never fell into the snare of collecting for collecting's sake, of acquiring more snuff boxes, more tea caddies, more Turners, than anyone else possessed. Within its limits—and Lord Leverhulme was interested primarily in the art and craftsmanship of his own country—the collections he made cover a liberal range, as indeed one would have expected from a man of his active mind.

The backbone of the collection—and this must be true of any representative collection of English art—is a remarkable series of distinguished works by 18th-Century portrait painters. Sir Joshua Reynolds is represented by two full-length portraits in his grandest manner, *Elizabeth Gunning, Duchess of Hamilton and Argyll* (Pl. 56a) and *The Hon. Mrs. Peter Beckford*. His less formal, more intimate, style is well revealed in *Mrs. Paine with her Two Daughters* (a companion picture to one in the Ashmolean Museum) and in a version of *Venus chiding Cupid*. More interesting, perhaps, because in a less-familiar vein are two landscapes by Reynolds after Rembrandt.

Reynolds' contemporary, Gainsborough, is represented by several works of which two are outstanding, *Ann Luttrell, Duchess of Cumberland* and *Mrs. Charlotte Freer*, the former being a study of exceptional profundity and subtlety, and the other showing the painter's delicacy of touch whilst still retaining adequate firmness.

Romney's grand portrait of the beautiful *Sarah Rodbard* (Pl. 56b) shows this painter at the height of his excellence as a romantic portraitist. On a less sumptuous scale, his picture of *Mrs. Oliver* depends much less upon the sensuous appeal of rich silk drapery and much more upon the truly painterly qualities of bold construction and thoughtful colouring.

For an English collection, the Scottish painters are exceptionally strongly represented. An Allan Ramsay of two solemn-faced sisters, austere and formal, suggests an early work of that master. Raeburn justifies the high reputation he still enjoys in his own land with two essentially masculine studies, one of *Thomas Telford*, the engineer, and the other of *James Edgar of Auchingrammont*. Hoppner, invariably decorative, but too often lacking in strength, rises superior to his usual limitations with a fine virile portrait of the Marquess of Hastings, who, in brilliant scarlet uniform, looks every inch a Governor. One cannot, however, overlook the delicate and charming portrait of *Elizabeth Howard, Duchess of Rutland*, from the Castle Howard collections. An unsuspected talent for authoritative picture construction is revealed by Francis Wheatley, whose *Woman in a Large Straw Hat* is a minor masterpiece, quite at variance with his more trivial yet more superficially attractive work.

Among the landscapes pride of place must be given to a number of magnificent works by Richard Wilson in his Italian manner. Of these *Castel Gandolfo: Lake Albano* is probably the most completely successful, but a version of *The White Monk* is also outstanding. Two other landscape painters are each represented by a single canvas, luckily of superlative quality. Constable's *East Bergholt Mill with Rainbow* is one of the painter's largest and most important *plein air* studies, a picture full of the variable rain-drenched light of a stormy day. Turner's *Falls of Clyde*, on the other hand, is one of those late works compounded of sensuous colour and tremulous light, passionate and ethereal at the same time.

It would have been surprising if Lord Leverhulme, collecting when he did, should not have been attracted by the Pre-Raphaelites: they were indeed among his earliest purchases. The best known of them all is probably Holman Hunt's *Scapegoat*, a miracle of uncompromising realism. In this collection the visitor will also find Millais' *Sir Isumbras at the Ford*, to which Ruskin took such virtuous exception; Madox Brown's *Cromwell on His Farm*; Rossetti's *Sybilla Palmifera* and a version of *The Blessed Damosel*, also a great many works by Burne-Jones. Too often overshadowed by larger and more imposing works are two small pictures worthy of note—Madox Brown's *Windermere* and Millais' restrained little *The Violet's Message*.

The earlier water-colour painters are less well represented than one could wish, but an attempt has latterly been made to strengthen this section, which now includes works by J. R. Cozens, Paul Sandby, Francis Towne, Girtin, Rowlandson, Ibbetson, Varley and John White Abbot. Most important, however, is a rare and lovely *East Bergholt Church* by the young Constable.

Later water-colourists are represented much more adequately. Outstanding amongst them is a series of pictures by Turner, ranging from the early topographical *Wells Cathedral* and *Hafod* through all stages of this master's development down to the misty loveliness of *Lucerne from the Walls*. One room is devoted entirely to the works of Peter de Wint, and nearly the whole of another to David Cox. Other men represented are Bonington, Cotman, Copley Fielding, W. J. Muller, Edward Lear, Russell Flint, Wilson Steer and many of their contemporaries.

Contemporary painting is admittedly less adequately represented than it merits. This is due simply to lack of space and not to any particular prejudice. Space has, however, been made for characteristic works by Dame Laura Knight, Sir D. Y. Cameron, Campbell

Taylor, Gerald Brockhurst, Edward Le Bas, Sir Alfred Munnings, and a few others.

The Lady Lever Art Gallery is not, however, devoted exclusively to pictures: it is, indeed, in other fields that it attains its unique distinction, and particularly in its array of English furniture. It can be claimed that nowhere outside of London can such a comprehensive collection of furniture be found. Four rooms are devoted exclusively to furniture, and all other rooms contain a number of pieces chosen to augment the pictures.

To Lord Leverhulme's predilection for English work, a number of exceptions must be made. First, an interest in Napoleon prompted him to collect furniture and other things associated with the Emperor, to which one room is devoted. Secondly, an instinctive appreciation of the perfection of Chinese ceramics led him to acquire a collection which is remarkable in size, range and quality.

Finally may be mentioned a group of early 15th-Century Catalan primitives, all, except one (and that the latest and least interesting) in a perfect state of preservation.

This, briefly and inadequately described, is the collection which the 1st Viscount Leverhulme amassed during the last forty or fifty years of an extremely full life, and from which the Lady Lever collection was formed.

In 1914 the foundation-stone of the present Gallery was laid, and in 1922 the Gallery, dedicated to the memory of his wife who had died nine years before, was completed and thrown open to the public. It was vested in Trustees in July 1923 and endowed by the donor. Standing in the village of Port Sunlight, it is a simple dignified building of classical appearance in Portland stone—a monument to the achievement of one man, and an inspiration to the many who come to visit it.

Opening hours: weekdays, 10 a.m. to 5 p.m. (6 p.m. summer). Sundays, 2 p.m. to 5 p.m. (6 p.m. summer). Admission is free.

SYDNEY L. DAVISON,
Curator

53.*a* GUARDI Campo di San Zanipolo *Oxford*

53.*b* CLAUDE LORRAINE Aeneas shooting the stag of Sylvia *Oxford*

54.a BASTIANO MAINARDI(?) Portrait of a Youth

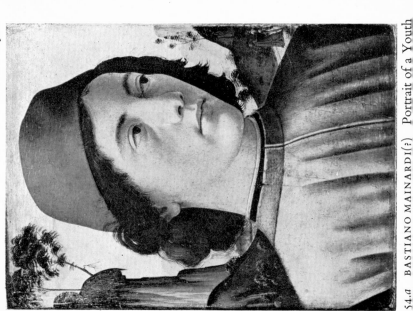

54.b GIOVANNI BELLINI(?) S. Ierome in the Wilderness

55.b WATTEAU Le Repos Gracieux

55.a REYNOLDS Mrs. Meyrick

56.a REYNOLDS
Elizabeth Gunning,
Duchess of Hamilton
Port Sunlight,
Lady Lever Art Gallery

56.b ROMNEY
Miss Sarah Rodbard
Port Sunlight,
Lady Lever Art Gallery

SHEFFIELD

THE Graves Art Gallery, Surrey Street, was founded through the generosity of the late Dr. J. G. Graves. In addition to giving generously towards the cost of the building, Dr. Graves presented a large collection of paintings, of which only a small part can be exhibited at any one time. The collection, which has been enlarged by other gifts, contains some important works of the 16th and 17th Centuries, including an *Infant Christ* by Murillo, a *St. Sebastian* by Anthonis Moro, a *Virgin and Child* attributed to Rubens, and a portrait of an old lady by Adriaen Beeldemaker. English landscapes include a fine work by Constable and several attributed to Richard Wilson.

The Graves Art Gallery at present also houses part of the collection of 19th-Century English paintings normally exhibited in the Mappin Art Gallery, which was seriously damaged during the war.

Open weekdays 10 a.m. to 8 p.m.; Sundays 2 to 5 p.m.

THE RUSKIN MUSEUM

The Ruskin Museum, Meersbrook Park, was founded by John Ruskin in 1875. The aim of the Museum is to illustrate the general doctrines of Ruskin, and its collections consist mainly of documents and copies made by or for Ruskin and connected with Italian art. It contains, however, two important Italian pictures, the *Madonna adoring the Child* by the excessively rare Florentine Quattrocento artist Andrea Verrocchio, and another attributed to Cosimo Rosselli. The collection also includes water-colours by Turner and Ruskin, and a small collection of engravings and medieval manuscripts. Among the former the Dürer collection is noteworthy, and of the manuscripts the most remarkable is the Missal Album of Lady Diana de Croy.

Open weekdays 10 a.m. to dusk; Sundays 2 to 5 p.m.

RICHARD SEDDON,
*Director of City Art Galleries
and Ruskin Museum*

SOUTHAMPTON ART GALLERY

Southampton Art Gallery was opened in 1939. In the same year it was closed for the war, re-opening in 1946. The Robert Chipperfield bequest, to which the Gallery owes its existence, and another bequest gave an adequate income for purchases which have been concentrated mainly on English contemporary painters, English painters of the 18th and early 19th Centuries and minor continental masters. Portraits and water-colours have not been sought as older collections are already rich in these, but amongst the water-colours is William Blake's *Ruth departing from Naomi* and there are sufficient portraits and water-colours to give the flavour of these two categories of English painting.

Contemporary paintings include *Red Landscape* by Graham Sutherland, one of his paintings of South Wales, *Portland Foreshore* by John Piper and amongst others hung are Matthew Smith, Augustus John, Stanley Spencer, Frances Hodgkins, Joseph Herman, Humphrey Spender and Frederic Gore.

There are also examples of the 'New English' painters such as Wilson Steer and the Camden Town Group is well represented: the Sickerts, in particular, being re-inforced by a loan from the Robert Emmons collection.

Among the minor masters is a *Martyrdom of St. Catherine*, the earliest dated canvas by Francesco Desiderio ('Monsù Desiderio') so far discovered, a portrait by Sofonisba Anguisciola and *Rebecca at the Well* by Domenico Feti.

Richard Wilson, George Morland, Phillip de Loutherbourg and John Martin are included, but the most important painting in the English section is *View of Southampton*, an early Constable which dates close to the year 1810.

French 19th-Century painting is represented by a large Sisley dated 1867, *In the Forest*, an oil painting by Forain, also large, *The Fisherman*, and includes examples by Camille Pissarro, Courbet and Lepine.

G. L. CONRAN

YORK ART GALLERY

THE City of York Art Gallery was opened in 1879. During the second world war it was damaged and only reopened in 1948. Its collection consists mainly of paintings of the English School with some good examples of Dutch, Flemish, French and Italian paintings.

Among artists of the English School during the 17th and 18th Century are the following: Reynolds, Lely, Laroon, Marlow, Devis, Ibbetson, Wotton, Wright of Derby, Morland, Mercier, Loutherbourg. In addition there are portraits of 16th, 17th and 18th Century by unknown artists. The English School is carried on into the 19th Century in works by Linnell, Dadd, Watts, Burne Jones, J. Holland, Greaves, Callow, Calcott, J. F. Herring. And among contemporaries or near contemporaries are Sickert, Gosse, Walker, Pryde, Le Bas, Dunlop, Hillier, Gilman, Maitland, Newton. A special collection of fifty works by William Etty, a native of York, includes fine examples of his work, such as *The Bridge of Sighs*, *Flowers of the Forest*, *Venus and Cupid*, *The Wrestlers*.

The few paintings of the French School include works by Baptiste, Gaspard Poussin, Dupré, Ribot, J. E. Blanche, Maufra and Camille Pissarro.

Dutch painting of the 17th Century can be seen in paintings by Ochtervelt and Jan Steen, and the few works of the Flemish School include one of the School of Breughel. The Italian group contains one rarity, the only known work by Girolamo Comi, as well as paintings by Salvator Rosa and a follower of Tiepolo.

A special collection of water-colours and drawings, exclusively of views of the city of York, numbers several hundred, from the 17th Century onwards.

Opening hours 10 a.m. to 5 p.m.; Sunday 2.30 to 5 p.m.

H. HESS,
Curator

PUBLIC PICTURE GALLERIES
NATIONAL TRUST COLLECTIONS

INCLUSION of the National Trust prefix to this heading is at first sight misleading since it is not one of the Trust's specific functions to own picture galleries. The Trust's primary functions are to hold open spaces and houses of historic or architectural importance in which there may indeed happen to be rare works of art, including pictures. Moreover, its historic buildings are seldom made into museums or galleries, for the Trust differs from the Government and local authorities in striving to put its houses to habitable purposes, either as private houses or public institutions. This consequently means that hours of public access must often be limited.

One difficulty in compiling this section is to decide what quantity or quality of paintings constitutes a gallery, for in many National Trust houses there may well hang among rows of indifferent family ancestors, one or two pictures only that rank as works of art or iconographical interest. For example, there are those fine portraits by Reynolds and Carl van Breda of Bennet Langton's family at Gunby Hall, Lincolnshire; the contemporary portrait of Queen Elizabeth and the splendid Gainsborough of Lady Buckinghamshire at Blickling, Norfolk; the fascinating masquerade portraits of the eccentric Sir Francis Dashwood at West Wycombe Park, Bucks; the composite Gainsborough-Reynolds portrait of Miss Sukie Trevelyan and the William Bell Scott and Ruskin decorative panels of the hall at Wallington, Northumberland; and even Miss Beatrix Potter's original water-colours for her children's books at Hill Top, Sawrey, Lancs. But, in order to refer to occasional specimens of good quality such as these we obviously cannot include whole masses of poor paintings in our section. Another difficulty is that sometimes pictures in National Trust houses do not belong to the Trust but to the donors of these houses, like Lord Sackville of Knole and Lord Faringdon of Buscot, or even to the tenants, like H.M. Government who bought the pictures and other contents of

Ham House from Sir Lyonel Tollemache. With the permission of the owners we shall, however, refer to selected picture collections on loan in National Trust houses to which the public resort.

It transpires that the number of National Trust picture collections that qualify for mention is fairly restricted. With few exceptions these collections do not reach that uniformly high standard we expect to find in our great national picture galleries. On the other hand, they offer their own rewards, often in the fascinating history of their formation and, usually, in their beautiful and gracious settings.

We shall deal with the Trust's picture collections as far as possible in the chronological sequence of their formation, bearing in mind, however, that several were the fruits of successive generations of one family. Of such sort the collection at Knole is pre-eminently representative.

KNOLE PARK, KENT:[1]

(Open Wednesdays, Thursdays, Fridays, Saturdays and Bank Holidays, except Boxing Day, November to March 10–12, 2–2.30: April to October 10–12, 2–4.30. Closed February).

There are, numerically, more pictures on view in the state-rooms at Knole than in any other National Trust house. The majority, as is to be expected, are portraits of the distinguished family which has lived here since Elizabethan times down to the present day. The first Sackville to come to Knole in 1566 was Thomas (a cousin of the great queen herself) later created Earl of Dorset. He before Shakespeare's day was the author of *Gorbuduc*, a long blank verse poem, of 'unbearable dullness' to quote his descendant, Miss Sackville-West. His portrait in the role of Lord High Treasurer, holding his wand of office, by Marc Gheeraedts the younger, stands on an easel in the great hall, in the company of later Sackville representatives, including the 4th Earl, wearing a red and gold embroidered doublet, by Van Dyck, and the 1st Duke of Dorset, as Lord Warden, heading a procession to Dover Castle, by John Wootton.

The Brown Gallery of great length is plastered with portraits of historical personages by unidentified artists of the early English

---

[1] All the pictures in the state-rooms at Knole are lent by Lord Sackville to the National Trust, which is responsible for their care and maintenance.

School, of which several are after Holbein. In the apartments called after Lady Betty Germain, an intimate friend of the Sackvilles, is her own prim little portrait taken when lady-in-waiting to Queen Anne. Other pictures here include landscapes and genre scenes by Teniers, Wouvermans and Berchem, mostly bought on the continent by the 3rd Duke of Dorset in the 1770's. The Spangle Dressing-Room contains a series of portraits by and after Lely: the billiard-room a desultory selection of Italian School paintings, collected by the 3rd Duke. In the Venetian Ambassador's bedroom is a portrait of the envoy, Niccolò Molino, by Daniel Mytens, dated 1622. Mytens is well represented at Knole and in the Leicester Gallery are several competent portraits by him and a less satisfactory likeness of James I seated, so legend affirms, on the very crimson velvet chair that still rests beside the monarch's picture and exactly matches in colour his rubicund countenance.

The remaining rooms contain the best pictures at Knole. In the ballroom hang portraits of nearly all the owners of Knole and their wives, by Van Somer, Mytens, Van Dyck (that of the 5th Countess being among his best), Van Loo (the 2nd Duke in the costume of a Roman Emperor), Mme Vigée le Brun and Gainsborough (3rd Duke). In the Crimson Room, besides another Gainsborough, a full-length Hoppner and a Romney after Reynolds, are 10 original Reynoldses, of which three were bought direct from the artist by the 3rd Duke. Of these the best known is the seated, cross-legged Chinese boy, Hwang-a-Tung (Pl. 63a). The Cartoon Gallery is so called after the set of 6 copies by Mytens of the Raphael Cartoons. These vast and clumsy canvases were presented by Charles I to the 1st Earl of Middlesex and brought to Knole by his daughter Frances when she married the 5th Earl of Dorset.

HAM HOUSE, SURREY: [1]

(*Open daily, weekdays* 10–6, *Sundays* 2.30–6)

Ham House was begun in 1610 for Sir Thomas Vavasour. In the middle of the 17th Century it was bequeathed to Elizabeth Countess

---

[1] All the pictures at Ham are now the property of H.M. Government and in the custody of the Victoria and Albert Museum.

of Dysart in her own right. This scheming woman had married in 1672 her second husband, the Duke of Lauderdale, notorious member of Charles II's Cabal Ministry, and as Duchess of Lauderdale enlarged and enriched Ham, which was, however, to pass in descent for nearly three centuries to the offspring of her first marriage to Sir Lionel Tollemache of Helmingham.

With the collection of late Stuart furniture for which Ham is renowned are many portraits of the Tollemache family. Duchess Elizabeth, so remarkable for her beauty and intellect, is represented in two portraits by Lely. In the Round Gallery the one shows her, just before the King's Restoration, at the height of her physical charms and is among Lely's most spirited and least conventional portraits. The other, entitled *Both Ye Graces in one Picture*, depicts her in later years as a far less amiable character seated beside the Duke her husband.

In the withdrawing-room hang the portraits of Maria Lewis, Countess of Dysart, and Louisa, Countess of Dysart, both copies after Reynolds and Hoppner by Constable, early commissions accepted by the artist with reluctance. In the great hall are portraits of Charlotte Walpole, Countess of Dysart, by Reynolds, Louisa Manners, Countess of Dysart, by Hoppner after Reynolds, and Henrietta Cavendish, by Kneller. In the miniature-room are miniatures of Queen Elizabeth by Hilliard and the *Young man against a background of flames* by Oliver, and over the chimneypiece an accomplished crayon-drawing of the Duke of Lauderdale by a little-known artist, Edmund Ashfield.

In the Gallery range a whole series of portraits by Lely, a Cornelis Jonson of the Duchess's father, William Murray, and a Joseph Michael Wright, signed and dated 1659, of Colonel John Russell. Twenty-two of the portraits in the Gallery were listed as hanging here in an inventory of 1679.

CHARLECOTE PARK, WARWICKSHIRE:
(Open April 1st to September 30th, daily, except Fridays, 11–6)
There have been in continuous descent Lucys at Charlecote certainly since the 13th and possibly since the 12th Century. The

present house was begun in 1558 by that Sir Thomas Lucy, J.P., identified in legend with Justice Shallow whom Shakespeare burlesqued so cruelly first in *Henry IV*, Part I, and then in the *Merry Wives of Windsor*. Death duties obliged the family within recent years to sell some of the best pictures from Charlecote, but there still remain enough portraits to afford an interesting social commentary upon an ancient county family from Elizabethan times down to the present century. In fact, every generation since Justice Shallow's reign is represented in the house.

In the great hall the visitor is confronted by the earnest faces of more than forty Lucys, several by Lely, Kneller and Dahl. They are dominated by the large family group by Cornelis Jonson of Sir Thomas III, his wife, children, their nurse, pet dogs and favourite hawk. Of particular interest are two oval portraits on copper, possibly by Isaac Oliver, of Sir Thomas III again and his close friend, Lord Herbert of Cherbury. According to Lord Herbert's autobiography the ovals were commissioned by him before 1610 and given to Lucy, who had saved his life in a shipwreck. There is a head and shoulders of George Lucy, painted in 1760 by Gainsborough for a sum of eight guineas.

In the dining-room is a large and typical parlour scene by Snyders, which once belonged to Mrs. Piozzi. In the Tapestry Room are contemporary portraits of Queen Mary (*c.* 1553), possibly by Lucas de Heere, that came from Kenilworth Castle, of Ambrose Dudley (*c.* 1565) brother of Lord Leicester, that came from Holland House, and a miniature of Admiral Richard Leveson by Isaac Oliver. In the drawing-room are a spectacular portrait of George Lucy painted while in Rome by Pompeo Battoni and an imaginative portrait of Richard I's Blondel by Nicolaus Frangipani, bought in 1836 at Mrs. Piozzi's sale.

STOURHEAD, WILTS:

(Open Wednesdays, Thursdays and Saturdays, 2.30–5.30)

With Stourhead we have a picture collection almost wholly formed in the late 18th and early 19th Centuries by two representatives of the Hoare family. They are Henry Hoare the younger and his grandson, Sir Richard Colt Hoare, an eminent antiquary and historian of Wiltshire. The Stourhead estate had been bought in 1714 by Henry's father (Henry the elder) who in 1722 built the centre block of the present house. The younger Henry did not succeed to the estate until 1741. Until his death in 1785 he contributed much to Stourhead by laying out the magnificent gardens and founding the picture collection. It is not easy to assess precisely which pictures, apart from family portraits inherited or commissioned, were bought by Henry. The greater part of the collection was certainly acquired by Sir Richard who has left us detailed records of his purchases. He was a man of taste, an omnivorous collector and patron of artists, especially artists of talent in the West Country, which gives a peculiar interest to his share of the contributions to Stourhead. Sir Richard in 1800 added the library and the picture gallery wings to house his collections which continued to accumulate until his death in 1838. Unfortunately, in the third quarter of the 19th Century Stourhead fell into neglect and in 1883 there was a sale at which several of the best pictures were dispersed.

The hall, which is the first room entered, displays a galaxy of family portraits, including each successive Hoare owner of Stourhead. Prominent among them are two huge canvases facing each other, the one (much admired by Horace Walpole) of Henry the younger by Dahl, mounted on a white horse by Wootton, the other of Sir Richard with his son by a protégé, Samuel Woodforde from Castle Cary. In the music-room the most interesting pictures are those commissioned by Sir Richard from the minor contemporary artists, Samuel Woodforde, John Rising, Sir A. W. Calcott, William Owen and Henry Thompson. The little dining-room is, like the hall, filled with family portraits, mostly pastels by Francis Cotes and William Hoare. Over the fireplace is a hunting scene by Wootton, representing Henry Hoare with his cousin, Benjamin Hoare of Boreham, and to the bottom left of it a profile of Augusta Hoare by Lord Leighton.

The large dining-room contains several full-length portraits by Allan Ramsay and Prince Hoare and over the fireplace an allegorical picture by Angelica Kauffmann. The Column Room displays part of a series of water-colour mountain scenes by A. L. R. Ducros, a

s

Swiss who worked in Italy between 1770 and 1805 and whose style had considerable influence upon the English water-colour School of the early 19th Century. They were bought by Sir Richard who dilates at some length upon them in the chapter upon Stourhead in his *History of Wiltshire*. The Italian Room chiefly comprises romantic Italian landscape views, of which two in the manner of Salvator Rosa are by Benjamin Barker of Bath and another by C. W. Bamfylde, a gentleman amateur from Hestercombe, Somerset. In the ante-room to the Gallery are a handsome Jacopo Bassano of the *Arrest of Christ*—one of the better old masters in the house —a good drawing of Westminster Bridge by Canaletto and the *Fortune Teller* by Caravaggio.

The Gallery, which Sir Richard added to the house, still contains a few of his best pictures to survive the sale of 1883 and a number of less important masters of a sort admired by the Georgian squirearchy. The best picture of the house, a small Nicolas Poussin group of *Hercules between Virtue and Vice*, hangs here. Other presentable pictures are two romantic landscapes by Gaspard Poussin, a Madonna by Trevisani, a triptych by the Fleming Jan Prévost and two classical scenes by J. L. Lagrenée. Others of interest, as illustrative of late Georgian connoisseurship are two Zuccharelli landscapes, two fairly typical Panninis and three huge canvases, an allegorical subject by Carlo Maratti, the *Adoration of the Magi* by Ludovico Cardi, and the *Emperor Augustus confronting the suppliant Cleopatra*, by Raphael Mengs, the friend of Winckelmann. Between the windows hang two large didactic subjects, entitled *Distress by Land* and the *Shipwrecked Mariner*, commissioned by Sir Richard from Henry Thompson, a pupil of Opie and one time Keeper of the Royal Academy.

ATTINGHAM PARK, SHROPSHIRE:

> (*Open Tuesdays and Thursdays*, 2.30–6.30 *from Easter to October*)

Mr. Noel Hill of an ancient Shropshire family built in 1783–5 on a lavish scale the present house on land he had inherited and called it Attingham. During the course of his house-building Hill became enobled as Lord Berwick. He died almost immediately and was succeeded in his title by three sons in turn. The eldest, Thomas Noel Hill, 2nd Lord Berwick, travelled as a very young man in Italy where he spent freely on pictures and works of art generally and so formed the nucleus of the Attingham collections. On his return home he found the space for his pictures inadequate and so commissioned John Nash to build him the beautiful picture gallery where today the majority of his surviving purchases are to be seen. But unfortunately he overspent himself and in 1827 was obliged to sell nearly all the contents of the house. Several of his pictures were bought in by his brother, William, who five years later became 3rd Lord Berwick. William Hill, who for long had been Minister at the courts of Sardinia and Naples, and was a friend of Byron, added considerably to the collections so that most of the pictures now at Attingham are his contribution. Before his death the majority had been made heirlooms, but his brother, the 4th Baron, by an arrangement with his trustees sold some and out of the proceeds purchased substitutes, including the colossal unidentified family group by Nicholas Maes. Thereafter little change took place, but the 8th Lord Berwick (who in 1947 bequeathed the property to the National Trust) made a few additions, notably the portrait in the drawing-room by E. P. S. Gerard of Caroline Murat, Queen of Naples, some of whose furniture had been brought to Attingham by the 3rd Baron.

The picture collection falls roughly under four heads. First, family and other portraits. Of these the earliest is a portrait after Holbein, of Lord Mayor Rowland Hill, and the finest, Sir Thomas Lawrence's full-length of Henrietta Maria Hill, as Marchioness of Ailesbury.

Second, 18th-Century commissions. Of these are two large allegorical groups by Angelica Kauffmann to the order of the 2nd Lord Berwick in 1793 and 1794 and, probably, the two rural scenes by Richard Westall.

Third, Italian pictures. This group is by far the most numerous. It comprises a Cesari Magni of the Holy Family with St. Elizabeth and St. John, a Bonifazio Veronese (*Christ and the Woman of Samaria*), a pair of dancing figures by Giulio Romano, a series of landscapes by Salvator Rosa, a composition by a follower of Caravaggio (*Soldiers Gambling*), Domenichino (portrait of Cardinal di Bonsi), Sebastiano del Piombo and a 16th-Century Venetian School painting (the *Concert*), held by some scholars to be an early copy of a lost Giorgione.

Fourth, a range of continental pictures—other than Italian—including a Van Dyck of a Genoese gentleman holding in one hand a paper addressed to the artist, several of the Spanish School, including a Ribera (*Death of Archimedes*) and a number of landscapes by Filippo Hackaert.

BUSCOT PARK, BERKSHIRE:[1]

(*Open Wednesdays and Thursdays 2–6*)

Buscot is a late 18th-Century house bought at the end of the 19th Century by the 1st Lord Faringdon and greatly improved by his grandson, the present peer. It contains a collection of pictures, numerically small—some 25—but all of interest and some of considerable importance. The majority were acquired by the 1st Baron and indeed are of a sort that particularly appealed to the discerning collector of late Victorian times.

The sitting-room, which is first entered, has 4 pictures, all by Reynolds, a pair of fairly conventional aristocratic portraits and a pair of sentimental child studies. The music-room comprises the Dutch section—Rubens' seated *Brigitta Spinola*, painted at Genoa in 1605, two Rembrandts and a Genoese Van Dyck of a man in a black cloak. The dining-room has a sketch for a landscape by Gainsborough of a lake and mountains in Wales, a portrait of Lord Liverpool by Lawrence and an unfinished portrait of Mr. Colman by Reynolds.

Around three walls of the central saloon, and fixed in panels are Burne-Jones' 'Briar Rose' canvases, recording the story of the sleeping beauty. The four rectangular scenes were bought at an exhibition in 1890, and the intervening panels later decorated on the site by Burne-Jones for the 1st Lord Faringdon.

The drawing-room contains a selection of Italian pictures, mostly

[1] All the pictures at Buscot are the property of Lord Faringdon.

collected by the present Lord Faringdon. There are the ends of a cassone painted by Michele da Verona: a superb *Virgin and Child with St. Peter and St. Cecilia,* by Palma Vecchio from the Fremantle collection: a *Madonna and Child with St. John* by Ridolfo Ghirlandaio from the Wantage collection: and the idyllic *Flight into Egypt* by Previtali, a picnic scene under a palm tree with the pharos of Alexandria reproduced in the background.

POLESDEN LACEY, SURREY:

> (*Open Saturdays and Sundays 11–1 and 2–6; Wednesdays, 2–6. Closed Bank Holidays*)

At Polesden Lacey we have a small but carefully chosen collection which can most accurately be described as Edwardian, even if its formation overlapped the last years of Queen Victoria's reign and the first of George V's. Certainly the choice of pictures is a credit to the eclectic tastes of a wealthy manufacturer, the Rt. Hon. William McEwen, and his daughter, the Hon. Mrs. Ronald Greville, a notable hostess, whose social zenith coincided with the first decade of this century. The sumptuous settings of crimson damask or heavily gilded *boiseries* against which many of the pictures hang are characteristic of this brief but most epicurean epoch.

The dining-room, with its rich brocade hangings, is a suitable background to Mrs. Greville's collection of English portraits (dominated by the impressive figure of her father by Benjamin Constant). Raeburn's *Paterson Children* and Lawrence's *Rural Amusement* or *The Two Pattison Boys,* are particularly good examples of those masters who were never more favoured than a generation ago. Jonathan Richardson's self-portrait is also of interest. In the corridor are shown the greater number of the pictures. Among the more important are portraits by Corneille de Lyon (two of Charles Brandon, Duke of Suffolk, and his wife, Mary Tudor), the Master of St. Severin and Carel Fabritius (a boy in a brown doublet and large brown hat), a splendid landscape by Jacob van Ruysdael (*The Beach at Muiden*) and works by Ter Borch (one, *The Introduction,* an outstanding picture (Pl. 63*b*)), Pieter de Hooch (the popular *Golf Players*), Aert van der Neer (*Town on a Frozen River*), Saloman van Ruysdael, Cuyp and Quentin Matsys. Of the Italians there is a triptych by Francescuccio Ghissi, a small panel by Domenico Ghirlandaio and a portrait bust of a man by Francesco Morone of Verona.

WIGHTWICK MANOR, STAFFORDSHIRE:

(Open every Thursday 10.30–12.30 and 2.30–5.30)

Wightwick Manor, close to Wolverhampton, was built in 1887–93 for Mr. Theodore Mander by Messrs. Grayson and Ould of Liverpool, two architects who worked under the influence of William Morris. Certainly the spirit of Morris prevails in the decorations, furnishings and collections formed in this remarkably interesting country house, first by Mr. Theodore Mander and then by his son, the donor and present occupier, Sir Geoffrey Mander. The pictures, of which the majority are the property of the National Trust (some few only being loans), are by members of the Pre-Raphaelite Brotherhood and their disciples.

In the drawing-room is a composite Pre-Raphaelite portrait of Mrs. William Morris by Ford Madox Brown, of which the face with the red hair of Mrs. Rossetti (Lizzie Siddall) was painted by D. G. Rossetti. Two chalk drawings by Ruskin, a water-colour of Rossetti's bedroom reflected in a girandole mirror by Treffry Dunn, and a self-portrait by Lizzie Siddall should be noted. In the hall, its walls hung with Flemish verdure tapestries, are four studies by Rossetti, lent by his niece, Mrs. Angeli. In the great parlour, its windows and roof painted by C. E. Kempe, hang Watts' huge portrait of Mrs. Nassau Senior, Burne-Jones' *Love among the Ruins* (from the Bearsted collection), a study of Rossetti's head for *Rienzi* by Holman Hunt and a rare oil painting—*A Candlemas dialogue*— by Christina Rossetti. The dining-room contains several portrait drawings by Rossetti and crayon portraits by Ford Madox Brown. There is also a large oak cabinet of which the panels of St. George riding in triumph (Swinburne having been the model) are painted by Treffry Dunn. Recent acquisitions include twelve designs for stained glass windows by Brown and Morris, Watts' drawing of Effie Gray and Sir John Millais' small oil of Effie Gray, as Mrs. Ruskin, bending over her needlework.

UPTON HOUSE, OXFORDSHIRE:

(Open every Wednesday and from July 1st to September 30th every Wednesday and Saturday 2–6)

Of all the picture collections in the National Trust's possession by far the largest and finest is that at Upton. It was formed practically in its entirety by the 2nd Viscount Bearsted who, shortly before his death in 1948, gave it with the house and gardens to the Trust. In the collection nearly every European School is represented, of which only a token number of the pictures can be referred to here.

Of the English School we should look for Hogarth's *Morning* and *Night*, two much reproduced brawl scenes in Covent Garden. Richard Wilson's view in Italy is an early landscape. There are several conversation pieces by Arthur Devis and a landscape, *Crossing the Ford* by Gainsborough, an early work in the manner of Nicolas Berchem. There are portraits by Reynolds, Romney, Lawrence and Raeburn; a slight study, *A Sunny Day at Dedham* by Constable and Stubbs' *Haymakers*, *Reapers* (Pl. 64a) *and Labourers* among the most moving scenes of English rural life. Sporting pictures by Herring, Ferneley, Sartorius, Stubbs and Ben Marshall are numerous and fine.

Of the Dutch School we may mention two girl portraits by Cuyp, a river scene by Jan van Goyen, the *Duet* or the *Corsage Bleu*, a genre picture of extreme elegance, by Gabriel Metsu, a series of small panels by Jan Steen, *Le Coup de Soleil*, a view of the undulating dune of Overveen by Jacob van Ruysdael and three pictures by Rembrandt, including the *High Priest at an Altar* wearing a golden robe and writing at a book by candlelight.

The early Netherlandish School probably includes the most important of Lord Bearsted's acquisitions. The series opens with three exquisite portraits by Roger van der Weyden, Hugo van der Goes and Hans Memlinc. The School of Louvain is represented by three panels by Dirk Bouts and a Madonna by his son, Aelbert. But Upton is unique among English private collections in that it includes works by two extremely rare artists, Jerome Bosch and Pieter Bruegel the Elder. The Bosch triptych of the *Adoration of the Magi* is a replica of the well-known painting in the Prado, and is accepted by most critics as being also from the hand of the master himself. Pieter Bruegel's *Death of the Virgin* (Pl. 64*b*) is a small grisaille panel of the highest quality to which is added the associative interest of having belonged to Rubens. Rubens himself is represented by a brilliant sketch of *Judas Maccabaeus praying for the Dead*, of which the finished picture is in the Museum at Nantes.

The early French School is represented by a miniature of St. Michel, being the forty-fifth leaf of Fouquet's *Book of Hours* for Etienne Chevalier, two equestrian portraits of François I and Henry II ascribed to Jean Clouet, two small male portraits by Corneille de Lyon and a series of miniatures of the story of Melusine from the atelier of Verard. The 18th Century is represented by a portrait of the artist's mother by Augustin: *Venus, Mars and Vulcan* by Boucher and several attitudinising girls by Greuze.

Of the German School we have a portrait of the Emperor Maximilian I by Bernard Strigel and a splendid miniature by Holbein of a gentleman of the Steelyard in a dark cloak which is inscribed 'Anno 1533', from the Gaell collection.

Lord Bearsted's pictures of the Italian School are no less important. The panel from Prince Orloff's collection of *The Last Supper* commissioned by Donna Giovanna di Bardi from the studio of Giotto is amongst the earliest. The *Madonna and Child with an Angel* by Filippino Lippi, the *Presentation of the Virgin* by Giovanni di Paolo and the *Sts. John and Luke* by Carlo Crivelli represent the quatrocento. Lorenzo Lotto's portrait of a young monk, Parmigiano's young man and Tintoretto's *Wise and Foolish Virgins* represent the cinquecento. Of the 18th-Century painters there are pictures by Canaletto (large view of the Doge's Palace from the Giudecca), Bellotto (a garden scene), Guardi (*Pope Pius VI blessing the populace in front of the Scuola di San Marco*) and Tiepolo (*Madonna and Child*).

Finally, the Spanish School boasts the *Stripping of Christ* by El Greco, a small autograph version of the picture in Toledo Cathedral, *St. Elizabeth of Hungary* by Murillo and two pictures by Goya, the portrait of Don Francisco Bayeu y Subias before an easel and *The Sermon*, the interior of a cathedral with a priest addressing the congregation.

ASCOTT HALL, BEDS

In 1950 Mr. Anthony de Rothschild made over to the Trust his important collection of paintings, mainly of the Dutch and English Schools. The outstanding masterpiece of the Collection is the *View of Dordrecht* by Aelbert Cuyp from the Holford Collection, one of the most romantic renderings of light effects in the whole of Dutch painting. At some period the picture had been cut in half, but the two parts are now re-united. The more intimate painting of street scenes of the same period is represented at its best in the *View of a Dutch Town* by Jan van der Heyden, and other aspects of Dutch landscape can be seen in the works of Hobbema, Wouvermans, Berchem, Wynants and Hackert. A particularly attractive painting of a Dutch interior was formerly attributed to Pieter de Hooch, till on being cleaned it was found to bear the signatures of Ludolf de Jongh, his most skilful imitator, whose works are of great rarity. The two paintings by Rubens, a *Madonna* and a portrait of Hélène Fourment, form a strong contrast with the Dutch canvases in their Baroque brilliance.

The Italian pictures are few in number, but include a magnificent *Madonna* by Andrea del Sarto and a fine Florentine Mannerist portrait, which has been attributed to Bronzino and Pontormo.

Finally, the collection includes an important group of English paintings, including two exceptionally fine Gainsboroughs of the Duchess of Richmond and of Thomas Needham, a very fine allegorical portrait of Miss Meyer as Hebe, and a vigorous Hogarth of an unidentified lady. The few sporting pictures include a Stubbs of the best quality.

In addition to these paintings the house contains an exceptional collection of porcelain, both Oriental and European.

SANDHAM MEMORIAL CHAPEL, BURGHCLERE:
   (*Open daily at all reasonable hours*)

It is so seldom that contemporary pictures or works of art are acquired by the National Trust without relation to an historic house that the Sandham Memorial Chapel is an interesting exception on this count. It was accepted in 1946 from Mr. J. L. Behrend solely because of the paintings by Mr. Stanley Spencer, A.R.A., on its interior walls. The chapel was built in 1926–27 expressly for Mr. Spencer's ambitious mural scheme. He spent six years at work unaided and his paintings are the realisation of designs made shortly after his demobilisation from the first world war in 1919. The subjects of the paintings emanate from Mr. Spencer's experiences during the war as an orderly in the R.A.M.C. He enlisted in 1915 and was transferred at his own desire to the Royal Berkshire Regiment, with whom he served until the armistice on the Salonica front.

The subject of the large painting behind the altar is the Resurrection on the Salonica front. The soldiers are shaking hands, helping one another out of barbed wire, cleaning their kit and greeting their horses and pets. In the middle distance Christ is surrounded by soldiers handing in the crosses which are no longer needed for marking their graves.

To the left and right of the entrance door are scenes of military life, the arrival of a convoy of wounded in motor-buses, kit inspection, 'stand-to' outside a dugout in Macedonia, a soldier washing his shirt on a rock, mules laden with hay, a map-reading lesson and so forth.

JAMES LEES-MILNE.

I V

Scotland

THE NATIONAL GALLERIES OF SCOTLAND

THE National Galleries of Scotland were constituted in their present form by the National Galleries of Scotland Act (1906), and comprise two distinct entities, the National Gallery of Scotland, consisting of the national collection of paintings, drawings and engravings other than those of primarily Scottish historical interest, and the Scottish National Portrait Gallery. Both collections are situated in the capital. The exhibition galleries of the National Gallery are on the Mound, but the prints and drawings, other than any that may happen to be on exhibition in the Mound galleries at any given moment, are housed provisionally in another building, where they are available to students. The Scottish National Portrait Gallery at present shares its building in Queen Street with the National Museum of Antiquities. Both Galleries are under a single Director and Board of Trustees, but have separate Keepers, and there is a special committee to advise on acquisitions for the Portrait Gallery.

None of these collections was created by the Act of 1906. They owe their existence to the active public spirit of a number of different bodies and individuals in the course of the 19th Century. Like the National Gallery in London, and in contrast to so many of the great national collections of the Continent, the Scottish National Gallery was not formed round the nucleus of the artistic treasures of a ruling House. No great royal collection ever existed in Scotland. Charles Stuart, the most brilliant and discriminating of royal collectors, assembled his treasures in the south, and what remains of this collection forms the basis, not of the Scottish or British national collections, but of that of the British Royal House.

In both capitals the national collections were the product of the enquiring spirit of the early 19th Century. The National Gallery of Scotland was assembled in basically its present form in 1859,

261

when the galleries which it originally occupied in the Mound building, which it then shared with the Royal Scottish Academy, were first opened to the public, but the three principal collections then gathered together had been formed earlier in the century.

Four separate bodies contributed to the establishment of this Gallery. The Honourable Board of Manufacturers, set up in 1727 to administer the Annuity paid to Scotland, under the Act of Union, in compensation for increased taxation, provided the building, on a site granted on generous terms by the city, and undertook the expenses of administration and upkeep out of the Annuity. This body had originally been concerned with the encouragement of Scottish trade and industry, but had become increasingly concerned with the visual arts, having established among its other activities the Trustees' Academy, the foremost art school in Scotland and the ancestor of the Edinburgh College of Art. No pictures of any significance were contributed by the Board. These were provided by three other bodies: the Royal Institution, the Royal Scottish Academy and the University of Edinburgh.

The body later known as the Royal Institution had been originally established in 1819 with the object of organising loan exhibitions of Old Masters. A little later it also organised a series of exhibitions of the work of contemporary artists, but in 1826 the artists, dissatisfied with their treatment by the Institution, seceded and founded the Scottish (later Royal Scottish) Academy. After this date the Royal Institution concentrated its energies and expended its funds (funds which the Academicians alleged had been principally drawn from the profits of the modern exhibitions) on the formation of a permanent national collection of Old Masters. This collection was opened to the public in 1831, in the building at the junction of the Mound and Princes Street now occupied by the Royal Scottish Academy, which had been erected in 1823 by the Board of Manufacturers and which also housed the Trustees' Academy and the exhibition galleries of the Royal Scottish Academy. In 1859, on its transfer to the new gallery the Royal Institution transferred its collection, consisting of 77 paintings, to the Board of Manufacturers, and its collecting activity ceased.

The Royal Scottish Academy, founded as we have seen in 1826, also established a permanent collection, intended primarily for the instruction of Scottish artists. This collection, consisting of 141 paintings, mainly by contemporary artists, was deposited on loan at the Board's new gallery in 1859, but the Academy continued to acquire further works from various sources. At the same time the University of Edinburgh deposited on loan the collection of 46 paintings and 37 bronzes which had been bequeathed by Sir James Erskine of Torrie in 1826, subject to a life interest of his brother who had died ten years later. The erection of the National Gallery by the Board provided a solution for the difficulty in which the University found themselves, owing to their limited accommodation, in fulfilling Sir James Erskine's stipulations as to the public display of his collections.

The establishment of the National Gallery in 1859 was in one sense a great step forward, but during the first fifty years of its existence it functioned under great disabilities. While the Board of Manufacturers defrayed the administrative expenses out of the Union Annuity, no official provision was made for expanding the collection by purchase, while the Royal Institution, having achieved the establishment of a substantial permanent collection ceased, as we have seen, to acquire further works. Thus, during the whole of the period when the strength of the London gallery was being built up by the brilliant purchasing policy of Eastlake and his successors, the Edinburgh gallery had to rely for its expansion entirely on private generosity. Dissatisfaction with this state of affairs, coupled with the urgent need for further hanging space, found expression ultimately in a parliamentary agitation in 1901, which led to the appointment of a departmental committee, whose recommendations in a severely modified form were embodied in the Act of 1906, to which reference has already been made. By this Act the Board of Manufacturers ceased to exist and was replaced, in relation to the National Gallery, by a smaller body of Trustees, while the Trustees' Academy became the Edinburgh College of Art and was transferred to an entirely new building provided by the City on the site of the old cattle market. This enabled the Royal Scottish Academy to move into the old Royal Institution building, which it still occupies, thus freeing the whole of the Mound galleries for the accommodation of the National Gallery collections. The consequent remodelling of its interior was completed in 1911, since when no substantial addition has been made to the exhibition space available. The ratio of exhibition space to the total collection is far from adequate and the excellent selection shown inevitably fails to give a complete picture of the range and interest of the collection as a whole. The provision of some further space is urgently necessary. In this connection the restraint of the authorities in not overcrowding the available space is to be commended.

On the occasion of its removal to the Royal Institution building in 1910 the Royal Scottish Academy presented to the National Gallery the whole of the collection deposited on loan in 1859, and a number of other works including the important collection of old-master drawings bequeathed to them by David Laing, LL.D., in 1879. This collection added to that bequeathed to the Gallery in 1881 by W. F. Watson forms the basis of the present print and drawing collection, a department of the Gallery of the greatest interest and too little appreciated. Since the Act of 1906 a certain amount of money has been available for purchase from Treasury sources and the bequest of £55,000 by James Cowan-Smith in 1919 has formed a valuable additional fund for this purpose, while generous help has also been forthcoming from the National Art-Collections Fund. But to a great extent the growth of the collection has been promoted by gifts and bequests of single pictures or small collections by private individuals. The generous scale of such gifts, especially in the matter of Scottish portraits, may be gauged from the fact that of the 29 Raeburns in the collection only 7 have been purchased and only 2 of the 11 Ramsays. The Gallery has also been fortunate in the extent to which its own collections have been strengthened by long-term loans, such as that of Van der Goes's wings of the *Holyrood Altar*, by His Majesty the King, and, since the war, by the loan of the finest pictures from the Bridgewater House collection by the Earl of Ellesmere, which has temporarily raised the Gallery's representation of old masters of the Continental Schools to the first rank.

The three collections forming the basis of the permanent collection have distinct characters. That of the Royal Institution, intended

57.*a* REMBRANDT Hendrickje Stoffels   *Edinburgh, National*
Gallery of Scotland

57.*b* RAMSAY Jean Jacques Rousseau   *Edinburgh, National*
Gallery of Scotland

58.*a*   JACOB VAN RUISDAEL   The Banks of a River   *Edinburgh, National Gallery of Scotland*

58.*b*   REV. JOHN THOMSON   Fast Castle   *Edinburgh, National Gallery of Scotland*

from the beginning as a public collection of old masters, consists mainly of gallery pictures of relatively large dimensions of the Flemish and Italian Schools of the Baroque period. Owing to the limited exhibition space available the interest of this collection is not fully conveyed by the exhibited series, but 4 of the finest paintings in the Gallery originate from it, the 3 Van Dycks bought in Genoa in 1830 and the great Tiepolo *Finding of Moses*, presented by Mr. Robert Clouston in 1845. The Royal Scottish Academy collection consisted mainly of works of contemporary Scottish and English painters, but some fine old masters, such as Ribera's *Mathematician* and Bassano's *Adoration* come from the same source. Perhaps in some ways the most significant of their purchases were a series of large compositions by Etty, evidently intended to foster a school of heroic figure painting in Scotland, and whose influence may be seen in some of the works of David Scott. Unfortunately their great size prevents the present exhibition of any of these works. In contrast to these two gallery collections, the Torrie collection was essentially domestic in character, consisting of cabinet pictures mainly of the Dutch School, a characteristic gentleman's collection of the period of the Regent and Lord Yarmouth. The great Ruisdael *Banks of a River* (Pl. 58a) is the finest Torrie painting. Before turning to describe in greater detail the contents of the Gallery under different Schools, one or two notable gifts and bequests should be mentioned here. In 1859, the year of the Gallery's opening, Robert Graham of Redgorton bequeathed Gainsborough's enchanting full-length of *The Hon. Mrs. Graham*, and two years later Lady Murray, a collateral descendant of Allan Ramsay, bequeathed an important series of Ramsay drawings, the *Portrait of His Wife* and a small but choice collection of French paintings including Watteau's *Fête Champêtre* and Boucher's *Portrait of Madame de Pompadour*. These paintings do not appear to have belonged to Ramsay himself as has sometimes been supposed but to have been acquired by his son. In 1892 Mr. William McEwan presented the outstanding Rembrandt of *Hendrikje Stoffels* (Pl. 57a). Among more recent acquisitions may be mentioned the great Constable of *Dedham Vale* purchased out of the Cowan-Smith Bequest, supplemented by generous aid from the National Art-Collections Fund in 1944.

T

Surveying the total collection as it now stands it may be considered to fall into two main sections: on the one hand, the collection of Scottish paintings, giving, as is proper in the National Gallery of Scotland, the most complete view anywhere obtainable of the development of painting in Scotland from the 17th to the 19th Century and, on the other, the general collection of English and Continental old masters, a collection which contains many fine works but which cannot claim to cover its field with any approximation to completeness.

The Scottish pictures, as the key collection of this School, deserve fuller attention than, perhaps, the absolute merit of the works would always justify. The School cannot, any more than that of England, claim to be one of the major branches of European painting, but it has produced a number of interesting painters. In the third and fourth decade of the 17th Century there were at least two good native portrait painters active in Scotland, George Jamesone (d. 1644) and John Scougall. Both worked in the contemporary Flemish manner. Jamesone's portrait of the *Countess Marischal* shows him as an adequate but not an inspired artist; Scougall's *Self Portrait* is a more interesting work, somewhat recalling the contemporary work of Sir Nathaniel Bacon in England. The latter part of the century was an unpropitious time for art in Scotland and the two artists from this period represented in the Gallery both lived and worked mainly on the Continent. William Gou Ferguson (*c.* 1633–*c.* 1690) shows both in his *Portrait* and his *Still Life* strong Dutch influence; James Hamilton (*c.* 1645–*c.* 1720) who worked in Flanders and Germany shows some individuality in his *Still Life* with its light tone and *trompe-l'œil* effect.

William Aikman (1682–1731) studied in Edinburgh under Sir John Medina (1659–1710), and settled there in 1712 after extensive travels in Europe and Asia Minor, but removed in 1723 to London. His *Self Portrait* is a competent work very much in the manner of Kneller, and illustrates the close cultural links between Edinburgh and London at the period of the Union. The modello for a ceiling decoration, now destroyed, at Gordon Castle, representing the *Rape of Proserpine*, by his contemporary John Alexander (*fl. c.* 1712– after 1745), is an interesting and unusual example of Baroque decoration in Scotland. With Allan Ramsay (1713–84) we first reach a painter of deservedly international reputation. He is well represented in the Gallery by 11 works of various dates, the finest of which are perhaps the *Portrait of his Wife*, with its almost pastel tone, and the penetrating *Rousseau* (Pl. 57*b*) painted for David Hume in 1766. Allan Ramsay, while working latterly mainly in London, always kept up a close connection with Edinburgh; his contemporary Gavin Hamilton (1723–98) lived and worked mainly in Rome. He is represented in the Gallery by a classical composition of the *Death of Hector*. John Runciman (1744–68), on the other hand, is a romantic painter who appears, as Delacroix did later, to have drawn inspiration from Rubens. His freely painted scenes from Shakespeare and the Bible have something of the freshness and vigour of Rubens' sketches. His *King Lear* (Pl. 59*b*), though inevitably falling below Shakespeare's conception, has at least caught something of its elemental force. His *Portrait of a Youth* has a directness which recalls the work of Hogarth. One cannot but feel that this painter, who died at the age of twenty-four, might, had he lived, have become the most interesting of all earlier Scottish painters.

The artist of the great age of Edinburgh was Sir Henry Raeburn (1756–1823), a painter who may at one time have been overpraised but is now unduly under-rated. His work is somewhat uneven, but he has a great grasp of character and his portraits are remarkable for the variety of the light-effects with which he experiments. The 29 examples of his work in the Gallery give a reasonably complete picture of his achievement, and this collection is strengthened by some important loans. The great full-length of *Col. Alastair Macdonell of Glengarry* combines an admirable portrayal of individual character with a rather theatrical setting in a way which would inevitably bring to mind the novels of Sir Walter Scott, even if one did not know that the sitter was said to have been the original of Fergus MacIvor. A more charming and intimate note is struck by the recently acquired *Rev. Robert Walker Skating on Duddingston Loch* (Pl. 60*a*), which is on an unusually small scale. Of his bust portraits the *Self Portrait* and the *Lord Newton* are perhaps the best. He is less often successful in his female portraits, but the bust of *Mrs. Scott Moncrieff* has always enjoyed great popularity.

Landscape painting in Scotland is a development of the latter part of the 18th Century. A good example of its earlier phase is the *Falls of Clyde* by Jacob More (More of Rome) (1740–93), where a Scottish subject is handled in an Italianate classical manner recalling Richard Wilson. Alexander Nasmyth (1758–1840) shows rather more Dutch influence in his *Windings of the Forth*, as does his son Patrick (1787–1831) in his delightful *English Landscape*, an excellent work which recalls Ruisdael and Koninks. The Rev. John Thomson of Duddingston (1778–1840) belongs rather to the classical tradition. In his best work such as the two views of *Fast Castle* (Pl. 58*b*) he shows a sense of architectural structure and breadth of design and handling which place him in the first rank of Scottish landscape painters.

The finest portrait painter of the next generation to Raeburn is Andrew Geddes (1783–1844), who studied in London. His *Portrait of his Mother* in the Gallery is justly famous, and while evidently inspired by Rembrandt is an entirely direct and genuine work. The same can hardly be said for his variation on Rubens' *Chapeau de Paille*, called *Summer*. On the other hand, his portrait of the miniaturist *Andrew Plimer* is an able and attractive work under the influence of Raeburn. Raeburn's influence is also seen in the beautiful early *Self Portrait* by Sir David Wilkie (1785–1841), better known for his genre pieces and historical compositions. Good examples of the former type are the *Pitlessie Fair* of 1804 and the *Bride at her Toilet* of 1838 and of the latter the study for *John Knox preaching before the Lords of Congregation*. A particularly interesting work of his has been recently added to the collection, the large-scale figure composition of the *Soothsayer of Martinique and the future Empress Josephine*, a composition with a breadth of design and handling which recalls the contemporary work of Delacroix. Many of Wilkie's paintings, especially his later works, have suffered much from his use of bituminous pigment in the shadows.

In dealing with 19th-Century Scottish painting it is naturally only possible to pick out some of the major works in the Gallery. The *Portrait of the Artist's Brother* by Robert Scott Lauder (1803–69) is a work in the Raeburn tradition but one of exceptional freshness and charm. Lauder has an important place in the history of Scottish painting from his influential position as Master of the Trustees' Academy. Perhaps the most interesting artist of this period, and one who can only be adequately studied in Edinburgh, is David Scott (1806–49). He was more ambitious than his contemporaries in attempting heroic compositions and had a vivid and striking imagination. His *Philoctetes* shows the influence of Etty's *The Combat* which had been purchased by the Royal Scottish Academy in 1831. In Rome, which he visited in 1832–33, he came in contact with the German painters of the Nazarene School and under their influence evolved a style anticipating that of the English Pre-Raphaelites, with whom his brother William Bell Scott was later associated. This style is well exemplified in his *Paracelsus* of 1838. His most popular paintings are the curious *Puck fleeing before the Dawn* and the *Traitor's Gate*, a picture which achieves a seriousness not often found in 19th-Century historical painting. An exact contemporary of David Scott was William Dyce (1806–64). Two of the three compositions by which he is represented in the Gallery, *Paolo and Francesca* and the important tapestry cartoon of the *Judgement of Solomon*, are, unfortunately, too large for permanent exhibition and his interesting early Raeburnesque style of portraiture and his later minute style, in which he shows himself the only 19th-Century artist to assimilate and successfully to exploit the advances of contemporary photography, are not represented in the permanent collections. His contemporary, Sir Daniel Macnee, though a lesser artist, achieved the Presidency of the Royal Scottish Academy. His *Lady in Grey*, while its debt to Reynolds' *Nelly O'Brien* is obvious, remains a charming work. The generation which grew up around the middle of the century and practised during its latter half are not so easy for us to admire today. The fairy fantasies of Sir Noel Paton, such as his well-known *Oberon* compositions, lack the delicacy and humour of the similar work of his English (or Irish) contemporary Richard Doyle, while the paper-thin costume pieces and the solider *Master Baby* of Sir William Orchardson (1831–1910) are equally distinguished by their vulgarity.

With the work of William McTaggart (1835–1910) we enter a different world altogether. Exaggerated claims have sometimes been made as to his achievement, but we are at least in contact with an absolutely sincere and genuine artist preoccupied with the same problems as his greater European contemporaries. The room in the Gallery devoted to his work well illustrates both his achievement and his limitations, his breadth of vision and freedom of technique, but also his fundamental lack of structure, a lack which has recently been emphasised by the hanging of Monet's *Poplars on the Epte* in the same room. There are also some interesting paintings by members of the group known as the Glasgow School among which the *Vegetable Stall* by W. Y. Macgregor (1855–1923) is a remarkably bold and direct piece of painting to have been executed, as it was, in 1884. The *Portrait of the Artist's Mother* by Sir James Guthrie (1859–1930) is another good piece of work. If McTaggart and the Glasgow School represent the Scottish equivalent to Impressionism, Post-Impressionism finds its reflection in the work of S. J. Peploe (1871–1935) and Leslie Hunter (1871–1931), both of whom are represented in the Gallery by characteristic works.

The representation of the English School in the Gallery is by no means complete but there are a number of fine and interesting works. The small painting of the murderess *Sarah Malcolm* by William Hogarth (1697–1764) is characteristically vigorous. The *Admiral Viscount Duncan* by Sir Joshua Reynolds (1723–92) is a fine portrait, while the *Lady Frances Scott* (1759), is not only one of his subtlest child portraits, without a trace of the sentimentality that sometimes spoils them, but particularly fascinating in its colour. Gainsborough's (1727–88) *Hon. Mrs. Graham* is a justly celebrated work, painted in 1775–76. The other full-length, of *Mrs. Hamilton Nesbit* (c. 1786), is not quite of the same quality, but is a fine work all the same. It is an indication of the lack of hanging space that this picture is not generally exhibited.

Turning to landscape we find two works by Richard Wilson (1714–82), one of which is excellent, and a beautiful *Scene in Wales* by John Crome (1769–1821). Turner (1775–1851) is represented by the delightful oil of *Summer Hill* exhibited in the R.A. in 1811, a picture which marks an interesting stage in the development from the purely topographical views of gentlemen's seats of the 18th Century. There is also a fine collection of Turner water-colours, bequeathed by Mr. Henry Vaughan in 1901, the exhibition of which is restricted by terms of the bequest to the month of January. Reference has already been made to the acquisition in 1944 of the great painting of *Dedham Vale* by Constable (1776–1837). This picture was exhibited at the R.A. in 1828. The influence of the Dutch masters of the 17th Century is perhaps more clearly visible in the composition of this work than is always the case with Constable's paintings. The brilliance of its pigment and technique has been recently revealed by an admirable cleaning. The water-colour of *A Shady Pool where Greta meets the Tees* by John Sell Cotman (1782–1842) is a characteristic and particularly beautiful work, while the *Buildings on a River* is a fine example of his rarer works in oils. The oil *Landscape* (with a white house) by Richard Parkes Bonington (1801–28) is a particularly fine painting which suggests the early period of Corot. Among other artists active in the early 19th Century, William Blake (1757–1827) is represented by three characteristic works. There is also a fine water-colour of *Guisborough Priory* by Thomas Girtin (1775–1802).

Later English painting is not seriously represented in the Gallery unless we count as English the American John Singer Sargent (1856–1925), whose *Lady Agnew of Lochnaw* is a characteristically flashy work. In piety, we should not overlook the picture of *Callum*, Mr. James Cowan Smith's favourite Dandie Dinmont, painted by John Emms (d. 1913), the only painting that accompanied Mr. Cowan Smith's Bequest of £55,000 for the purchase of works for the Gallery, its acceptance and exhibition in the Gallery being the condition of the money bequest.

None of the Continental Schools present any even approximately complete series, but the Gallery contains many interesting and attractive Continental works and a few masterpieces. There is nothing particularly striking among the earlier Italians but the little triptych with the Crucifixion in the centre ascribed to Bernardo Daddi (*c.* 1290– after 1355) is a good specimen of Florentine painting of the next generation to Giotto. From the 15th Century there are some cassone panels and similar works of which the most interesting is the Florentine cassone with a story from Boccaccio. Another interesting Florentine work is the little predella panel with the *Last Supper* catalogued as by Andrea del Castagno (1423–57), but given by Berenson to his 'Carrand Master'. Qualitatively the best of the 15th-Century Florentine works is the *Holy Family with Angels*, by Filippino Lippi (1457–1504), an exquisite little work in particularly beautiful preservation. The so-called *Court of Apollo* by Pietro Perugino (1445–1513) is an interesting and rather puzzling fragment. There are several rather problematical North Italian works of the 15th Century, including the *Noli Me Tangere* ascribed to Zoppo (*c*. 1433–78), formerly in the Simon collection in Berlin, the *Madonna of the Bridge*, an exquisite Ferrarese work the catalogue attribution of which to Ercole de' Roberti (1450–96) does not seem entirely satisfactory, and the *Flagellation*, formerly ascribed to Bianchi Ferrari but now catalogued as by Bramantino (1475–1536), an attribution also open to question. The little *Christ in the Temple* ascribed to Bernardo Butinone (active 1454–1507), though quite a minor work, is one of considerable charm and contains one of the nicest cats in Italian painting. Venetian painting of about 1500 is represented by the very interesting small unfinished *Madonna and Saints* ascribed to Cima da Conegliano (*c*. 1459–1517), a work which is extremely informative as to the technical practices of its school and period. In the absence of major works in the permanent collection (for Poussin's copy of the *Feast of the Gods* by Bellini really tells us more about Poussin) the presence of the early Lotto *Madonna and Saints* among the Bridgewater House pictures is a welcome supplement.

The great masters of the earlier 16th Century are not represented in the permanent collection, the catalogue attribution to Michelangelo of the wax copies from the Medici tombs being an impertinence, but this gap is splendidly filled, at present, by the Bridgewater House Raphaels. Similarly among the Venetians, while the early *Adoration* by Bassano (1510–92), and his male portrait sometimes given to Tintoretto, and the *Mars and Venus* and the fragment of a *Donor and a Saint* by Paolo Veronese (1528–88) are excellent specimens of their respective masters, they fall naturally into the background beside the 4 wonderfully representative Titians and the Tintoretto *Entombment* from Bridgewater House. Italian painting of the 17th Century was well represented in the Royal Institution collection, as has already been said, especially the Genoese School, but few of these works are now exhibited. In some ways the finest Italian work in the Gallery is the great *Finding of Moses* by Giovanni Battista Tiepolo (1696–1770), an artist who may be regarded as the epilogue to the grand style of Italian painting or, as Ruskin viewed him, as 'the first of the Moderns'. The *Finding of Moses* is certainly his major work in any British gallery even in its mutilated state without the *Halberdier* which was cut from the right-hand side in the 19th Century. Fortunately it can now be seen complete since Mr. Ronald Tree has generously placed the *Halberdier* on loan at the Gallery. Both parts have been recently cleaned and the present effect of the painting is immensely impressive. There is also a lovely little sketch for one of the frescoes of *Antony and Cleopatra* in the Palazzo Labia at Venice by the same artist. Of the same period there are some drawings and paintings by Francesco Guardi (1712–93).

Before passing to the Northern Schools we might notice 4 excellent works of Spanish painting, the *St. Michael* by an anonymous artist of the 15th Century, a wonderful piece of decorative Gothic design with a pink rock in the background highly suggestive of Graham Sutherland, the *St. Jerome* by El Greco (1545–1614), the *Portrait of a Mathematician* by Jusepe de Ribera (1588–1656), who should perhaps be counted rather among the Italians, and the tapestry cartoon *El Medico* (1780) by Goya (1746–1828), a work showing the influence of the younger Tiepolo.

The Flemish School in the 15th Century is represented in the permanent collections by works of mainly secondary quality, but this is somewhat redeemed by the loan of the wings of the *Holyrood Altar* by H.M. the King. These are not only the most important of all Scottish historical paintings (indeed they may be considered the beginning of the historical series which we study in the Scottish National Portrait Gallery), but they are works of outstanding quality. The quality is indeed perhaps more apparent in the religious parts of the paintings than in the royal portraits, interesting as these are. These panels, ascribed to Hugo van der Goes (1435(?)–1482(?)), are splendid specimens of monumental Flemish painting of the second half of the 15th Century, and it is an interesting reminder of the wide popularity of Flemish painting at this period that the Uffizi contains an altar by the same painter

commissioned by the Portinari family of Florence. It is unfortunate
that exigencies of space prevent the exhibition of these two wings
in the same room and necessitate their placing where the backs do
not receive a favourable light. There are two good specimens of
the Italianate style in Flemish painting in the early 16th Century,
the *Deposition*, by Joos van Cleef (1484–1540) and the *Way to
Calvary* by Bernard Van Orley (*c.* 1491–1542). There is no specimen in the Gallery of the work of Brueghel or his school but there
is an interesting little *Landscape* by Paulus Bril (1554–1626) signed
and dated Rome, 1616. But the real masterpieces of Flemish painting are the three great Van Dycks purchased in Genoa for the
Royal Institution. The *Lomellini Family*, the purchase of which
was advised by Wilkie, is one of the finest of all his portrait groups
both as regards the portrayal of character in the sitters and as
regards the splendour of the design and execution. The single full
length of an *Italian Nobleman* is almost as fine, if somewhat overshadowed by the Lomellini group. The *St. Sebastian*, though less
immediately attractive, is also a work of the greatest interest. All
these works can be dated to his stay in Genoa during the years
1623–27. There is no comparable work by Rubens, but the recently
acquired study of a *Saint's Head* is a good specimen of his brilliant
technique.

The representation of the Dutch School is considerably fuller.
There are three characteristic works by Frans Hals (1580/1–1666).
The picture of *Verdonck*, a Haarlem humorist, dating from before
1623 is painted in a manner which recalls the *Laughing Cavalier* of
1624. It is an interesting example of the recovery of the original
form of a work by modern cleaning. When the picture entered the
Gallery the man had a red cap and held a wine-glass in his hand.
Investigations carried out by Dr. de Wildt in 1927 revealed these
to be later additions and a careful cleaning showed the original
hair and ass's jaw-bone beneath. The pair of portraits of a man and
his wife are rather later in date and are typical of the artist in their
technical ability and in their dullness. The painting of *Hendrikje
Stoffels* by Rembrandt (1606–69) (Pl. 57a) is one of the masterpieces
of the Gallery which can bear comparison with analogous works
in any collection, and has the advantage of having undergone a

revealing and sympathetic cleaning. In this case the *Self Portrait* from Bridgewater House is a valuable supplement but in no sense puts the Edinburgh example in the shade. An interesting Rembrandtesque portrait is that of a young man with his face illuminated from below catalogued as by Ferdinand Bol (1616-80) but sometimes ascribed to Jan Lievens (1607-74) which passed at one time as a portrait of Wallenstein by Rembrandt.

The Physician and Patient is an excellent example of the work of Jan Steen (1626-79) and there is a characteristic family group by Nicolas Maes (1632-93). The *Still Life* by Willem Kalf (1621/2-1693) is an unusually simple and satisfying composition. Special interest attaches to the large paintings of *Christ in the House of Martha and Mary* by Vermeer as a specimen of this artist unusual both in scale and handling. This picture, more than any other genuine work of the artist, seems to have suggested to the Dutch forger Van Megeren the lines along which he developed the new style of Vermeer with which he so successfully deceived so many experts. Turning to landscape we find the fascinating little coast scene ascribed now to Hercules Seghers (1590-1640(?)) but formerly given to Rembrandt. It is interesting to note the affinities between this picture and Crome's *Scene in Wales* in another part of the Gallery. The two works by Jan van Goyen (1596-1656) are very attractive and show the delicate 'handwriting' of his brushwork which makes them almost like drawings. Undoubtedly the finest Dutch landscape and absolutely one of the finest pictures in the Gallery is the great *Banks of a River* by Ruisdael (Pl. 58a). This is an early work and is beautifully simple in its composition and calm in its treatment. Beside this work the other Ruisdael and the three characteristic pictures by Hobbema (1638-1709) appear rather trivial. Nineteenth-Century Dutch painting is represented on the one hand by a number of characteristic works by Jacob Maris (1837-99) and one by his youngest brother Willem (1844-1910), and by Anton Mauve (1838-90) and on the other by *Les Oliviers* by Vincent van Gogh (1853-1890). Although this picture cannot be considered one of his most exciting works, there do not appear to be any adequate grounds for the suggestion recently put forward that it is a forgery.

Among the French pictures the only one from the 17th Century deserving special mention is the copy by Poussin (1594–1665) of the *Feast of the Gods* by Giovanni Bellini, now in Washington. This work is not only exceedingly beautiful but of the greatest interest as a documentation of Poussin's preoccupation with Venetian painting during his early years in Rome, and as showing that his interest was not confined to Titian. Perhaps indeed the classical qualities of Bellini touched a deeper chord in his nature than Titian ever reached. Here again the Bridgewater House collection with the Chantelou *Sacraments*, the *Moses striking the Rock* and Claude's *Burning Bush* forms at present an invaluable supplement to the permanent collection. The high quality of the French 18th-Century paintings is mainly due to the bequest of Lady Murray in 1861, though some important works have come from other sources. The *Fête Champêtre* by Watteau (1684–1721) is a particularly fascinating work with a lovely sense of light and atmosphere. It is interesting to contrast it with the same painter's *Pastoral*, also an exquisite work, but more of a decorative Rococo caprice. How far, for all their charm, Watteau's immediate followers fell behind him can be clearly seen in the *Toy Windmill* by Lancret (1690–1743) or the *Ladies Bathing* by Pater (1695–1736). François Boucher (1703–70) is represented by the admirable small portrait of *Madame de Pompadour*. Another side of French painting altogether is well represented in the *Still Life* and *Vase of Flowers* by Chardin (1699–1779), the latter in its freshness and directness of approach looking forward to the work of French painters more than a hundred years later. Among the works by Greuze (1725–1815) the genre *Interior of a Cottage* and the *Portrait of a Boy* are at least a refreshing change from his habitual subject matter. There is an interesting series of 19th-Century landscapes. Many of the works by Corot (1796–1875) belong to his disagreeable late period but the *Entrée du Bois* is a fresh and charming work and the *Portrait of his Mother* is an unusual and interesting picture. The Barbizon School is well represented by works by Diaz (1808–76), Troyon (1810–75), Daubigny (1817–78) and Harpignies (1819–1916), mostly originating from the bequest of Mr. Hugh A. Laird in 1911. The *Seine à Bercy*, from the same collection, by Lepine (1836–92) is an unusually fine and sensitive work, recalling the best type of early Corot. Fantin-Latour (1836–1904) is represented by characteristic flower and fruit pieces. The *Self Portrait* of Honoré Daumier (1808–1879) is a particularly attractive work in quite a different style.

The group of paintings by the Impressionists and Post-Impressionists is not large but some of the works are of outstanding quality. The Camille Pissarro (1830–1903) of the *Marne at Chennevières* is not only a work of extraordinary beauty in itself but exceptionally interesting, since it dates from 1864/5 and is one of the few early paintings that escaped the destruction of the artist's studio and its contents during the war of 1870. The *Poplars on the Epte* by Claude Monet (1840–1926) cannot claim any specially prominent place in this artist's extensive *œuvre*, but it is a worthy example. The *Diego Martelli* by Degas (1834–1917), on the other hand, is a particularly fine work. Reference has already been made to *Les Oliviers* by Van Gogh (1853–90). A finer example of Post-Impressionism is supplied by the *Jacob Wrestling with the Angel* of Gauguin (1848–1903) (Pl. 59a). This is historically an important picture in the artist's development, painted in Brittany in 1889, and showing signs of his recent contact with Van Gogh. It has a nervous vitality that is sometimes lacking in his more stylised later compositions.

In addition to the paintings there is, as we have seen, quite an extensive collection of prints and drawings. This collection has attracted little notice, even from students, but is of considerable interest. As with the paintings the series of works by Scottish artists naturally aspires to greater completeness than any other section. The collection of drawings by Allan Ramsay, bequeathed by Lady Murray, is particularly outstanding. Among English works reference has already been made to the Turner water-colours bequeathed by Mr. Vaughan, and other good 18th- and 19th-Century water-colours are in the collection. While there are perhaps no outstanding masterpieces in the Dutch and Flemish sections the former presents a really admirable series of good drawings by minor masters. Of the Italian School, there are a few interesting sheets from the 15th Century. That ascribed to Lorenzo di Credi (1459–1537), and containing studies for the Pistoia altar, though rejected by Berenson appears to be an extremely interesting product of

Verrocchio's studio. The main strength of the series, however, as with the paintings lies in the 17th and 18th Centuries. There is an excellent and characteristic pen and bistre study by Tiepolo. The representation of the French School is, by contrast, rather disappointing. One might have hoped that the excellence of the French pictures in Lady Murray's Bequest would have been matched by drawings of comparable quality, but this does not prove to have been the case. The most outstanding French 18th-Century drawing *Une Souris dans la Lune* by Fragonard (1732–1806) comes not from that source but from the Watson Bequest. The print collection contains numerous older sheets of interest but is perhaps chiefly distinguished by its very important series of works by English, Scottish and French masters of the 19th and 20th Centuries.

As has been said, the Scottish National Portrait Gallery is a separate entity of the National Galleries of Scotland. Its foundation was due to the energy and generosity of J. R. Findlay, of the *Scotsman*, a member of the Board of Manufacturers who anonymously offered to the Board £10,000 in 1882, for the purpose of establishing such a gallery, on the condition that an equal sum was found by the Government. This sum having been voted by Parliament, Mr. Findlay again anonymously offered, in 1884, to erect a building to accommodate the Gallery and the National Museum of Antiquities if a site were provided. A site in Queen Street being secured by joint contributions from the Board of Manufacturers and the Treasury, the present unfortunate building was erected and opened to the public in 1889, when Mr. Findlay was made known as the anonymous donor. Since that time the collection, originally small and very incomplete, has steadily grown. It now forms a remarkable documentation of Scottish history.

Authentic historical portraits earlier than the 16th Century are rare in all Northern European countries and those of James III, his Queen, Margaret of Denmark, their son and daughter and Sir Edward Boncle, on the *Holyrood Altar* of Van der Goes, painted *c.* 1473, are unique in Scotland. These wings are housed as we have seen in the National Gallery on the Mound, on loan from H.M. the King, but they form the beginning of the historical series con-

tinued in the Queen Street Gallery. One point that they bring
before us is the frequency with which royal portraits, especially
when by famous foreign artists, are not painted from the life. In
the *Holyrood Altar* this may be clearly seen in the contrast of the
rather lifeless royal heads, no doubt done after drawings by another
artist, with the vivid head of Sir Edward Boncle evidently from the
life. A similar accomplished portrait not from the life is the *Margaret
Tudor* (1489–1541) by Mabuse (1472(?)–1535). The most interesting portrait of the later 16th Century is the Cobham version of the
'Sheffield' portrait of *Mary Queen of Scots* painted by P. Oudry in
1578. This is a portrait of considerable character, though it does not
wholly explain the fascination that the sitter exercised on her contemporaries. The miniatures of this period seem often more successful than major works in conveying character and that of *Bothwell*,
dated 1566, seems to bring us very much closer to one of the actors
in the drama. The unattractive face of James VI and I may be seen
in various stages from boyhood up. Perhaps the most attractive of
the earlier 17th Century portraits is the anonymous one of *William
Drummond of Hawthornden*. The portraits of *Charles I* and *Henrietta
Maria* are not outstanding, but the portrait of the young *Charles II
as Prince of Wales* by William Dobson (1610–46) (Pl. 60b) is a work
of high artistic quality as well as great historical interest. The
anonymous portrait of the *Marquis of Argyll* (1598–1661) is a work
full of character. From the troubled times of the latter part of the
century the miniature of *John Graham of Claverhouse, Viscount
Dundee* (1649(?)–89) by David Paton (*fl.* 1650–1700) is again
notable, not only from the eminence of the sitter, but the quality
of the work. There is an interesting collection of Jacobite portraits
including the charming pair of *Prince Charles Edward and his Brother*
as boys painted by Antoine David in 1732.

The intellectual figures who made Edinburgh so famous in the
18th Century are well represented. There is an excellent portrait
of David Hume the philosopher and historian (1711–76) by Allan
Ramsay, and also a fine Ramsay *Self Portrait*. The collection of
portraits of Burns includes all the most important authentic original
portraits of the poet including the well-known and charming one
done by Alexander Nasmyth in 1787. In the next generation the

collection of portraits of Sir Walter Scott (1771–1832) is more extensive though not quite so complete. Of particular interest are the miniature done at Bath when he was five and the splendid sketch by Geddes painted about 1818, which is one of the artist's finest works, comparable to the *Portrait of his Mother* in the National Gallery. From later in the 19th Century we have very complete series of portraits of a somewhat more local appeal, such as the chief protagonists in the disruption of the Church in 1843, but also interesting portraits of such internationally famous figures as Thomas Carlyle (1795–1881) and Robert Louis Stevenson (1850–1895). In addition to the painting collection, the National Portrait Gallery has a very extensive collection of engravings and of photographs of Scottish portraits in other places, and also a unique collection of the 'calotypes' of his Scottish contemporaries taken by the pioneer photographer, the artist David Octavius Hill (1802–70) in the middle of the century. There is also a large collection of casts from portrait gems by James Tassie (1735–99). These collections are conveniently arranged and readily available to students.

The Galleries are open on weekdays from 10 a.m. to 5 p.m. but during the darkest period of winter close at 4 p.m. Sundays 2 to 5 p.m. (or 4 p.m. in winter). During the Festival fortnight they are usually also open from 6 to 9 p.m.

GILES ROBERTSON

59.*a* GAUGUIN Jacob wrestling with the Angel

59.*b* JOHN RUNCIMAN King Lear *Edinburgh, National Gallery of Scotland*

Edinburgh, National Gallery of Scotland

60.*a* RAEBURN Rev. Robert Walker, D.D., skating on Duddingston Loch

Edinburgh, Scottish National Portrait Gallery

60.*b* DOBSON Charles II

GLASGOW: CORPORATION
ART GALLERY AND MUSEUMS

THE first recorded account of a civic art acquisition by Glasgow dates from early in the 17th Century. The Town Council, in 1618, commissioned a portrait of James VI of Scotland (James I of England). On several subsequent occasions there are comparable entries in the Minutes of the Burgh—these probably indicating a sense of loyalty to the reigning monarch rather than a consciousness of art value. John Scougall (1645–1730) supplied portraits of Queen Anne, King William III and Queen Mary II. Allan Ramsay provided full-length paintings of King George II, King George III and the 3rd Duke of Argyll. The records also contain evidence of some interest in picture conservation. In 1742 one John Williamson was paid £6 sterling for 'enlargeing washing and mending of nine whole-length pictures'.

In 1730 the University of Glasgow, through the appointment of Francis Hutcheson to the Chair of Moral Philosophy, became indirectly responsible for the creation of an interest in art appreciation. Hutcheson had already published his essay, *Inquiry into the Original of our Ideas of Beauty and Virtue*, and to his class came Robert Foulis, and his brother Andrew. Hutcheson encouraged the brothers to become printers and they were latterly established as 'Printers to the University'. Their travels abroad in search of books also brought them into contact with pictures, and after several years of deliberation their plan to encourage an interest in art matured. In 1754, fifteen years before the formation of the Royal Academy, they established in Glasgow an Academy of Art, which was the first of its kind in Britain. A collection of pictures was acquired, the University lent part of their new library for the training of students, and from 1761 to 1775 an annual exhibition of works of art was held, not only in the halls of the College but in the quadrangles. At one time it was hoped that the Government would give a grant towards expenses, but this did not materialise and by 1776 Foulis, hard pressed by his creditors, was compelled to write 'finis' to a noble experiment. It is interesting to recall that Robert Foulis is credited with stimulating an art interest in his friend, Dr. William Hunter, who eventually bequeathed his collection of pictures to the University.

After a long interval an 'Institution for the Promoting and Encouraging of the Fine Arts in the West of Scotland' was founded. It held two exhibitions and then died, probably of 'appellicitis'—too long a name! The Glasgow Dillettanti Society had a longer innings and a series of rules for the visitors. Among these was a caution, 'not on any account to touch the pictures', a notice which is not so much of a novelty as the one of an exhibition in Kirkcaldy, 'Visitors are requested to bring their opera glasses.' The West of Scotland Academy was next upon the scene. Its first exhibition was in 1841 and after a gallant effort it succumbed with its thirteenth exhibition.

The Glasgow Art Collection as it exists today owes its origin to Archibald McLellan, Coachbuilder, Deacon-Convener of the Trades House, and a City Magistrate. McLellan was born in 1796 and from the age of twenty-seven collected pictures, 'illustrative of the characteristics and progress of the various schools of painting in Italy, Germany, Spain, the Low Countries and France'. He travelled much abroad, spent his money liberally on his hobby, giving as much as £1,000 for one picture (a large sum for a Glasgow man to spend upon art in those days). He believed in art's refining influence and he bought, not for profit, but to hand over his treasures to his native city. On McLellan's death in 1854 it was found impossible to give effect to his bequest. His gifts to the City had involved his affairs to the extent of £44,500. After much deliberation the Town Council agreed to liquidate the deceased magistrate's debts by paying £15,000 for the art collection, and £29,500 for the building.

The Galleries in which the paintings were hung were frequently used for dancing, concerts, lectures, etc., and the collection generally was not highly regarded by the public. Moreover, the care and maintenance of an art collection seems to have been looked upon by the civic authorities with some reluctance, for they took little interest in the matter. Gradually the idea that the collecting and display of works of art might be a desirable civic enterprise developed into active and enthusiastic planning. The interest of art experts at home and abroad in several of the masterpieces acquired by McLellan and the addition of important items by public-spirited citizens were probably responsible for the awakening.

Eventually a series of makeshifts in the shape of adapted buildings terminated in the opening, in 1901, of the present Art Gallery and Museum in the Kelvingrove Park. For fifty years the Corporation has increasingly regarded the civic art possessions and their conservation as essential features in a well-run city. The will and a sufficiency of deeds have more than balanced the caution and errors of judgment. For example Glasgow purchased the *Portrait of Carlyle* by Whistler in 1891. The chief credit for this enlightened decision must be given to the artists who formed the famous 'Glasgow School of Painters'. They memorialised the city magistrates who, some months before France acquired *Portrait of My Mother*, made Glasgow the first city in Britain to give official recognition of Whistler's importance as an artist. Incidentally, the University of Glasgow conferred on Whistler the Honorary Degree of LL.D. Perhaps as a sequel to these gestures, a most interesting collection of Whistler's work is to be found today in the Hunterian Museum.

The West Galleries, five in number, contain examples from the Continental schools of painting. Gallery 1 is hung with Italian paintings and then in order come Flemish, Dutch and French Schools, with a small gallery arranged to exhibit, for purposes of comparison, a selection from all Schools.

The Giorgione, *Adulteress brought before Christ* (Pl. 61*b*) is among the greatest of Glasgow's art possessions. The discussion as to whether this picture was painted by Giorgione or by Titian has probably been going on since 1672. The painting is incomplete; the head of a missing figure on the right is believed to be in the Sachs collection in New York.

The fine **Botticelli** *The Annunciation* is a late work, and it is interesting to recall in passing that about the time it was painted Isabella d'Este's agent was describing Botticelli as 'one who works more willingly and has no hindrances as the aforesaid'. The 'aforesaid' was Botticelli's brilliant pupil, Fillipino Lippi to whom the

Tondo *Virgin, Child and St. John with Angels* (cautiously labelled School of Botticelli) is now generally attributed.

Two important works, from the Burrell collection, are *The Virgin and Child* by Bellini, formerly in the Palazzo Barberini in Rome, and *The Judgment of Paris* by Domenico Veneziano. The latter is part of a marriage chest, and is among the first Italian paintings of classical subjects representing nude figures. The Dolci *Salome with the Head of St. John the Baptist*, the Schiavone *The Ordeal of Tuccia*, the Zuccarelli *A Pastoral Landscape with Figures*, the Canalettos and some others may not measure up to the description of 'great', but they help to emphasise an unusually rich range of times and style in Italian painting.

Temporary wall screens are used to display smaller pictures. One which has recently attracted the attention of critics is *The Nativity* by Francesco Francia. It is one of three panels which formed the predella of the altar-piece of the *Madonna Enthroned* now in the Bologna Gallery, while a second panel *Baptism of Christ* is in the Keller collection, New York. A third panel has been identified in a picture which recently appeared on the market—the subject being —*Flight into Egypt*. The attribution to Antonello da Messina of an *Adoration of the Magi* has been challenged, but in spite of the fact that it was exhibited in London in 1892 as a Flemish painting, the present label appears to be justified. Recently Dr. Grete Ring claims it for the French.

One of the most important pictures in the Flemish collection is *The Virgin by the Fountain* which at one time was attributed to Mabuse but which is now generally accepted as a work by Bernard Van Orley.

Rubens' *Nature Adorned by the Graces* is a fairly early work, and was probably painted about 1615. Recent research has shown that it was originally in the collection of the Duke of Buckingham, who may have purchased it direct from Rubens when sitting for his portrait. On the Duke's death in 1628 it was sold at Antwerp. Later it was purchased in Paris by the painter, Sir James Thornhill; it remained for several years in England—exercising a powerful influence on the work of several painters—and after a period in Amsterdam it returned to Britain and was eventually bequeathed to Glasgow. Comparison of the flowers and fruit should be made with those in *Nymphs bringing Offerings to Venus*, a fine example of the work of Jan 'Velvet' Brueghel. When this picture was exhibited at the exhibition of Flemish and Belgian art in the Royal Academy in 1927 it was suggested that the figures were by Hendrick van Baelen.

The Fruit-Seller by Jacob Jordaens was painted about 1650 and is connected with one of a series of eight designs for tapestries of *Scenes from Country Life*. At one time it was in the collection of Lucien Bonaparte. The Flemish collection also contains several works by Teniers and a typical small landscape by Bril.

Among the most widely known of famous paintings in the Glasgow collection is *A Man in Armour* by Rembrandt (Pl. 62a.) It was bequeathed in 1877 by Mrs. Graham-Gilbert, widow of John Graham-Gilbert, R.S.A. It is first recorded in the Fraula collection, Brussels, in 1738. It eventually passed to Sir Joshua Reynolds who has this comment to make concerning its qualities:

> Rembrandt, who thought it of more consequence to paint light than the objects that are seen by it, has done this in a picture of Achilles which I have. The head is kept down to a very low tint, in order to preserve this due gradation and distinction between the armour and the face; the consequence of which is that upon the whole the picture is too black.

The model in *The Painter's Study* by Rembrandt has been identified by Bode and Hofstede de Groot as the earliest known study of Hendrickje Stoffels. *The Slaughterhouse* by the same artist is a similar study to one in the Louvre, and is in an excellent state of preservation.

Christ riding into Jerusalem is the only known example of a religious painting by Cuyp and has been much improved in tone by its recent cleaning.

The McLellan Bequest has made the Dutch collection rich in pictures by Kalf, Ruisdael, Hobbema, Van de Velde, Bakhuysen, De Heem, Van Ostade and many others.

The *St. Victor and a Donor* (Pl. 62b) is placed in the small gallery containing a selection of pictures of all Schools. This has been done partly because it is constantly subjected to discussions concerning its title and attribution. It has been included in exhibitions of Flemish art (as by Van der Goes) and of French art (as by Maître de Moulins).

During the last ten years, partly with the help of the Hamilton Trustees and the McInnes Bequest, the group of 19th- and 20th-Century French paintings has become an outstanding feature of the collection. The Delacroix, *Adam et Eve Chassés du Paradis* is a study for one of the subjects in the Chambres des Députés in Paris. Daumier is represented by two notable paintings from the Burrell collection, *Le Meunier, son fils et l'âne* and *Le Bon Samaritain* and a range of smaller canvases. *Le Bon Samaritain* is probably the painting which was commissioned for a provincial church in 1849 by the Director of the Beaux-Arts, rejected and then lost sight of for many years. The Barbizon School and the Impressionists are present in fair numbers. The names of Degas (Pl. 61a) Van Gogh, Cézanne, Seurat, Gauguin, Picasso, Matisse, Braque, Bonnard, Vuillard, Derain, Utrillo all appear in the catalogue although it would be misleading to suggest that the work of each of them is, in any way, adequately or completely represented.

Limitations of gallery space make it possible to show only a portion of British paintings in the collection. The four East Galleries are arranged in the following order: (1) Early Scottish and English paintings; (2) the Glasgow School; (3) 19th-Century School; and (4) Contemporary paintings.

The paintings in the first gallery are mainly portraits. The most important Scottish painters of the 17th Century shown are Jamesone (who according to tradition was a pupil of Rubens) and Scougall. While it is a matter of regret that Allan Ramsay is so inadequately represented his quietly distinctive *Portrait of the Third Duke of Argyll* in his robes of the Lord Justice General of Scotland is a fine example of his work.

Allan Ramsay's pupil, David Martin, is represented by the excellent character study of Provost Murdoch. It was this David Martin who gave his young contemporary Raeburn some hints on painting, and pictures to copy, although Raeburn is generally regarded as a 'self-taught' artist. His portraits of *Mrs. William Urquhart, William Jamieson, Jun.* and *Mrs. Anne Campbell* reveal the great Scottish portrait painter in characteristic style. David Allan, who studied at the old Foulis Academy, is represented by a charming *Portrait of a Lady*. Of English portraiture of this period there are examples by Reynolds, Romney and Hoppner. The *Portrait of Mary Queen of Scots* attributed to various 16th-Century painters was owned from about 1585 by the family of the Earl of Morton, from whom it was acquired in 1269.

The Gainsborough *A Woody Landscape near Bath* recently presented to the collection by the Trustees of the Hamilton Bequest forms an important link between the landscapes of Richard Wilson (of which there are 6) and the *Hampstead Heath* by John Constable.

Other pictures worthy of inspection are the two still-lifes by the 17th-Century Scottish painter, W. Gow Ferguson, who lived most of his life in Holland; the two Wilkies, *The Cottar's Saturday Night*, and *Cardinals, Priests and Roman Citizens washing the Feet of the Poor*; and the Zoffany *The Minuet*.

A small gallery is devoted to the works of the artists who created the Glasgow School. The aim of the group which was established between the years 1880 and 1885 was to reject all sentimentality and anecdote and give pictorial art a full independence. Early traditional influences can be seen in some of the pictures on view, but painters like W. Y. Macgregor, Henry, Hornel, Roche, Walton, Lavery and Cameron developed a personal style. Some unfortunately abandoned their early spirit of adventure.

Outstanding among the paintings of the 19th Century is the *Portrait of Carlyle* produced during Whistler's finest period. It was first exhibited in London in 1874. The story of its acquisition by Glasgow has already been referred to. It is interesting to compare the *Modern Italy—the Pifferari* by Turner, who is claimed to have anticipated the works of the French Impressionists, with *The Paps of Jura* by William McTaggart. McTaggart (1835–1910), with the exception of a brief visit to Paris when a student, and two short tours of the Continent later on, lived all his life in Scotland. Quite independently he developed for himself a technique comparable to that of the French Impressionists.

Other pictures permanently on view are McCulloch's *Glencoe*;

Sam Bough's *Burns' Cottage*; Pettie's *Two Strings to her Bow*; Lavery's *House of Commons* with a companion piece *House of Lords*.

Contemporary paintings include Sickert's *Portrait of Hugh Walpole* and *Dieppe Harbour*; Steer's *Nidderdale*; and Augustus John's *Portrait of William Butler Yeats*. There are representative paintings by Nash, Nevinson, Wyndham Lewis, Spencer, Lowry and Hitchens. Of Scottish painters there are works by the four Scottish colourists, Peploe, Hunter, Cadell and Fergusson. The practice of showing works by younger contemporary artists is linked to a policy of circulating these to exhibitions in various schools throughout the city.

It has already been indicated that the picture galleries occupy the upper floor of the building. The ground floor is devoted to the display of items under the general heading of Museum exhibits and under the particular descriptions appropriate to each section: armour, shipbuilding and engineering, archæology, natural history, etc.

Reference must be made to the Burrell collection, the gift of which to the city in 1944 marked an event of outstanding importance. Sir William and Lady Burrell intimated their desire that Glasgow should possess, for all time, their collection of tapestries, pictures, porcelain, stained glass, silver, etc. In addition, funds amounting to £450,000 have been given to the city to provide for a special gallery to house the collection and to add to it. It will be some time before the new gallery can be erected, and meanwhile items from the collection (excluding textiles) are on view from time to time. Some of the pictures have also been circulated throughout Britain under the auspices of the Arts Council.

Glasgow is often described as the commercial capital of Scotland, but it is appropriate here to remember that the full civic motto runs thus: 'Let Glasgow Flourish by the preaching of the Word'. Inasmuch as this is a recognition of spiritual values, the Art Gallery is attempting to live up to the level of its high calling.

T. J. HONEYMAN,
Director

61.*a* DEGAS Duranty *Glasgow, City Art Gallery*

61.*b* GIORGIONE The Adulteress brought before Christ
Glasgow, City Art Gallery

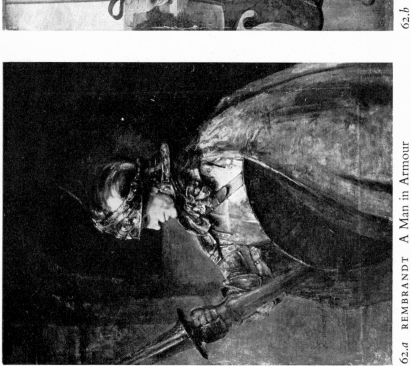

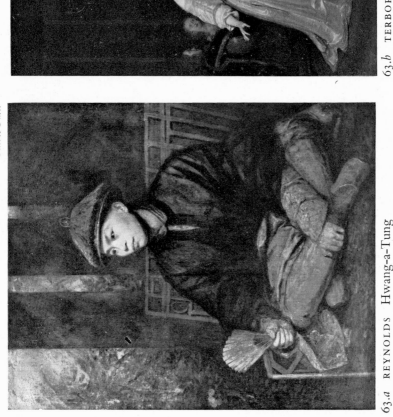

63.a REYNOLDS Hwang-a-Tung

63.b TERBORCH The Introduction

64.a STUBBS The Reapers   *National Trust, Upton House*

64.b PIETER BRUEGEL THE ELDER   *National Trust,*
      Death of the Virgin   *Upton House*

GLASGOW: THE ART COLLECTIONS
OF THE UNIVERSITY

EVER since the early 19th Century, when the Hunterian Museum was finally brought from London to Scotland, the University of Glasgow has possessed an art collection of considerable importance. In the annals of medicine its founder, William Hunter, is famous as an obstetrician and as the British pioneer in the enlightened methods of the teaching and investigation of anatomy. Within his own profession his work has perhaps been overshadowed by the brilliant achievements of his younger brother John, but the diversity of his activities, and the range of his friendships in the worlds of politics, science, literature and art, make him much more typical of the cultivated society of 18th-Century London. His museum was in many ways a mirror of his interests. The scientific collections were many and extensive, including zoological, geological and ethnological specimens and a valuable selection of anatomical and pathological preparations; the library of printed books and manuscripts, among them the famous York Psalter, was one of the finest of the age; and the cabinet of coins and medals was, except for the British Museum's, unrivalled in Britain. The picture gallery comprised only one small section, but its 54 paintings include some of the first rank.

Hunter had originally intended that his museum should form part of a medical school in London which, subject to the grant of a site on Crown Land, he was willing to establish at his own expense. The offer, however, was short-sightedly refused in 1765 by Grenville's Whig administration. Disappointed and deeply hurt, Hunter turned his thoughts to the University of Glasgow, where, before taking up his medical career, he had been a student of Arts and Divinity. The idea of himself returning to teach in Glasgow, expressed in a letter to his friend William Cullen, never materialised. But there can be little doubt that the slight he had received in London greatly influenced his decision to leave the collections to his old University. At his death in 1783, the Museum, much larger and more important than when offered to London eighteen years earlier, passed for a period of years to his nephew and heir, Matthew Baillie; in 1807 Baillie relinquished his interest and, by sea and by road, it made its way to Glasgow.

In the century and a half since the Museum came to Glasgow many paintings, drawings and prints have been added, but Hunter's picture gallery still comprises the main body of the University's art collections. Not all of it can pass the severe tests of modern connoisseurship; some of the grander attributions which Hunter believed in, Titian and Correggio for instance, cannot now be accepted. Like many others of his time, Hunter, in his conscious role as a collector, placed great emphasis on the art of the 17th Century; but it was perhaps with the work of his contemporaries that his choice was most uniformly successful. The Museum is justly famous for three magnificent Chardins, *Le Garçon Cabaretier*, *La Récureuse* (Pl. 44*b*) and *Une Dame prenant son Thé*; and there are several other 18th-Century pictures nearly equally worthy of notice. One of these, a portrait of Hunter himself as a young man, is by Allan Ramsay. Others seem to have come into the collection by the way. Reynolds' highly dignified portrait of *Lady Maynard* and Roslin's delightful *Lady Hertford* were, in all probability, gifts by distinguished patients, and three remarkable paintings of big game by Stubbs, a moose, a nylghau and a pigmy antelope, were specially commissioned as illustrations for natural history researches. With this group might also be included four Kneller portraits of eminent physicians and men of science, acquired from the collection of Dr. Richard Mead, the best of which, *Dr. Arbuthnot*, is of exceptionally high quality.

Some of the finest of the paintings by earlier masters belong to the Dutch and Flemish Schools of the 17th Century. The most notable is a Rembrandt sketch for the Munich *Entombment*, and two of the most attractive are an airy, open, landscape by Philips Koninck and a delicate little *Landscape with a Hawking Party* attributed to Lucas van Uden. The Italian pictures of the *seicento*, which have had attached to them many of the names fashionable in Hunter's time, include an interesting Salvator Rosa, *Laomedon Detected*, and, among the slighter things, a curious little Grimaldi landscape, *Tobit and the Angel*. The most interesting French picture of the period is a market scene, *A Woman Selling Fruit*, reasonably attributable to Louis Le Nain.

During the 19th Century, by gifts and by purchases, Hunter's Gallery was slowly added to. One of the most interesting of the bequests is an impressive portrait formerly believed to be by Sebastiano del Piombo, but in recent years more plausibly attributed to Salviati. Of the many officially commissioned portraits a few, including two Raeburns, have other than historical importance. A comparatively recent purchase is Augustus John's portrait of Viscount Montgomery.

In 1936 the University received a gift which in its own way almost rivals the Hunterian Bequest. It was made by Miss R. Birnie Philip and consists of a large collection of paintings, drawings and prints by her brother-in-law, James McNeill Whistler. It includes 39 oil paintings, most of them unfinished but all of great interest; and there are no fewer than 102 pastel drawings, 15 water-colours, 57 etchings and 98 lithographs. In addition, there are several personal memorials, among them a number of letters to the artist, the manuscript of the famous '*Ten o'Clock*' lecture, etching tools, many etching plates, and blue and white china and garnet jewellery designed by Whistler for his wife. Miss Birnie Philip's valuable gift is, in extent and scope, so important as to make Glasgow a necessary centre for Whistler studies.

The Hunterian Bequest and the Birnie Philip gift include a number of prints. In 1940 these were considerably augmented when the engravings and etchings collected by Professor W. R. Scott were given to the University. But in the years following 1939 the collection was completely transformed by the presentation by Dr. James A. McCallum of nearly 4,000 prints which he had himself brought together. The McCallum collection covers all periods; it begins with Schongauer and, through Dürer, Rembrandt, Goya and many others, comes down to the present day, to Muirhead Bone and Picasso. As something of a supplement to it there are about 200 drawings, mainly of the British School and including examples by Gainsborough, Rowlandson and Turner. In the past few years further gifts of prints and drawings have followed Dr. McCallum's; two of the most important are the extensive series of prints after Turner, from the collection of the late A. Acland Allen, and the Davidson Bequest of drawings and designs by Charles Rennie Mackintosh. In 1949 the University instituted a Department of the History of Art; the newly acquired print collection, no less than the older galleries of paintings, provides valuable material which can be closely related to its teaching.

Tentative plans have been made for a new gallery to contain the collections. In the meantime they are, somewhat inadequately, housed in two rooms of the Hunterian Museum in the main University buildings and in a nearby Print Room.

The Museum is open to the public throughout the year, from Mondays to Fridays from 10 a.m. to 5 p.m. and on Saturdays from 10 a.m. to 12 noon. The prints are available for purposes of study on Wednesdays from 1 p.m. to 5 p.m. There is a brief handbook containing a list of the pictures; a full catalogue is at present in the course of preparation.

A. McLAREN YOUNG,
Curator and Lecturer in Fine Art

BERWICK-UPON-TWEED ART GALLERY

THIS Gallery was opened in May 1949 and consists of 42 pictures given by Sir William Burrell. Although a comparatively small collection it has some important pictures and is particularly strong in 19th-Century French artists. Daubigny's *Cap Gris Nez* is one of his best works and George Michel is represented by a fine and characteristic landscape. Degas' *Danseuses Russes* is a good example of his late manner with its startling colours. The Dutch 19th-Century School can be seen in paintings by Anton Mauve and Bosboom. There are, too, portraits by Thomas Hudson, Opie, Sir Henry Raeburn, Sir John Lavery and Allan Ramsay. Mention should also be made of 3 water-colours by the Northumbrian artist Crawhall.

The Gallery is open each weekday from 10 a.m. to 7 p.m.

INDEX OF ARTISTS

Printed in Great Britain by
Butler & Tanner Ltd.,
Frome and London